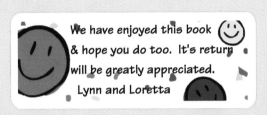

We have enjoyed this book
& hope you do too. It's return
will be greatly appreciated.
Lynn and Loretta

D1445511

THE TEACHINGS OF

Howard W. Hunter

THE TEACHINGS OF

HOWARD W. HUNTER

Fourteenth President of
The Church of Jesus Christ of Latter-day Saints

EDITED BY CLYDE J. WILLIAMS

DESERET
BOOK

Salt Lake City, Utah

Reprinted in 2002 by
The Church of Jesus Christ of Latter-day Saints
Salt Lake City, Utah

English approval: 9/01

Originally published in 1997 by Bookcraft, Inc., Salt Lake City, Utah

Library of Congress Catalog Card Number: 97-70099

ISBN 1-57008-310-X

Printed in the United States of America

CONTENTS

SIGNIFICANT DATES IN THE LIFE OF HOWARD W. HUNTER

1907   Born 14 November in Boise, Idaho, to John William (Will) and Nellie Marie Rasmussen Hunter.

1911   Contracts polio and recovers (but will suffer from back pains the rest of his life).

1920   Baptized in indoor swimming pool in Boise on 4 April.
        Ordained a deacon by Bishop Alfred Hogensen on 21 June.

1923   Earns rank of Eagle Scout on 11 May.

1924   Organizes Hunter's Croonaders dance band after learning several instruments and performs throughout Boise and in nearby towns.

1927   On 5 January sets sail aboard SS *President Jackson,* with Hunter's Croonaders as ship's orchestra, for a two-month Oriental cruise.
        Father, Will Hunter, is baptized on 6 February.

1928   Meets Clara May (Claire) Jeffs on 8 June.

1929   The Great Depression begins.

1931   Marries Claire Jeffs in the Salt Lake Temple on 10 June.

1934   Son Howard William (Billy) Hunter Jr. born on 20 March.
        During the summer enrolls at Southwestern University, taking prerequisite courses for law school.
        Son Billy dies on 11 October at age six months.

1935   Called as stake Scout leader and appointed assistant district commissioner of Los Angeles Metropolitan Area Scout Council.

1936   Son John Jacob Hunter born on 4 May.

1938   Son Richard Allen Hunter born on 29 June.

1939   Graduates cum laude, third in his class, from law school on 8 June.
        Takes California bar exam on 23–25 October; passes.

1940   Admitted to California bar, bar of U.S. District Court for Southern California, and bar of U.S. Circuit Court of Appeals.
        Begins own law practice in April.

Called as bishop of newly organized El Sereno Ward, Pasadena Stake, on 27 August at age 32.

1941   Serves concurrently as Scoutmaster and bishop during wartime shortage of male leadership.

1948   Called as a high councilor.

1950   Called as president of the Pasadena Stake on 25 February at age 42. Designates Monday night as family home evening for Pasadena Stake members.

1952   Called as chairman of Southern California regional council of stake presidents.

1953   Sealed to parents on 14 November, his forty-sixth birthday, in the Arizona Temple.

1959   On 9 October called to the Quorum of the Twelve at age 51 by President David O. McKay.
Ordained an Apostle and set apart as a member of the Quorum of the Twelve by President McKay on 15 October.

1961   In January appointed as chairman of the advisory board for New World Archaeological Foundation, based at BYU.
During the Christmas season, visits Holy Land with Claire and Elder Spencer W. Kimball and wife, Camilla.

1964   Assigned as president of Church's Genealogical Society in January.

1969   In August coordinates first Church-sponsored World Conference on Records and the concurrent World Convention and Seminar on Genealogy in Salt Lake City.

1970   Organizes Church's 500th stake, in Fallon, Nevada.
Called as Church Historian and recorder.

1974   Assigned to help oversee funding and building of the Orson Hyde Memorial Garden in Jerusalem.

1975   Organizes fifteen stakes from five stakes in Mexico City on one weekend.
Accompanies BYU International Folk Dancers on seventeen-day tour of China in May.
Claire hospitalized with a collapsed lung in July.

1979   In April is authorized by First Presidency to negotiate purchase of property for BYU's Jerusalem Center for Near Eastern Studies. Oversees a decade of complex negotiations before center's completion in 1989.
Attends Mount of Olives dedication of Orson Hyde Memorial Garden; receives Medal of the City of Jerusalem from Mayor Teddy Kollek on 24 October.

1980   Hospitalized for removal of benign tumor on 4 June.
        Suffers heart attack on 23 July.

1981   Wife, Claire, suffers cerebral hemorrhage in May.

1982   Claire suffers another cerebral hemorrhage on 7 April.

1983   Claire dies on 9 October.

1984   Organizes stake in California.
        Elected chairman of the board of Beneficial Life Insurance Company.

1985   In February visits Jerusalem to defuse opposition to construction of
           BYU Jerusalem Center.
        Set apart as Acting President of the Quorum of the Twelve on 10
           November due to President Marion G. Romney's ill health.

1986   Undergoes coronary bypass surgery on 12 October.

1987   In March seeks treatment for back and leg pain related to spinal bone
           deterioration.
        Undergoes surgery for bleeding ulcer on 8 April.
        Undergoes back surgery on 4 June, limiting use of his legs.

1988   Set apart as President of the Quorum of the Twelve on 2 June, after
           the death of President Romney.

1989   Dedicates BYU Jerusalem Center in May.

1990   Marries Inis Bernice Egan on 10 April in the Salt Lake Temple.
        In December is hospitalized with pneumonia.

1991   In the summer is hospitalized in Salt Lake City after aspirating food
           into lung.
        In August dedicates Panama for the preaching of the gospel.

1992   On 12 September dedicates Austria for preaching of the gospel.
        In November is hospitalized for internal bleeding.

1993   Endures a threatening intruder while speaking at BYU Marriott Cen-
           ter on 7 February; is unharmed.
        In May undergoes gall bladder surgery and suffers near-fatal reaction
           to medications; recovers some days later.

1994   President Ezra Taft Benson dies on 30 May.
        Ordained the fourteenth President of the Church on 5 June at age
           86.
        On 26 June speaks in Nauvoo, Illinois, marking next day's 150th an-
           niversary of Joseph, Hyrum Smith martyrdom.
        On 1 October is sustained as prophet, seer, revelator, and President
           of the Church in a solemn assembly opening the 164th Semian-
           nual General Conference.

Dedicates Orlando Florida Temple on 9 October.

Presides over inauguration of Eric B. Shumway as president of BYU—Hawaii on 18 November.

On 11 December presides over creation of Church's 2,000th stake: the Mexico City Mexico Contreras Stake.

1995   Dedicates the Bountiful Utah Temple in January.

Hospitalized for exhaustion on 12 January; prostate cancer had recurred and spread to the bones.

Passes away at home on 3 March.

Much of this chronology was taken from the *Ensign,* April 1995, pp. 11, 13–14, 17.

PREFACE

The apostolic ministry of Howard W. Hunter spanned from 1959 to 1994. He served as Acting President of the Quorum of the Twelve from 1985 till the death of President Marion G. Romney in 1988, and then as President of the Twelve till June of 1994, when he was ordained the fourteenth President of the Church. President Hunter served as President of the Church for nine months, the shortest term of any prophet in this dispensation. Yet despite his short service as prophet, President Hunter left a spiritual legacy for all to emulate.

In compiling *The Teachings of Howard W. Hunter,* well over 300 talks were located. They span in time from 1941, when President Hunter was a bishop in Southern California, to March 1995, when President Hunter died. Some of these addresses were given in meetings for the Church's Genealogical Society and often dealt with methods and progress in the work of gathering data. Most of these talks did not contain doctrinal material. President Hunter also spoke at business conventions and other settings where the talks were not doctrinally oriented. A few other talks were not available because of the private setting in which they were given, such as temple president seminars. Some 240 talks were used in selecting the teachings of President Hunter.

A bibliography of LDS writings on Jesus Christ and the New Testament was published in *BYU Studies* in 1995 (see vol. 34 no. 3). It showed that President Howard W. Hunter had spoken more on the Savior and New Testament gospel themes than any other General Authority up to that time. For readers who want to become more Christlike and understand those matters that pertain to eternal goals, *The Teachings of Howard W. Hunter* has much to offer. President Hunter speaks of how to apply the gospel in our daily lives. He gives powerful and comforting counsel to couples concerning marriage and family responsibilities.

Those who have had to endure much of suffering and trials will find President Hunter is one who can relate and offer answers from the seedbed of his own suffering. Concerning this aspect of President Hunter's life, President Boyd K. Packer humorously remarked, "I once asked President Hunter if he had a doctor's book, and if so I wanted to borrow it. He asked why. I said, 'I want to keep it. It seems to me you read through it looking for some major affliction you haven't had, wonder what it would be like, and decide to try it.' " ("President Howard W. Hunter—He Endured to the End," *Ensign*, April 1995, p. 28.) President Gordon B. Hinckley declared, "I believe that [his suffering] went on longer and was more sharp and deep than any of us really knew. He developed a high tolerance for pain and did not complain about it. That he lived so long is a miracle in and of itself. His suffering has comforted and mitigated the pain of many others who suffer. They know that he understood the heaviness of their burdens. He reached out to these with a special kind of love." ("A Prophet Polished and Refined," *Ensign*, April 1995, p. 33.)

For those who desire to sense more deeply the importance and power of temples and temple work in our own lives, President Hunter offers wise counsel and prophetic promises. He shows how the temple provides us with the eternal perspective we need in mortality and should be our ultimate earthly goal.

In his quiet and unassuming way, President Hunter was one who endeavored to humbly go about life's primary task of living a Christlike life. His efforts in this lifelong goal are reflected clearly in his teachings, and they became the major focus of most everything he taught. "President Howard W. Hunter lived as he taught, after the pattern of the Savior whom he served," declared President Thomas S. Monson. "One day in a moment of quiet reflection, President Hunter shared with me his personal philosophy with the expression, 'I feel ours is the mission to serve and to save, to build and to exalt.' He was truly a prophet, a seer, and revelator for our time." ("President Howard W. Hunter: A Man for All Seasons," *Ensign*, April 1995, p. 33.)

On 5 September 1994 the mayor of Jerusalem, Teddy Kollek, was interviewed about his association with President Howard W.

Hunter over the previous several years. His response is very telling of how President Hunter affected people: "With all my high regard for the Mormon Church and its members and the way you all behave—and I saw you individually and I saw you when almost 2,000 came here for the opening of the Orson Hyde Garden . . . —he is even quieter, if possible, more simple, more direct than all of you. And that is very impressive." (As quoted in Mark Scott, "Reflections on Howard W. Hunter in Jerusalem: An Interview with Teddy Kollek," *BYU Studies* 34, no. 4 [1994–95], p. 14.) It is this quiet yet impressive spirit which emanates from the teachings of Howard W. Hunter that will make this volume a powerful force in the lives of those who use it.

In the production of this book, the compiler is especially grateful to Mike Bolander and Jeff Brady, whose help and expertise have greatly assisted in the arranging and organizing of this work. Thanks are given to Dean Robert L. Millet for his helpful suggestions and continued encouragement. Gratitude is expressed to Randall Dixon and the staff at the Church Historical Department for their help in the early stages of this project. The editors at Bookcraft have been especially helpful in the final preparation of the volume. I am blessed to have a wife and children who have been very supportive and have encouraged me to complete this work.

Finally, I am thankful to have had the privilege of studying the teachings of Howard W. Hunter. His example of quiet, humble dedication has been an inspiration. I concur with the resounding words of Elder Jeffrey R. Holland: "Howard W. Hunter was foreordained in the councils of heaven before this world was, and he has been made, fashioned, molded into a prophet of God, as each of his predecessors have been and as each of his successors will be. He has not simply outlived others, nor has he gone through what he has gone through by accident. He is a man of velvet and steel. He [was] called of God." (Church Educational System Book of Mormon Symposium, 9 August 1994, p. 4.)

1

THE
GODHEAD

God the Eternal Father

Who really loves God? He loves the Lord with all his heart who loves nothing in comparison of him, and nothing but in reference to him, who is ready to give up, do, or suffer anything in order to please and glorify him. He loves God with all his soul, or rather with all his life, who is ready to give up life for his sake and to be deprived of the comforts of the world to glorify him. He loves God with all his strength who exerts all the powers of his body and soul in the service of God. He loves God with all his mind who applies himself only to know God and his will, who sees God in all things and acknowledges him in all ways. (65–02, p. 512)

All nature testifies of a God. I, too, know that God lives. There is ample evidence of this fact, but concrete proof is not necessary to those who have faith. All nature portrays the existence of a supreme being. In this material world, we have learned that every building has a builder and everything that is made has a maker. As we look at this Tabernacle, the great organ that has been played for us, the clock on the wall, the camera that carries the image to the world, the lights, the microphones before me, we realize that each of these had its maker. Outside those things made by man, all of nature whispers to my reasoning that there was a creator. I know this to be God. (68–05, pp. 105–6)

There must be a regulating hand in an orderly universe. There is an exactness of order in the universe of which we become conscious. The days come and the nights follow. The tides rise and fall with regularity, the recurring lunar cycle of the moon is exact; the seasons come and go in the sequence of nature. The stars in the sky follow exact repeated orders; the planets and their satellites perform precisely in their relation to their suns. The biologist sees the wonders and the beauty of plant and animal life, and the chemist discovers the mysteries of the elements of the earth; but with or without scientific training, every person becomes aware of a vast universe in which there is intricate exactness in all nature.

When we observe the phenomena of the heavens and the earth, we can come to only one conclusion: these are the effects of some great cause. There can be no design without a designer and nothing built without a builder. For every effect there is a cause. There must be a guiding hand to regulate the universe in its precise order. Are we compelled to admit the reality of a Supreme Being? Millions of people in the world have this deep and abiding conviction. (70–01, p. 33)

Finding the reality of God requires faith and effort. Is God a creation of man's mind, or is man a creation of God? Men struggle with many fundamental questions, but the question as to whether or not God is a reality should take precedence. The approach to the solution of this query differs from that given to scientific research. We are not dealing with a subject of the material realm, but rather of the spiritual.

In order to find God as a reality, we must follow the course which he pointed out for the quest. The path is one that leads upward; it takes faith and effort, and is not the easy course. For this reason many men will not devote themselves to the arduous task of proving to themselves the reality of God. On the contrary, some take the easy path and deny his existence or merely follow the doubter's course of uncertainty. These are the atheists, infidels, free thinkers, skeptics, and agnostics. (70–01, p. 33)

A knowledge of God's reality does not come without effort. It is the general rule that we do not get things of value unless we are willing to pay a price. The scholar does not become learned unless he puts forth the work and effort to succeed. If he is not willing to do so, can he say there is no such thing as scholarship? Musicians, mathematicians, scientists, athletes, and skilled people in many fields spend years in study, practice, and hard work to acquire their ability. Can others who are not willing to make the effort say there are no such things as music, mathematics, science, or athletics? It is just as foolish for man to say there is no God simply because he has not had the inclination to seek him.

History tells us there is a God. Science confirms the fact there is a Supreme Being. Human reasoning persuades us that there is a God. His own revelations to man leave no doubt as to his existence. In order for an individual to obtain unwavering knowledge of the reality of God, he must live the commandments and the doctrines announced by the Savior during his personal ministry. "Jesus answered them, and said, My doctrine is not mine, but his that sent me. If any man will do his will, he shall know of the doctrine, whether it be of God, or whether I speak of myself." (John 7:16–17.) In other words, those who are willing to make the search, apply themselves, and do God's will, will have the knowledge come to them of the reality of God. (70–01, p. 34)

A knowledge of God adds meaning to life. When a man has found God and understands his ways, he learns that nothing in the universe came by chance, but all things resulted from a divinely prearranged plan. What a rich meaning comes into his life! Understanding which surpasses worldly learning is his. . . . If all men could find God and follow his ways, the hearts of men would be turned in love toward their brothers, and nations would be at peace. (70–01, p. 34)

Jesus Christ and the Atonement

Christ did at least two things no other person could do. The great standard! The only sure way! The light and the life of the world! How grateful we should be that God sent his Only Begotten Son to earth to do at least two things that no other person could have done. The first task Christ did as a perfect, sinless Son was to redeem all mankind from the Fall, providing an atonement for Adam's sin and for our own sins if we will accept and follow him. The second great thing he did was to set a perfect example of right living, of kindness and mercy and compassion, in order that all of the rest of mankind might know how to live, know how to improve, and know how to become more godlike. (94–08, p. 5)

Only Christ could serve as the perfect model. The world is full
of people who are willing to tell us, "Do as I say." Surely we have
no lack of advice givers on about every subject. But we have so few
who are prepared to say, "Do as I do." And, of course, only One in
human history could rightfully and properly make that declaration.
History provides many examples of good men and women, but
even the best of mortals are flawed in some way or another. None
could serve as a perfect model nor as an infallible pattern to follow,
however well intentioned they might be.

Only Christ can be our ideal, our "bright and morning star"
(Revelation 22:16). Only he can say without *any* reservation,
"Follow me, learn of me, do the things you have seen me do" . . .
(see Matthew 11:29; 16:24; John 4:13–14; 6:35, 51; 7:37; 13:34;
14:6; 3 Nephi 15:9; 27:21). (94–01, p. 64)

Christ was perfect because he wanted to be. It is important to
remember that Jesus was capable of sinning, that he could have
succumbed, that the plan of life and salvation could have been
foiled, but that he remained true. Had there been no possibility of
his yielding to the enticement of Satan, there would have been no
real test, no genuine victory in the result. If he had been stripped
of the faculty to sin, he would have been stripped of his very
agency. It was he who had come to safeguard and ensure the
agency of man. He had to retain the capacity and ability to sin had
he willed so to do. As Paul wrote, "Though he were a Son, yet
learned he obedience by the things which he suffered" (Hebrews
5:8); and he "was in all points tempted like as we are, yet without
sin" (Hebrews 4:15). He was perfect and sinless, not because he had
to be, but rather because he clearly and determinedly wanted to
be. As the Doctrine and Covenants records, "He suffered temptations but gave no heed unto them" (D&C 20:22). (76–02, p. 19)

Jesus is the Son of God. I am grateful today for my affiliation
with a people who have a firm conviction that God lives, that Jesus
is the Christ; and I bear witness to you that the story of the babe
born in the manger at Bethlehem is not a myth of the past, but
that Jesus, the Son of God, was born of Mary into mortality; that
he lived among men; that he died upon the cross and was resurrected; that he actually and truly lives today; and that he is a personal being and is the Savior of the world. (59–04)

We must not deny the divinity of Christ. Although [Christ's] teachings and attributes have been of inestimable value to the human family, they must be considered as by-products of those things that really command our veneration and our worship—his atonement for our sins and his resurrection from the dead. Unfortunately, too many men have worshipped at the shrine of Christ's attributes and ethics but have denied the divinity of their Redeemer. (83–05, p. 70)

The Savior never gave expecting to receive. Never did the Savior give in expectation of receiving. He gave freely and lovingly, and his gifts were of inestimable value. He gave eyes to the blind, ears to the deaf, and legs to the lame; cleanliness to the unclean, wholeness to the infirm, and breath to the lifeless. His gifts were opportunity to the downtrodden, freedom to the oppressed, forgiveness to the repentant, hope to the despairing, and light in the darkness. He gave us his love, his service, and his life. And most important, he gave us and all mortals resurrection, salvation, and eternal life. We should strive to give as he gave. To give of oneself is a holy gift. (See Spencer W. Kimball, *The Wondrous Gift* [Salt Lake City: Deseret Book Co., 1978], p. 2.) (94–20)

We should understand and accept the Savior's offer to take his yoke upon us. Christ issued a profound invitation in what Elder James E. Talmage has appropriately called "one of the grandest outpourings of spiritual emotion known to man" (*Jesus the Christ,* 3rd ed. [Salt Lake City: The Church of Jesus Christ of Latter-day Saints, 1916], p. 258). These are the words of the Master used in making this appeal:

"Come unto me, all ye that labour and are heavy laden, and I will give you rest.

"Take my yoke upon you, and learn of me; for I am meek and lowly in heart: and ye shall find rest unto your souls.

"For my yoke is easy, and my burden is light." (Matthew 11:28–30.) . . .

"Take my yoke upon you," he pleads. In biblical times the yoke was a device of great assistance to those who tilled the field. It allowed the strength of a second animal to be linked and coupled with the effort of a single animal, sharing and reducing the heavy labor of the plow or wagon. A burden that was overwhelming or perhaps impossible for one to bear could be equitably and comfortably borne by two bound together with a common yoke. His yoke requires a great and earnest effort, but for those who truly are converted, the yoke is easy and the burden becomes light.

Why face life's burdens alone, Christ asks, or why face them with temporal support that will quickly falter? To the heavy laden it is Christ's yoke, it is the power and peace of standing side by side with a God that will provide the support, balance, and the strength to meet our challenges and endure our tasks here in the hardpan field of mortality.

Obviously, the personal burdens of life vary from person to person, but every one of us has them. Furthermore, each trial in life is tailored to the individual's capacities and needs as known by a loving Father in Heaven. Of course, some sorrows are brought on by the sins of a world not following the counsel of that Father in Heaven. Whatever the reason, none of us seems to be completely free from life's challenges. To one and all, Christ said, in effect: As long as we all must bear some burden and shoulder some yoke, why not let it be mine? My promise to you is that my yoke is easy, and my burden is light. (90–07, pp. 17–18)

The Savior took upon himself more than our sins. Christ knows the full weight of our sins, for he carried it first. If our burden is not sin nor temptation, but illness or poverty or rejection, it's the same. He knows. Alma saw his day, and testified:

"And he shall go forth, suffering pains and afflictions and temptations of every kind; . . . he will take upon him the pains and the sicknesses of his people. . . .

"And he will take upon him death, that he may loose the bands of death which bind his people; and he will take upon him their infirmities." (Alma 7:11–12.) (89–03, p. 115)

The Savior suffered for our sins, and sicknesses, in part to perfect his mercy. We are indebted to the prophet Alma for our knowledge of the full measure of His suffering: "He shall go forth, suffering pains and afflictions and temptations of every kind; and this that the word might be fulfilled which saith he will take upon him the pains and the sicknesses of his people.

"And he will take upon him death, that he may loose the bands of death which bind his people; and he will take upon him their infirmities, that his bowels may be filled with mercy, according to the flesh, that he may know according to the flesh how to succor his people according to their infirmities." (Alma 7:11–12.)

Think of it! When his body was taken from the cross and hastily placed in a borrowed tomb, he, the sinless Son of God, had already taken upon him not only the sins and temptations of every human soul who will repent, but all of our sickness and grief and pain of every kind. He suffered these afflictions as we suffer them, according to the flesh. He suffered them all. He did this to perfect his mercy and his ability to lift us above every earthly trial. (88–03, pp. 16–17)

Without the Atonement there would be no hope of eternal life. Modernists dispute that the Master voluntarily offered himself to atone for the sins of mankind, and they deny that there was in fact such an atonement. It is our firm belief that it is a reality, and nothing is more important in the entire divine plan of salvation than the atoning sacrifice of Jesus Christ. We believe that salvation comes because of the Atonement. In its absence the whole plan of creation would come to naught. . . .

Without this atoning sacrifice, temporal death would be the end, and there would be no resurrection and no purpose in our spiritual lives. There would be no hope of eternal life. (68–05, p. 106)

Spiritual maturity comes when we understand the Atonement. I am grateful for the knowledge we have that God lives, that he is our Eternal Father and that his Son, Jesus Christ, is the Savior of the world. When we come to the point where we understand the atoning sacrifice of the Master, we are approaching a spiritual maturity. I don't think spiritual maturity ever comes to us until we understand the true significance of the atoning sacrifice of the Master by which he gave his life that we might have life everlasting. When we understand the principle, we realize this is the greatest of love—that the Master laid down his life for us, that the grave will not be the end, but that we will live again. We have the additional joy of knowing that not only will we live again after death, but we will have those with us that we love if we have accomplished in mortality those ordinances that make those relationships permanent throughout eternity. Of course, we must so live our lives that we can have the fulfillment of those ordinances which are performed. (79–06)

The gospel of Jesus Christ is the greatest message we will ever hear. The message I speak of . . . is simple and beautiful and magnificent. . . . [It] has been referred to as the greatest, the most exciting, the most significant and important that we will ever hear. It has to do with the "good news"—the gospel of Jesus Christ.

Specifically, it is that Jesus of Nazareth, the same who was born of Mary in Bethlehem some two thousand years ago, is the Savior of all mankind. We know, and testify to the world, that he lived a truly perfect and exemplary life, that he suffered for our sins in the Garden of Gethsemane, that he gave his life for us by being crucified on a cross, and that he was resurrected after three days—as he said he would be. The final part of this good news is that he will return at some future time to gather in his own. (83–01, p. 15)

What does it mean to rely upon the merits of the Savior? Nephi asks, "After ye have gotten into this strait and narrow path, I would ask if all is done? Behold, I say unto you, Nay; for ye have not come thus far save it were by the word of Christ with unshaken faith in him, [now, note these words:] relying wholly upon the merits of him who is mighty to save." (2 Nephi 31:19.) What does it mean to rely wholly on the merits of our Savior? It means that no man or woman can receive eternal life without the Atonement of Jesus Christ being fully efficacious in one's life. (88–04)

The Atonement was an act of supreme love. We must always remember that the Atonement of Jesus Christ was a foreordained assignment by our Heavenly Father to redeem his children after their fallen state. It was an act of love by our Heavenly Father to permit his Only Begotten to make an atoning sacrifice. And it was a supreme act of love by his beloved Son to carry out the Atonement.

I have stood in the Garden of Gethsemane on many occasions. I've contemplated in my mind the suffering, the agony of the Savior. That agony that was experienced when our Heavenly Father permitted him, in a way our minds cannot even comprehend, to take upon himself the pain and sins of all mankind. My soul was filled with sorrow as I've thought of his great sacrifice for mankind.

I've stood beneath Golgotha, the place of the skull, and contemplated the humiliation of the crucifixion which led to our Savior's mortal death, but which brought to pass his and all mankind's immortality. And again my soul has been subdued.

And I've stood in front of the garden tomb and imagined that glorious day of resurrection when the Savior emerged from the tomb alive, resurrected, immortal. In that contemplation my heart has swelled with joy.

Through these experiences I've felt to pour out my soul in thanksgiving and appreciation to our Heavenly Father for the love which he and his Son have given to us through the glorious atoning sacrifice. (88–04)

2

THE PLAN
OF SALVATION

Salvation is an individual matter. The atonement that Christ wrought was in behalf of every individual. However, each must work out his or her own salvation, for we are not saved collectively. The worthiness of one's friends or family will not save him or her. There must be an individual effort. While it is true that worthy couples will obtain ultimate exaltation in the celestial kingdom, each man and each woman sealed in an eternal relationship must be individually worthy of that blessing. (89–02, p. 76)

The Premortal Existence

The brotherhood of man is literal. The brotherhood of man is literal. We are all of one blood and the literal spirit offspring of our eternal Heavenly Father. Before we came to earth we belonged to his eternal family. We associated and knew each other there. Our common paternity makes us not only literal sons and daughters of eternal parentage, but literal brothers and sisters as well. This is a fundamental teaching of The Church of Jesus Christ of Latter-day Saints. (79–01, p. 32)

Agency played an important part in the premortal world. Part of our reassurance about the free, noble, and progressing spirit of man comes from the glorious realization that we all existed and had our identities, and our agency, long before we came to this world. To some that will be a new thought, but the Bible teaches clearly just such an eternal view of life, a life stretching back before this world was and stretching forward into the eternities ahead.

God said to Jeremiah, "Before I formed thee in the belly I knew thee; and before thou camest forth out of the womb I sanctified thee, and I ordained thee a prophet unto the nations" (Jeremiah 1:5). At another time God reminded Job that "all the sons of God shouted for joy" (Job 38:7) before there was yet any man or woman on the earth God was creating. The Apostle Paul taught that God the Father chose us "before the foundation of the world" (Ephesians 1:4).

Where and when did all of this happen? Well, it happened long before man's mortal birth. It happened in a great premortal existence where we developed our identities and increased our spiritual capabilities by exercising our agency and making important choices. We developed our intelligence and learned to love the truth, and we prepared to come to earth to continue our progress.

Our Father in Heaven wanted our growth to continue in mortality and to be enhanced by our freedom to choose and learn. He also wanted us to exercise our faith and our will, especially with a new physical body to master and control. But we know from both ancient and modern revelation that Satan wished to deny us our independence and agency in that now-forgotten moment long ago, even as he wishes to deny them this very hour. Indeed, Satan violently opposed the freedom of choice offered by the Father, so violently that John in the Revelation described "war in heaven" (Revelation 12:7) over the matter. Satan would have coerced us, and he would have robbed us of that most precious of gifts if he could: our freedom to choose a divine future and the exaltation we all hope to obtain.

Through Christ and his valiant defense of our Father's plan, the course of agency and eternal aspirations prevailed. In that crucial, premortal setting, a major milestone was passed, a monumental victory was won. As a result, we would be allowed to continue to pursue what President David O. McKay once described as the "eternal principle of progress." (In Conference Report, April 1940, p. 118.) (89–06, pp. 17–18)

There are premortal principles that affect mortality. From those passages of scripture [Acts 17:26, Deuteronomy 32:8, Acts 10:34–35] we learn these basic principles: First, all men on earth are of one blood—we stem from common ancestors, Adam and Eve; second, God, our Father, in his omniscient wisdom, determined premortally the nation in which we were to live; third, nationalities are apparently circumscribed in relation to the House of Israel; fourth, our Father does not favor one people over another, but accepts all those of every nation who fear him and work righteousness. (79–01, p. 33)

We developed spiritual talents before we came to earth. While on earth, we are dual beings comprised of a physical body and a spirit. Our bodies are of recent origin and come to us from mortal elements. Our spirits were begotten by God and have had an extensive period of growth and development in the spirit world, where we came to know God and to comprehend the nature of spiritual realities. Some of our Father's sons developed spiritual talents to a marked degree, and they were foreordained to spiritual callings in mortality whereby their talents would be utilized to administer salvation to our Father's children. (83–06)

A Mortal Versus an Eternal Perspective

Mortality is the schoolroom of eternity. We know where we have been and we know where we are going. We know also that the mortal existence is the schoolroom of eternity where we come to learn the lessons the Lord would have us learn and to be tried and tested. We are told that we are not to question the ways of the Lord because he in his great wisdom has reasons for that which comes to us in life. Ours is not to question but to have faith in him—an unfailing faith, a faith that endures to the end. (61–04)

We know where we came from. Holy writ tells us that we were born the spiritual children of our Heavenly Father, that we dwelt with him in a spiritual existence before our birth into mortality. The divine object of our coming to earth is to obtain a body of flesh and bones, to learn by the experiences which come to us in this mortal life the difference between good and evil, and to accomplish those things which the Lord commanded. Thus this life is the schoolroom of our journey through eternity. There is work to do and lessons to learn that we might prepare and qualify ourselves to go into the spiritual existence to follow. (61–07, p. 963)

All things are spiritual to the Lord. The Lord makes no distinction between temporal and spiritual commandments, for he has said that all of his commandments are spiritual (see D&C 29:34–35). When we understand the plan of life and salvation, this becomes evident to us. Mortality is just one part of our eternal life. . . .

Man distinguishes between the temporal and the spiritual, probably because living in mortality between the spiritual pre-existence and the spiritual life hereafter, he fails to recognize the full significance of his activities during the years he spends on earth. To the Lord everything is both spiritual and temporal, and the laws he gives are consequently spiritual, because they concern spiritual beings.

Every phase of our life, therefore, becomes the concern of the Church. The great welfare program of the Church demonstrates this principle. The Church is interested in our social and our recreational needs, education, family life, our business affairs, and all that we do.

There is no way we can separate the activities of worship on the Sabbath day from the many pursuits of the weekday by calling one religious and the other temporal. Both are spiritual. God has ordained them thus, for they consist of our thoughts and actions as we wend our way through this part of eternity. Thus our business transactions, our daily labors, our trade or profession, or whatever we do become part of living the gospel. (61–07, pp. 962–63)

All have spiritual sight. Each of us has spiritual eyes which are the counterpart of our natural eyes. We were first created spiritually and then our bodies were created as the covering of our spirit. We are told that in our first estate we walked by sight. This was through the vision of our spiritual eyes, because we had not yet been given bodies with natural eyes.

All men have spiritual sight, but are not always privileged to use such sight unless quickened by the Spirit of the Lord. (60–11)

We need a gospel perspective to make life-changing resolutions. In working with most of us, God has our vision or perspective come line upon line and precept upon precept, here a little and there a little, until the complete picture is before us.

When an individual has the light of the gospel, certainly progression in the right direction is made much, much easier. Our paths may frequently be strewn with difficulties and uncertainties, but the Light of Christ, illuminating the way, still gives assurance that the direction is correct. So it goes without saying that life-changing resolutions need a gospel vision or perspective, they need to be built on a foundation of stone, the rock of revelation. Resolutions without this underpinning are likely to be shortsighted and short-lived. So we should ponder gospel principles carefully as we plot our course through this year and throughout our lives. (92–01, p. 43)

Today is part of eternity. Too often we think about eternity as something that is a long way off. Eternity is today and for a long time. Eternity was this morning, eternity is this afternoon. Eternity will be tonight and tomorrow and the days that follow and the years that make their course. We are on that road today, and shouldn't those moments be filled with sweetness in planning, in loving, and all of the things that make life beautiful? (79–07)

There is a distinction between immortality and eternal life. Immortality and eternal life are sometimes erroneously used interchangeably, but they are separate and distinct. Immortality is a gift to all men whether they have pursued good or evil in this earth life. This comes as the result of the atoning sacrifice of the Master, whereby all men shall be resurrected and live again. Eternal life, on the other hand, will be received only by those who live the fullness of the gospel and keep the commandments of the Lord (see D&C 29:43–44; 14:7). (80–02)

As we evaluate our lives we should consider the conditions under which we labored. As we evaluate our lives, it is important that we look, not only at our accomplishments, but also at the conditions under which we have labored. We are all different and unique individuals; we have each had different starting points in the race of life; we each have a unique mixture of talents and skills; we each have our own set of challenges and constraints to contend with. Therefore, our judgment of ourselves and our achievements should not merely include the size or magnitude and number of our accomplishments; it should also include the conditions that have existed and the effect that our efforts have had on others. (82–02, p. 20)

Man has great potential. My spiritual reasoning tells me that because God is an exalted being, holy and good, that man's supreme goal is to be like him. (60–07, p. 5)

We are eternal beings passing through an earthly estate. We are children of God, our Eternal Father. We are eternal beings, at the present time passing through an earthly estate, one of the several successive estates of a continuing eternal existence. Life did not begin with birth into this mortal sphere nor does it end with death. As children of God we lived with him in a premortal state, and there we were taught and prepared to come to earth where we would receive bodies and be given the opportunity for spiritual growth. (80–02)

Physical Death and the Resurrection

Death is a part of living. Death is part of life. Dying is part of living. As we go through life we know this event will come to each of us. The time of the event is the only uncertainty. We should each live so when that time comes we will be prepared to meet our maker and have him say to us, "Well done my good and faithful servant."

Brigham Young once said, "Build to make it last for a thousand years, but live each day as though it were to be the last." . . .

Occasions such as this challenge each of us to reflect upon our lives. Are we ready to follow this same course? We think of the things we have put off, the kindness we intended to express, the letters we were going to write. Are our lives in order through righteous living and keeping the commandments? Our resolution should be to so order our lives that we will be ready and not found wanting. (61–04)

Death is part of living and a continuation of our eternal existence. (90–01)

When death comes, will we be ready? In the quiet of this chapel today, our souls have been on their knees. We have contemplated the uncertainties of life and the certainty of death. Each of us in his turn will follow the same course—only the point of time is the difference. Will we be ready? Will the things we intend to accomplish be completed? Will we make right the little wrongs and replace the harsh words with kindness before our call comes? Will we accept the fullness of the gospel of Jesus Christ by following his teachings, keeping his commandments, being of service to our fellowman, ready to enter the tomb, partake of the glorious resurrection, and stand at the judgment as worthy servants? (84–01)

The resurrection is the greatest of all the Savior's miracles. Surely the resurrection is the center of every Christian's faith; it is the greatest of all of the miracles performed by the Savior of the world. Without it, we are indeed left hopeless. (88–03, p. 16)

What is the nature of a resurrected being? Now follows one of the most misunderstood and controversial statements made by Paul:
"So also is the resurrection of the dead. It is sown in corruption; it is raised in incorruption:
"It is sown in dishonour; it is raised in glory: it is sown in weakness; it is raised in power:
"It is sown a natural body; it is raised a spiritual body. There is a natural body, and there is a spiritual body." (1 Corinthians 15:42–44.)
Because Paul distinguishes between a natural body and a spiritual body, and had previously referred to the seed planted in the ground, a false conclusion is reached from the analogy. It is argued that the seed itself is not harvested—it dies in the ground and there comes forth a new plant; therefore, this is so with the body which is buried in the ground—it comes forth a spiritual body, something new and different. This appears to be strengthened by the fact that Paul adds: "Now this I say, brethren, that flesh and blood cannot inherit the kingdom of God. . . . " (1 Corinthians 15:50.)
Now let me point up the fallacy of this reasoning by this statement from scripture:
"And the spirit and the body are the soul of man.
"And the resurrection from the dead is the redemption of the soul." (D&C 88:15–16.)

There is a separation of the spirit and the body at the time of death. The resurrection will again unite the spirit with the body, and the body becomes a spiritual body, one of flesh and bones but quickened by the spirit instead of blood. Thus, our bodies after the resurrection, quickened by the spirit, shall become immortal and never die. This is the meaning of the statements of Paul that "there is a natural body, and there is a spiritual body" and "that flesh and blood cannot inherit the kingdom of God." The natural body is flesh and blood, but quickened by the spirit instead of blood, it can and will enter the kingdom.

The best example of the validity of this position—and which portrays the truth of the resurrection—is the happening which we commemorate at this Easter season, when Jesus came forth from the tomb, the first fruits of the resurrection. The record tells us he appeared to many and they recognized him, the most specific example occurring that first Easter day when ten of the Twelve were together, and "Jesus himself stood in the midst of them, and saith unto them, Peace be unto you.

"But they were terrified and affrighted, and supposed that they had seen a spirit.

"And he said unto them, Why are ye troubled? and why do thoughts arise in your hearts?

"Behold my hands and my feet, that it is I myself: handle me, and see; for a spirit hath not flesh and bones, as ye see me have.

"And when he had thus spoken, he shewed them his hands and his feet." (Luke 24:36–40.)

Not a spirit, but a body reunited with the spirit—a spiritual body as defined by Paul. (69–05, pp. 107–8)

The Resurrection is a historical fact. The testimony of those who saw [Jesus] as a living person after his death has never been contradicted. He appeared at least ten or eleven times: to Mary Magdalene and the other women in the garden, to the two disciples on the road to Emmaus, to Peter at Jerusalem, to the apostles when Thomas was absent and again when he was present, to the apostles at the Sea of Galilee, and on a mountain to over 500 brethren at once, to James the brother of the Lord, and to the apostles at the time of the ascension.

We can come to only one conclusion: the resurrection is a historical fact amply proved by authenticated documentary evidence and the testimony of competent witnesses. The man-made theories devised to discredit are without substantiation, and any discrepancies in the narrative are too slight to be given weight. . . .

I bear witness that Jesus is the Christ, the resurrection and the life, and he that believeth in him, though he were dead, shall live. (63–02, p. 513)

The resurrection is the most crucial doctrine of Christianity. The doctrine of the resurrection is the single most fundamental and crucial doctrine in the Christian religion. It cannot be overemphasized, nor can it be disregarded.

Without the resurrection, the gospel of Jesus Christ becomes a litany of wise sayings and seemingly unexplainable miracles: but sayings and miracles with no ultimate triumph. No, the ultimate triumph is in the ultimate miracle: for the first time in the history of mankind, one who was dead raised himself into living immortality. He *was* the Son of God, the Son of our immortal Father in Heaven, and his triumph over physical and spiritual death is the good news every Christian tongue should speak. (86–02, p. 16)

The empty tomb is the monument of the eternal triumph. Against the medals and monuments of centuries of men's fleeting victories stands the only monument necessary to mark the eternal triumph—an empty garden tomb. (86–02, p. 15)

The Savior conquered that which no other could. Alexander the Great, king of Macedon, pupil of Aristotle, conqueror of most of the known world in his time, was one of the world's great young leaders. After years of exercising military pomp and prowess and after extending his kingdom from Macedonia to Egypt and from Cyprus to India, he wept when there seemed to be no more world to conquer. Then, as evidence of just how ephemeral such power is, Alexander caught a fever and died at thirty-three years of age. The vast kingdom he had gained virtually died with him.

Quite a different young leader also died at what seems such an untimely age of thirty-three. He likewise was a king, a pupil, and a conqueror. Yet he received no honors from man, achieved no territorial conquests, rose to no political station. So far as we know, he never held a sword nor wore even a single piece of armor. But the

Kingdom he established still flourishes some two thousand years later. His power was not of this world.

The differences between Alexander and this equally young Nazarene are many. But the greatest difference is in their ultimate victories. Alexander conquered lands, peoples, principalities, and earthly kingdoms. But he who is called the Perfect Leader, he who was and is the Light and Life of the world—Jesus Christ the Son of God—conquered what neither Alexander nor any other could defeat or overcome: Jesus of Nazareth conquered death. (86–02, p. 15)

3

PRINCIPLES OF
THE GOSPEL

The plan of salvation is the gospel of Jesus Christ. The gospel, as brought to the earth by the Savior, is the good news of salvation; therefore, the plan of salvation is the gospel of Jesus Christ. . . .

As we study the scriptures carefully, the understanding comes to us that the basic elements or principles of the gospel taught by the Master consist of the following steps:

1. We must develop within ourselves a faith in Jesus Christ, that he is the Son of God and Savior of the world.

2. We must repent of wrongdoings and be willing to follow his teachings.

3. We must be baptized according to instruction for a remission of past sins.

4. We must receive the Holy Ghost by the laying on of hands.

5. We must continue in righteous living to the end of mortal life. (75–01, p. 37)

Ethics alone cannot lead one to exaltation. If we should eliminate from our religious beliefs the doctrine of the atonement and resurrection of Jesus Christ and the resurrection of mankind, there would be nothing left but a code of ethics. The propositions of ethics may be noble, but they lack those elements of the gospel that lead men to eternal exaltation. Philosophy and theology may be interesting and give us lofty concepts, and we may become inspired by profound thinking, but Christian faith is based upon the simplicity of the gospel, the example, the life, and the teachings of Jesus Christ. . . . In a society of turmoil, immorality, freethinking, and questioning of the reality of God, we reach out for the simplicity of the gospel of Jesus Christ—the gospel which gives to us comfort, hope, a desire for righteousness, and peace in one's heart. (69–05, p. 108)

Obedience

Surely the Lord loves, more than anything else, an unwavering determination to obey his counsel. (82–03, p. 58)

The principle of obedience allows for agency. Obedience is often referred to as the first law of heaven. It is a requirement and therefore a principle of the gospel for which all persons will be held accountable. Like other principles of the gospel, we will not be compelled, however, to be obedient against our will. The basic principle of free agency gives us the election to obey or disobey. (78–02)

Obedience is the most genuine way to show our love for God. We need to keep the commandments of God, and we need to encourage all to do so. Obedience is the most genuine way to show our love for God. "If ye love me, keep my commandments" (John 14:15), the Savior taught. (94–06, pp. 72–73)

Belief alone is not sufficient. When speaking to the multitudes [the Savior] said:

"Not every one that saith unto me, Lord, Lord, shall enter into the kingdom of heaven; but he that doeth the will of my Father which is in heaven" (Matthew 7:21).

As I read these words, it seems to me that the Lord is saying: Just because a person may acknowledge my authority and love me, or have a belief in my divine nature, or merely express faith in my teachings, or the atoning sacrifice I made, does not mean he shall enter the kingdom of heaven or attain a higher degree of exaltation. By implication he is saying: Belief alone is not sufficient. Then he expressly adds, "but he that doeth the will of my Father." In other words, he that labors and prunes the vineyard that it may bring forth good fruit. (90–01)

Obedience must always precede knowledge. You will remember when Adam was driven from the Garden of Eden he offered sacrifices. "An angel of the Lord appeared unto Adam, saying: Why dost thou offer sacrifices unto the Lord? And Adam said unto him: I know not, save the Lord commanded me." (Moses 5:6.) Then the angel explained to him the meaning of sacrifices. Obedience must always precede knowledge. If we are obedient to our assigned responsibility, knowledge will follow. We are prone to discount things we cannot understand. Few of us understand the power of the atomic bomb, the heat, the destruction; nevertheless it is a reality. (54–03)

Live in obedience to the gospel. If all men would live in obedience to [gospel] principles in their daily lives and in their dealings with each other, and if this same code would prevail among those who are in leadership among the peoples and nations of the world, righteousness would prevail, peace would return, and the blessings of the Lord would be showered down upon his children.

Righteous living must start in the lives of individuals. Each of us has the duty. (61–07, p. 963)

There is no happiness in the violation of laws. Should we observe the law because we are commanded to do so, or should we obey the law because of a real desire?

I recall a young man in our stake when I served as a stake president. He traveled around with a crowd which thought it was smart to do things that were not right. On a few occasions he was caught in some minor violations.

One day I got a call from the police station and was told he was being held because of a traffic violation. He had been caught speeding, as he had on a few other occasions prior to this time. Knowing the things he was doing might prevent him from going on a mission, he straightened up, and when he was nineteen years of age he received his call.

I shall never forget the talk we had when he returned. He told me while he was in the mission field he had often thought of the trouble he had caused by the mistaken belief that the violation of little things was not important. But a great change had come into his life. He had come to the realization that there was no happiness or pleasure in violation of the law, whether it be God's law or whether it be the laws which society imposes upon us.

He said to me, "When I drive a car now and the speed limit is sixty miles an hour, I feel it is morally wrong to drive a single mile faster."

I was impressed by the great change that had come over this young man while he served on his mission and studied moral principles. How unfortunate it is that he had to learn his lesson the hard way, but what a great blessing comes when there is the realization that one cannot be in violation and feel good about that conduct. (62–13, p. 3)

The Ten Commandments involve two major categories. The Decalogue or the ten laws were inscribed on two tablets of stone. Just how they were arranged is not known, but most students divide them into two sets. The first division consists of those laws which are concerned with man's relation to God. These are: no other gods, no graven images, no blasphemy, and keep the Sabbath. Some have included honor thy parents, while others have put this in the category of the last five, which are the laws encompassing a system of moral duties to others—thou shalt not kill, commit adultery, steal, bear false witness, or covet.

Apparently the Savior had these two groups of laws in mind, the first defining man's duty to God and the second providing for a duty to neighbors, when the lawyer asked him: "Master, which is the great commandment in the law?

"Jesus said unto him, Thou shalt love the Lord thy God with all thy heart, and with all thy soul, and with all thy mind.

"This is the first and great commandment.

"And the second is like unto it, Thou shalt love thy neighbour as thyself.

"On these two commandments hang all the law and the prophets." (Matthew 22:36–40.)

This clear, concise, unmistakable restatement of the Decalogue reduces the ten laws, the "thou shalt nots," as they are often called, to two simple admonitions containing the element of love—love the Lord and love thy neighbor. (65–02, p. 512)

Laws govern our growth. The laws governing mental or social or spiritual development are as immutable and unswerving in their spheres as are the laws governing physical development. . . .

It is a foolish thing, a self-deceiving thing, to attempt to reap success to any endeavor by cramming or by any shortcut method. You cannot force the physical growth process overnight; neither can you force the mental growth process. People grow mentally, socially, emotionally, and spiritually only to the degree they obey on a daily basis the laws governing such growth.

The Lord tells us this clearly and powerfully:

"There is a law, irrevocably decreed in heaven before the foundations of this world, upon which all blessings are predicated—

"And when we obtain any blessing from God, it is by obedience to that law upon which it is predicated." (D&C 130:20–21.) (66–01, p. 6)

Obedience requires that we search the scriptures to know the law. In order to be obedient to the law of the gospel and be obedient to the teachings of Jesus Christ, we must first understand the law and ascertain the will of the Lord. This is accomplished best by searching and studying the scriptures and the words of the prophets. In this way we become familiar with what God has revealed to man. (78–02)

The supreme test is our willingness to be totally obedient. This brings us to the supreme test. Are we willing to become totally obedient to God's law? There comes a time in our lives when a definite decision must be made.

Obedience is not tested when life is calm and pleasant and when we are deriving spiritual satisfaction from doing good; but when thoughts or pressures persuade us to act in a way contrary to God's commandments, then obedience is put to the test. (78–02)

Prerequisites to obtaining eternal life. If keeping the commandments is a prerequisite to the obtaining of eternal life, then some of the things that a man must do are as follows:

1. Have a belief in Jesus Christ and accept the principles of his gospel.

2. Be baptized, receive the Holy Ghost, and live to be worthy of his companionship.

3. Receive the Melchizedek Priesthood, magnify an assigned office therein, and merit this promise of the Lord—"All that my Father hath shall be given unto him" (D&C 84:38).

4. Enter into and keep the new and everlasting covenant of marriage.

5. Keep all the commandments and endure to the end.

One of the purposes of this mortal life is to give us the opportunity to prepare to meet God and go on with him in eternal life by living the fullness of the gospel law. (80–02)

The Lord tells us how to encourage more faithful living of the commandments. Our world cries out for more disciplined living of the commandments of God. But the way we are to encourage that, as the Lord told the Prophet Joseph in the wintry depths of Liberty Jail, is "by persuasion, by long-suffering, by gentleness and meekness, and by love unfeigned; . . . without hypocrisy, and without guile" (D&C 121:41–42). (94–08, p. 2)

Acquiring Faith

Faith is centered in Jesus Christ. Faith in the Lord Jesus Christ brings us to a knowledge of the reality of his atoning sacrifice. We have need to be taught and to understand this first principle. (75–01, p. 39)

Faith is required for a divine reason. Faith is the assurance of the existence of a truth even though it is not evident or cannot be proved by positive evidence.

Suppose that all things could be proven by demonstrative evidence. What then would become of the element of faith? There would be no need for faith and it would be eliminated, giving rise then to this query: If faith is the first step or principle of the gospel and is eliminated, what happens to the gospel plan? The very foundation will crumble. I submit that there is a divine reason why all things cannot be proven by concrete evidence. (75–01, p. 38)

One must have faith to discover God. Whether seeking for knowledge of scientific truths or to discover God, one must have faith. This becomes the starting point. Faith has been defined in many ways, but the most classic definition was given by the author of the letter to the Hebrews in these meaningful words: "Now faith is the substance of things hoped for, the evidence of things not seen" (Hebrews 11:1). In other words, faith makes us confident of what we hope for and convinced of what we do not see. The scientist does not see molecules, atoms, or electrons, yet he knows they exist. He does not see electricity, radiation, or magnetism, but he knows these are unseen realities. In like manner, those who earnestly seek for God do not see him, but they know of his reality by faith. It is more than hope. Faith makes it a conviction—an evidence of things not seen. (74–05, p. 97)

Faith is a requirement in a righteous life. Faith has always been a necessary condition of a righteous life. (62–12, p. 914)

A definition of faith. The classic example of faith is ascribed to the Apostle Paul in his Epistle to the Hebrews: "Now faith is the substance of things hoped for, the evidence of things not seen" (Hebrews 11:1).

This statement does not presuppose a perfect knowledge, but describes faith as that which gives to one an assurance or a confidence in things which are yet in the future. These things may be in existence, but it is through faith they are realized. Faith gives a feeling of confidence in that which is not visible or susceptible of positive proof. . . .

Those who lose or lack faith, live in the past—there is loss of hope for the future. What a great change comes into the life of one who finds an abiding faith to give assurance and confidence. (62–12, pp. 914–15)

Faith can stand in the place of tangible evidence. There is no positive, concrete, tangible evidence that God lives, yet millions have a knowledge that he does through that faith which constitutes the evidence of things unseen. Many say to the missionaries, "I would accept of baptism if I could believe that Joseph Smith was visited by the Father and the Son." For this fact there is no positive, concrete, tangible evidence, but to those who are touched by the Spirit, faith will stand in the place of such evidence of things unseen. Remember the words of the crucified Master as he stood before Thomas: "Blessed are they that have not seen, and yet have believed" (John 20:29).

To believe is to see.

I add my witness to the testimonies of the thousands of missionaries that God does live, that Jesus is the Savior of the world, that those who will believe through faith will be caused to see. (62–12, p. 915)

Honest doubts can be resolved. I have sympathy for young men and young women when honest doubts enter their minds and they engage in the great conflict of resolving doubts. These doubts can be resolved, if they have an honest desire to know the truth, by exercising moral, spiritual, and mental effort. They will emerge from the conflict into a firmer, stronger, larger faith because of the struggle. They have gone from a simple, trusting faith, through doubt and conflict, into a solid substantial faith which ripens into testimony. (60–10, p. 948)

Everyone, to a degree, lives by faith. Hopes and desires often fail to materialize with many of us because we lack faith—the one great motivating force which makes all things possible.

Everyone, to a degree, lives by faith. In the spring the farmer plows his fields and sows them with seed. It is his hope, of course, that the seed will grow, mature and produce a harvest. But it is more than hope. It is faith that motivates him to plant his field. Without faith he would never commence. This is true of all our pursuits in life. We would never take the first step in any activity nor pursuit unless we had faith that we would succeed. (60–01, p. 42)

Faith is complete confidence. The classic definition of Paul that "faith is the substance of things hoped for, the evidence of things not seen" (Hebrews 11:1) was explained by the Prophet Joseph Smith in these words: "From this we learn that faith is the assurance which men have of the existence of things which they have not seen, and the principle of action in all intelligent beings." (Lectures on Faith, Lecture First, paragraph 9.) James Moffatt uses these words in his translation of the Bible: "Now faith means we are confident of what we hope for, convinced of what we do not see" (Moffatt's Translation). We cannot have faith without belief, but we may believe and still lack faith. Faith is complete confidence, and nothing is impossible to the person who backs hope and desire with faith. (60–01, p. 42)

Faith is the road to exaltation. Faith in God is the beginning of true religion. "Without faith it is impossible to please him: for he that cometh to God must believe that he is, and that he is a rewarder of them that diligently seek him." (Hebrews 11:6.)

The supreme achievement of life is to find God and to know that he lives. Like any other worthy accomplishment, this can only be obtained by those who will believe and have faith in that which at first may not be apparent. This is the road to exaltation. (60–01, p. 43)

There are four pillars of our faith. As I have contemplated the foundation laid by the early Saints, I have reviewed with reverence the sacrifice and devotion which they showed for the cause of truth. The pillars of their faith are still resident with us as a people today. We, like the early Saints, believe and testify, as the first pillar of our faith, that the Prophet Joseph Smith did indeed see the Father and the Son in the grove of trees in the spring of 1820. Said he, "I had actually seen a light, and in the midst of that light I saw two Personages, and they did in reality speak to me" (JS—H 1:25). . . .

We share with our early brothers and sisters a witness and testimony of the Book of Mormon, Another Testament of Jesus Christ. This represents the second pillar of our faith. It is through reading and studying the Book of Mormon, and prayerfully seeking confirmation of its contents, that we receive a testimony that Joseph Smith was a prophet of God and that the Church of Jesus Christ has been restored to the earth. How thankful we are for the efforts of President Ezra Taft Benson in encouraging us to read and study this sacred book.

Through the instrumentality of the Prophet Joseph and the visitation of heavenly messengers, the sacred and holy priesthood was restored to the earth. This represents the third pillar of our faith. Without the holy priesthood, exaltation would not be possible inasmuch as the necessary ordinances and covenants come through the use of that sacred power. . . .

Lastly, there comes the pillar of faith related to salvation for the dead. The temple and its ordinances became Joseph's chief concern in Nauvoo (quotes D&C 128:9, 15). . . .

May we each live our lives in such a way as to be worthy to receive a temple recommend and enter into the temple to provide opportunity for salvation for the dead and for the personal blessings of temple worship which will come into our lives. (94–04, pp. 54–55)

The Power of Faith

Faith is the most powerful force in transforming human nature. As man's thoughts turn to God and the things that pertain to God, man undergoes a spiritual transformation. It lifts him from the commonplace and gives to him a noble and Godlike character. If we have faith in God, we are using one of the great laws of life. The most powerful force in human nature is the spiritual power of faith. Jesus said: "According to your faith be it unto you" (Matthew 9:29). (60–04, pp. 124–25)

To believe is to see. If we turn back to the ninth chapter of John, we read of another incident that took place in Jerusalem in which a man who had been born blind received his sight. It was the Sabbath day, and Jesus was apparently in the vicinity of the temple when he saw the blind man, and his disciples asked him:

"Master, who did sin, this man, or his parents, that he was born blind?

"Jesus answered, Neither hath this man sinned, nor his parents: but that the works of God should be made manifest in him.

"I must work the works of him that sent me, while it is day: the night cometh, when no man can work.

"As long as I am in the world, I am the light of the world." (John 9:2–5.)

Jesus then spat on the ground and made clay of the spittle mixed with the dust of the earth. He anointed the eyes of the blind man with the clay and told him to go wash in the pool of Siloam. If this had been Thomas, would he have gone as he had been commanded or would he have asked the question: "What good can come from washing in the stagnant waters of that dirty pool?" or "What medicinal properties are there in saliva mixed with the dust of the earth?" These would seem to be reasonable questions, but if the blind man had doubted and questioned, he would still be blind. Having faith, he believed and did as he was directed. He went and washed in the pool and came back seeing. To believe is to see.

A miracle had taken place. (62–12, p. 915)

By faith and prayer we see spiritual things more clearly.
Sometimes prejudices half close our eyes to spiritual truths and obscure them from our view. As we live the purer life, through faith
and prayer, our eyes are opened wider. The Apostle [Paul] defined
faith as "seeing things not seen" (see Hebrews 11:1), that is, we
see by the spirit those things not visible through natural light. We
are told repeatedly in scripture that the Lord shall be unto each of
us an everlasting light. Christ said: "I am the light of the world: he
that followeth me shall not walk in darkness but shall have the
light of life" (John 8:12).
  This is the light that causes us to see. This is the light that
caused Paul to see. (60–07, p. 5)

Miracles and blessings come by faith. Miracles are wrought by
faith, and the Lord blesses those who have faith in him. He who
will not have faith and will not believe until he has proof will not
receive the blessings which are promised. The Lord said: "Ask, and
it shall be given you; seek and ye shall find; knock, and it shall be
opened unto you: For every one that asketh receiveth; and he that
seeketh findeth; and to him that knocketh it shall be opened"
(Matthew 7:7–8). Merely to ask, seek, or knock without accompa-
nying faith, one will not receive, find, or have the door opened.
The Doctrine and Covenants is more explicit; it adds the words *in
faith*: "Whatsoever ye shall ask in faith, being united in prayer according to my command, ye shall receive" (D&C 29:6). And again
in the Doctrine and Covenants it is stated: "Remember that without faith you can do nothing; therefore ask in faith" (D&C 8:10).
(74–03, p. 27)

Repentance and Resisting Temptation

*A personal testimony of the Savior and his atonement can help
us avoid temptation.* Strive to build a personal testimony of Jesus
Christ and the atonement. A study of the life of Christ and a testimony of his reality is something each of us should seek. As we
come to understand his mission, and the atonement which he
wrought, we will desire to live more like him. We especially en-

courage the young men and young women to come to know the reason for the atoning sacrifice of our Lord. When temptations come, as they surely will, an understanding of the Savior's agony in Gethsemane and his eventual death on the cross will be a reminder to you to avoid any activity that would cause the Savior more pain. Listen to his words, "For behold, I, God, have suffered these things for all, that they might not suffer if they would repent; But if they would not repent, they must suffer even as I" (D&C 19:16–17). (94–11)

Individually and collectively we can withstand temptation. Is it just for an individual, or can a body of people withstand the temptations of Satan? Surely the Lord would be pleased with the Saints if they stood before the world as a light that cannot be hidden because they are willing to live the principles of the gospel and keep the commandments of the Lord.

With faith, and prayer, and humility, and sources of strength from an eternal world, we are able to live unspotted in the midst of a world of temptation. (76–02, p. 19)

Satan tempts us when we are weak and vulnerable. When Jesus had completed the fast of forty days and had communed with God, he was, in this hungry and physically weakened state, left to be tempted of the devil [see Matthew 4:3–10]. That, too, was to be part of his preparation. Such a time is always the tempter's moment—when we are emotionally or physically spent, when we are weary, vulnerable, and least prepared to resist the insidious suggestions he makes. This was an hour of danger—the kind of moment in which many men fall and succumb to the subtle allurement of the devil. (76–02, p. 17)

We must not accept Satan's terms. Jesus knew that if he were faithful to his Father and obedient to every commandment, he would inherit "all that [the] Father hath" (D&C 84:38)—and so would any other son or daughter of God. The surest way to lose the blessings of time or eternity is to accept them on Satan's terms. (76–02, p. 18)

Resistance to evil weakens when we are alienated from God. When man sins he suffers its painful effects. There are few chapters in [the scriptures] that do not contain some reference to what sin is or does. The predominant conception of the nature of sin in these books is that of a personal alienation from God. . . . The vanishing resistance to evil in the world is caused by this personal alienation from our Heavenly Father. (66–03, p. 516)

Repentance is homesickness of the soul. When the prodigal boy, in that parable which most perfectly tells the story of the sinning and repentant life, "came to himself," his first words were, "I will arise and go to my father" (Luke 15:18). While he is yet afar off the waiting father sees him coming and is moved with compassion. Repentance is but the homesickness of the soul, and the uninterrupted and watchful care of the parent is the fairest earthly type of the unfailing forgiveness of God. The family is, to the mind of Jesus, the nearest of human analogies to that divine order which it was his mission to reveal. (60–04, p. 125)

The path of repentance leads to perfect forgiveness. To those who have transgressed or been offended, we say, come back. The path of repentance, though hard at times, lifts one ever upward and leads to a perfect forgiveness. (94–14, p. 8)

Three steps lead to evil. This is the usual course of a man's life as he turns toward evil. First, he is a silent observer, then he becomes a consenting spectator, and finally he is an active participant. (64–02, p. 1087)

Baptism and Spiritual Rebirth

Baptisms must be performed by proper authority. Children in the Church are baptized when they are eight years old. They may be baptized in a lovely, modern, tiled baptismal font in a beautiful new building or on the shores of an icy lake or in a small stream or pond. But their baptism is always performed by one holding the Holy Priesthood of God, and it is always by immersion. (71–09, p. 11)

We should seek to have Christ "formed" in us. In Paul's short letter to the Galatians, he showed great concern over their apparent disbelief and their forsaking of his teachings regarding Christ.

He wrote to them: "But it is good to be zealously affected always in a good thing, and not only when I am present with you. My little children, of whom I travail in birth again until Christ be formed in you." (Galatians 4:18–19.) In other words, Paul expressed himself as suffering pain and anxiety until Christ be "formed" in them. This is another way of saying "in Christ," as that expression is used by Paul repeatedly in his writings.

It is possible for Christ to be born in men's lives, and when such an experience actually happens, a man is "in Christ"—Christ is "formed" in him. This presupposes that we take Christ into our hearts and make him the living contemporary of our lives. He is not just a general truth or a fact in history, but the Savior of men everywhere and at all times. When we strive to be Christlike, he is "formed" in us; if we open the door, he will enter; if we seek his counsel, he will counsel us. For Christ to be "formed" in us, we must have a belief in him and in his atonement. Such a belief in Christ, and the keeping of his commandments, are not restraints upon us. By these, men are set free. This Prince of Peace waits to give peace of mind which may make each of us a channel of that peace. (72–04, pp. 67–68)

It is only in the changing of a man's heart—a second birth—the changing of an individual, that the root strength comes to change a people or a nation. (66–01, p. 10)

Forgiveness

All of us need the saving grace of the Lord. The parable of the Prodigal Son [Luke 15:11–32] typifies the condition of too many of our fellow men, who mistakenly feel that squandering their inheritance in riotous living will bring them happiness. But it also portrays those who make another type of mistake—feeling that their righteousness makes them superior to their less-disciplined brethren. Both brothers in the parable desperately need the Lord to free them of their burdens. This is the message of the parable.

We learn from this parable that all of us, regardless of our status or condition, have an absolute need of the Lord's saving grace. We are all dependent on him for peace in this life and for eternal life. (90–08)

We can take full advantage of the Atonement in our lives. Given the freedom to choose, we may, in fact, make wrong choices, bad choices, hurtful choices. And sometimes we do just that, but that is where the mission and mercy of Jesus Christ comes into full force and glory. He has taken upon himself the burden of all the world's risk. He has provided a mediating atonement for the wrong choices we make. He is our advocate with the Father and has paid, in advance, for the faults and foolishness we often see in the exercise of our freedom. We must accept his gift, repent of those mistakes, and follow his commandments in order to take full advantage of this redemption. The offer is always there; the way is always open. We can always, even in our darkest hour and most disastrous errors, look to the Son of God and live. (89–06, p. 18)

We can know that we have received forgiveness of our sins. There is a great example in the Book of Mormon that illustrates how we can know we have received a forgiveness of our sins. King Benjamin had given a great sermon which announced the mission and Atonement of Christ. He then witnessed the effect of his message on the members of the Church. First they viewed themselves in their own carnal state, that is their worldly state, even less than the dust of the earth. Next, they cried to the Lord and said, "O have mercy, and apply the atoning blood of Christ that we may receive forgiveness of our sins, and our hearts may be purified." And the result of their prayer was this: "The Spirit of the Lord came upon them, and they were filled with joy, having received a remission of their sins, and having peace of conscience, because of the exceeding faith which they had in Jesus Christ" (Mosiah 4:2–3). (88–04)

We should be patient and forgiving of ourselves as well as others. It has always struck me as being sad that those among us who would not think of reprimanding our neighbor, much less a total stranger, for mistakes that have been made or weaknesses that might be evident, will nevertheless be cruel and unforgiving to themselves. When the scriptures say to judge righteously, that means with fairness and compassion and charity. That's how we must judge ourselves. We need to be patient and forgiving of ourselves, just as we must be patient and forgiving of others.

Of course, continual repentance followed by continual transgression isn't pleasing to the Lord, so we do have to be serious and responsible about our commitments. But God is usually more willing to forgive us than we are willing to forgive ourselves. It may not surprise you to know that God loves us more than we love ourselves. We are his creation, spirit children of a celestial birth, and we stand in the image of him whom we rightly call our Father. We ought never to be destructive in our criticism of others, but perhaps our greatest caution needs to be regarding the tendency to be destructive in the criticism we apply to ourselves. (92–01, p. 41)

4

SPIRITUAL
DEVELOPMENT

Developing spirituality is not easy. Developing spirituality and attuning ourselves to the highest influences of godliness is not an easy matter. It takes time and frequently involves a struggle. It will not happen by chance, but is accomplished only through deliberate effort and by calling upon God and keeping his commandments. (79–02, p. 25)

The development of spiritual capacity does not come without effort. We must take time to prepare our minds for spiritual things. The development of spiritual capacity does not come with the conferral of authority. There must be desire, effort, and personal preparation. This requires, of course, as you already know, fasting, prayer, searching the scriptures, experience, meditation, and a hungering and thirsting after the righteous life.

I find it helpful to review these admonitions from Almighty God:

"If thou shalt ask, thou shalt receive revelation upon revelation, knowledge upon knowledge, that thou mayest know the mysteries and peaceable things—that which bringeth joy, that which bringeth life eternal" (D&C 42:61).

"Ask the Father in my name, in faith believing that you shall receive, and you shall have the Holy Ghost, which manifesteth all things which are expedient unto the children of men" (D&C 18:18).

"Let the solemnities of eternity rest upon your minds" (D&C 43:34).

"Treasure up in your minds continually the words of life, and it shall be given you in the very hour that portion that shall be meted unto every man" (D&C 84:85).

"Search diligently, pray always, and be believing, and all things shall work together for your good, if ye walk uprightly and remember the covenant wherewith ye have covenanted one with another" (D&C 90:24).

"God shall give unto you knowledge by his Holy Spirit, yea, by the unspeakable gift of the Holy Ghost" (D&C 121:26).

These are promises that the Lord will surely fulfill if we prepare ourselves.

Take time to meditate, ponder, and pray on spiritual matters. (83–06)

Prayer and Fasting

We need to develop habits of personal and family prayer. As part of your private religious behavior, pray every day, night and morning. Let your heart be drawn out to the Lord continually as Amulek wisely counseled (see Alma 34:27). Pray as families both night and morning. What great blessings come into the lives of children who hear their parents petition the Lord for their welfare. Surely children who come under the influence of such righteous parents will be better protected against the influences of the adversary. (94–11)

Prayer is essential to our salvation. Prayer has changed many lives. It has had an effect on our lives, both yours and mine. Prayer is that which brings us in close communion with God. It is the very beginning of our relationship with God. It has existed from the beginning, for an angel spoke to Adam in the Garden of Eden and said to him, "Wherefore, thou shalt do all that thou doest in the name of the Son, and thou shalt repent and call upon God in the name of the Son forevermore" (Moses 5:8).

Prayer has always been a basic and essential element of salvation and exaltation. Without the help of God, we are nothing. Through prayer we can seek him. We are told that if we will seek him we shall find him. (see Matthew 7:7–8) (63–07, pp. 4–5).

God answers prayers. Every seeker receives; every seeker finds. Yet not every asker receives what he asks; not every seeker finds what he seeks. As an earthly father gives good gifts to his children, so God gives good things to those that ask him—not always what they ask, for they often ask amiss, but something far better than that which they ask for or seek. Those who would obtain exactly what they ask must confine their will to God's and ask for things which they know he is willing to give. (63–07, p. 5)

Prayer is powerful. Prayer has changed the course of history. It has been a great influence for good in the lives of many people.

Are you thankful for your blessings? Do you express your appreciation to the Lord? Do you seek him for guidance so that you might take the right path? Do you ask him for wisdom and for knowledge? Of course the older folks who are cramming for their final examinations need prayer in their lives, but you who still face the real problems of life need prayer and answers to prayer, for your peace of soul and mind and for your guidance. . . .

If you feel discouraged, prayer will rekindle courage and ambition within you. If you are ill, prayer will make you well. If you hold ill feelings, prayer will bring understanding to your soul. Prayer will unlock the treasure-house of your righteous desires. Prayer will keep you in tune with God.

The words spoken for the benefit of Thomas B. Marsh are applicable to each of us: "Pray always, lest you enter into temptation and lose your reward. Be faithful unto the end, and lo, I am with you." (D&C 31:12–13.)

I bear witness that God lives, that he hears and answers our prayers. (63–07, p. 7)

There is no spiritual progress without prayer. There can be no spiritual progress and no growth without prayer. The absence of prayer in our work, in our preparation, in our leadership and teaching, is a form of atheism. Prayer and the living of the gospel will give us the spirit of our calling. (66–02)

We should remember to pray always. Henry Ward Beecher once said, "It is not well for a man to pray cream and live skim milk." (*Proverbs from Plymouth Pulpit,* ed. William Drysdale [New York: Appleton, 1887], p. 192.) That was a century ago. There is now before us a danger that many may pray skim milk and live *that* not at all.

Our modern times seem to suggest that prayerful devotion and reverence for holiness is unreasonable or undesirable, or both. And yet, skeptical "modern" men have need for prayer. . . . If prayer is only a spasmodic cry at the time of crisis, then it is utterly selfish, and we come to think of God as a repairman or a service agency to help us only in our emergencies. We should remember the Most High day and night—always—not only at times when all other assistance has failed and we desperately need help. If there is any element in human life on which we have a record of miraculous success and inestimable worth to the human soul, it is prayerful, reverential, devout communication with our Heavenly Father. (77–04, p. 52)

Efficacious prayer requires that our thoughts first turn to God. Jesus was careful to place the petition "Hallowed be thy name" at the very forefront of his prayer (see Matthew 6:9). Unless that reverent, prayerful, honorable attitude toward God is uppermost in our hearts, we are not fully prepared to pray. If our first thought is of ourselves and not of God, we are not praying as Jesus taught. (77–04, p. 52)

Prayer is a necessity. Prayer is the utterance of the soul to God the Father. We do well to become more like our Father by looking up to him, by remembering him always, and by caring greatly about his world and his work.

Dr. Alexis Carrel, recipient of the Nobel Prize in physiology and medicine, once said, "Today as never before, prayer is a binding necessity in the lives of men and nations. The lack of emphasis on the religious sense has brought the world to an age of destruction. Our deepest source of power and perfection has been left miserably undeveloped." (*Reader's Digest,* March 1941, p. 36.)

If men are no longer awed by the thought of a holy God and are, as Mormon said of the people of his day, "without principle, and past feeling" (Moroni 9:20), then we face a fearful time. (77–04, pp. 53–54)

We must pray for those who offend us. I was interested in the story told today about the one who prayed and prayed for another and eventually a good feeling and a good spirit came. As it was told, I thought about an occasion when I was a bishop. One of the brethren in the ward came to me with bitterness in his soul toward

another man. I said to him, "My brother, if you will go home and
pray for him every morning and every night, I'll meet you two
weeks from today at this same time and then we will decide what
should be done." You already know his conclusion when he came
back in two weeks. He said, "He needs some help." I said, "Are
you willing to help him?" His answer was, "Yes, of course." All the
venom was gone and all the bitterness was gone. This is the way it
is when we pray for one another.

When we try to help those who have offended us, when we
pray for those who have unrighteously used us, our lives can be
beautiful. We can have peace when we come into a unity with the
Spirit and with each other as we serve the Lord and keep his commandments. (79–10)

Fasting brings us in tune with God. To discipline ourselves
through fasting brings us in tune with God, and fast day provides
an occasion to set aside the temporal so that we might enjoy the
higher qualities of the spiritual. As we fast on that day we learn and
better understand the needs of those who are less fortunate.
(85–03, p. 74)

Following the Savior

*If our lives are centered in Christ, nothing can go perma-
nently wrong.* I am aware that life presents many challenges, but
with the help of the Lord, we need not fear. If our lives and our
faith are centered on Jesus Christ and his restored gospel, nothing
can ever go permanently wrong. On the other hand, if our lives are
not centered on the Savior and his teachings, no other success can
ever be permanently right. (95–02)

Christ is our example. To be a light is to be an exemplar—one
who sets an example and is a model for others to follow. This became our challenge when we accepted the priesthood and by implication it became our covenant to follow Christ, the great exemplar. We have the responsibility to learn of him, the things he
taught and the things he did during his earthly ministry. Having
learned these lessons we are under commandment to follow his example and these are some of the examples he set for us:

1. Christ was obedient and valiant in the premortal life, thus gaining the privilege of coming into mortality and receiving a body of flesh and bones.

2. He was baptized in order that the door to the celestial kingdom would be opened.

3. He held the priesthood and received all the saving and exalting ordinances of the gospel.

4. Jesus served for about three years in a ministry of teaching the gospel, bearing witness of the truth, and teaching men what they must do to find joy and happiness in this life and eternal glory in the world to come.

5. He performed ordinances including the blessing of children, baptisms, administering to the sick, and ordinations to the priesthood.

6. He performed miracles. At his command the blind were given sight, the deaf heard, the lame leaped, and the dead returned to life.

7. In conformity with the mind and will of the Father, Jesus lived a perfect life without sin and acquired all of the attributes of Godliness.

8. He overcame the world, that is, he bridled every passion and has risen above the carnal and sensual plane so that he lived and walked as guided by the Spirit.

9. He brought to pass the Atonement, thereby ransoming men from the death caused by the fall of Adam.

10. Now, resurrected and glorified, he has gained all power in heaven and in earth, has received the fullness of and is one with the Father.

If we are to follow the example of Christ and walk in his footsteps, we must seek to do the same things after the pattern he set. (80–02)

Is there room for the Savior in our lives? On that night in Bethlehem there was no room for him in the inn and this was not the only time during the thirty-three years of his sojourn in mortality that there was no room for him. Herod sent soldiers to Bethlehem to slay the children. There was no room for Jesus in the domain of Herod so his parents took him to Egypt. During his ministry there were many who made no room for his teachings— no room for the gospel he taught. There was no room for his miracles, for his blessings, no room for the divine truths he spoke, no room for his love or faith. He said to them, "The foxes have holes, and the birds of the air have nests; but the Son of man hath not where to lay his head" (Matthew 8:20).

Even in our day, although two thousand years have passed, there are many who say the same thing that was said on that night in Bethlehem. "There is no room, no room" (see Luke 2:7). We make room for the gifts, but sometimes no room is made for the giver. We have room for the commercialism of Christmas and even pleasure-seeking on the Sabbath day, but there are times when there is not room for worship. Our thoughts are filled with other things—there is no room. (81–04)

Jesus Christ is the only beacon on which we can rely. The message of . . . The Church of Jesus Christ of Latter-day Saints is that there is but one guiding hand in the universe, only one truly infallible light, one unfailing beacon to the world. That light is Jesus Christ, the light and life of the world, the light which one Book of Mormon prophet described as "a light that is endless, that can never be darkened" (Mosiah 16:9).

As we search for the shore of safety and peace, whether we be individual women and men, families, communities, or nations, Christ is the only beacon on which we can ultimately rely. (92–05, p. 18)

We will be happiest when we follow the Savior's example. Each one of you is a son or daughter of our Father in Heaven. You, therefore, have divine potential. As members of The Church of Jesus Christ of Latter-day Saints, you are given a singular opportunity to develop that potential. Membership in his Church brings with it sacred responsibilities and limitless opportunities. We are happiest and most productive when we seek to know more of our Father in Heaven and his Son Jesus Christ, our beloved Redeemer. Life is fuller and more worthwhile when we seek to understand their teachings and apply them consistently in our life. Jesus Christ is in charge of the affairs of this earth. He unwaveringly does the will of the Father. When we are obedient to the commandments of the Savior, we are obedient to the commandments of our Father in Heaven. When we follow his example, we are the happiest. (90–09)

We should ask ourselves, "What would Jesus do?" Let us follow the Son of God in all ways and in all walks of life. Let us make him our exemplar and our guide. We should at every opportunity ask ourselves, "What would Jesus do?" and then be more courageous to act upon the answer. We must follow Christ, in the best sense of that word. We must be about his work as he was about his Father's. We should try to be like him, even as the Primary children sing, "Try, try, try" (*Children's Songbook*, p. 55). To the extent that our mortal powers permit, we should make every effort to become like Christ—the one perfect and sinless example this world has ever seen. . . .

We must know Christ better than we know him; we must remember him more often than we remember him; we must serve him more valiantly than we serve him. Then we will drink water springing up unto eternal life and will eat the bread of life.

What manner of men and women ought we to be? Even as he is (see 3 Nephi 27:27). (94–01, p. 64)

We must think more often of the Savior. I have chosen for my brief text . . . the words of an ancient and sacred hymn, which are attributed to Bernard of Clairvaux and estimated to be nearly nine hundred years old. With the rest of the Christian world, the members of The Church of Jesus Christ of Latter-day Saints sing reverently:

> Jesus, the very thought of thee
> With sweetness fills my breast;
> But sweeter far thy face to see
> And in thy presence rest.
> ("Jesus, the Very Thought of Thee," *Hymns,*
> 1985, no. 141.) . . .

How often do we think of the Savior? How deeply and how gratefully and how adoringly do we reflect on his life? How central to our lives do we know him to be?

For example, how much of a normal day, a working week, or a fleeting month is devoted to "Jesus, the very thought of thee"? Perhaps for some of us, not enough.

Surely life would be more peaceful, surely marriages and families would be stronger, certainly neighborhoods and nations would be safer and kinder and more constructive if more of the gospel of Jesus Christ "with sweetness" could fill our breasts.

Unless we pay more attention to the thoughts of our hearts, I wonder what hope we have to claim that greater joy, that sweeter prize: someday his loving "face to see / And in [his] presence rest." (93–02, pp. 63–64)

We must give more attention to the example of Jesus Christ. I would invite all members of the Church to live with ever-more attention to the life and example of the Lord Jesus Christ, especially the love and hope and compassion he displayed.

I pray that we might treat each other with more kindness, more courtesy, more humility and patience and forgiveness. We do have high expectations of one another, and all can improve. Our world cries out for more disciplined living of the commandments of God. But the way we are to encourage that, as the Lord told the Prophet Joseph in the wintry depths of Liberty Jail, is "by persuasion, by long-suffering, by gentleness and meekness, and by love unfeigned; . . . without hypocrisy, and without guile" (D&C 121:41–42). (94–03)

Christ invites us to follow him. Christ's supreme sacrifice can find full fruition in our lives only as we accept the invitation to follow him. This call is not irrelevant, unrealistic, or impossible. To follow an individual means to watch him or listen to him closely; to accept his authority, to take him as a leader, and to obey him; to support and advocate his ideas; and to take him as a model. Each of us can accept this challenge. Peter said, "Christ also suffered for us, leaving us an example, that ye should follow his steps" (1 Peter 2:21). Just as teachings that do not conform to Christ's doctrine are false, so a life that does not conform to Christ's example is misdirected, and may not achieve its high potential destiny. (94–08, p. 2)

We should follow the light of the world. While it will be a beautiful sight to see the lights of Christmas on this square, it is more important to have human lives illuminated by an acceptance of him who is the light of the world. Truly we should hold him up as our guide and exemplar.

On the eve of his birth angels sang "and on earth peace, good will toward men" (Luke 2:14). If men would follow his example, it would be a world of peace and love toward all men. (94–21)

Our responsibility today is to reflect the gospel as taught by Christ. What is our responsibility today as members of The Church of Jesus Christ of Latter-day Saints? It is to see that our individual lives reflect in word and deed the gospel as taught by our Lord and Savior, Jesus Christ. All that we do and say should be patterned after the example of the one sinless person to walk the earth, even the Lord Jesus Christ. (94–22)

Avoid being a secret follower of Jesus. Among our own people, in our communities, in our nation and throughout the world, there are secret followers of Jesus and half-hearted Christians—onlookers who have a noncommittal attitude. Why is it that so many will not commit themselves?

Joseph of Arimathea was only a secret disciple because of what others would think of him. He would not risk his social position nor the respect of his associates. It is fear that causes men to be noncommittal. They are afraid to declare their loyalty and assume active responsibility. The easy way is to let someone else be the leader and assume the responsibility. The world needs men who are willing to step forward and declare themselves. The world needs men who will lift the load of responsibility to their shoulders and carry it high under the banner of Jesus Christ—men who are willing to defend the right openly. (60–10, p. 949)

Following the Savior will bring unmeasured blessings. We sense that our people everywhere are striving more diligently to live Christlike lives, which is our charge. Following the Savior will bring us unmeasured blessings, protection, and opportunities. The doctrines that the Savior taught contain the answers to our problems, both personally and collectively. No message is more needed in the world. Individuals and nations can find peace and prosperity by hearkening to the words of the Master. Of this I bear solemn witness. (95–02)

We should pattern our life after the Master's. If we can pattern our life after the Master, and take his teaching and example as the supreme pattern for our own, we will not find it difficult to be consistent and loyal in every walk of life, for we will be committed to a single, sacred standard of conduct and belief. Whether at home or in the marketplace, whether at school or long after school is behind us, whether we are acting totally alone or in concert with a host of other people, our course will be clear and our standards will be obvious. We will have determined, as the Prophet Alma said, "to stand as witnesses of God at all times and in all things, and in all places that [we] may be in, even until death" (Mosiah 18:9). (90–03, p. 60)

Now is the time for people to stand up boldly for Christ. How can men of conscience ignore the teachings of the Master in their daily affairs, in business, or in government? We stand by and wink at many things because we fear to do anything about them. We may be against crime or communism, but what do we do about it? We may be against corruption in government or against juvenile delinquency, but what do we do about it? We may have a belief in the gospel of Jesus Christ, but what are we doing about it? We need to push fear into the background and come forward with a definite, positive declaration, and assume responsibility. . . .

Can we stand on the sidelines and merely observe? This is a day for action. This is the time for decision, not tomorrow, not next week. This is the time to make our covenant with the Lord. Now is the time for those who have been noncommittal or who have had a halfhearted interest to come out boldly and declare belief in Christ and be willing to demonstrate faith by works. (60–10, p. 949)

We must fix our eyes on the Savior to overcome the waves of unbelief. It is my firm belief that if as individual people, as families, communities, and nations, we could, like Peter, fix our eyes on Jesus, we too might walk triumphantly over "the swelling waves of disbelief" and remain "unterrified amid the rising winds of doubt" (see Matthew 14:22–33). But if we turn away our eyes from him in whom we must believe, as it is so easy to do and the world is so much tempted to do, if we look to the power and fury of those terrible and destructive elements around us rather than to him who can help and save us, then we shall inevitably sink in a sea of conflict and sorrow and despair.

At such times when we feel the floods are threatening to drown us and the deep is going to swallow up the tossed vessel of our faith, I pray we may always hear amid the storm and the darkness that sweet utterance of the Savior of the world: "Be of good cheer; it is I; be not afraid" (Matthew 14:27). (92–05, p. 19)

Testimony

The strength of The Church of Jesus Christ of Latter-day Saints and the power by which it is making rapid growth is the individual testimony of its members. (56–01)

A testimony comes by living the gospel. Action is one of the chief foundations of personal testimony. The surest witness is that which comes firsthand out of personal experience. When the Jews challenged the doctrine Jesus taught in the temple, he answered, "My doctrine is not mine, but his that sent me." Then he added the key to personal testimony: "If any man will do his will, he shall know of the doctrine, whether it be of God, or whether I speak of myself" (John 7:16–17). . . .

Merely saying, accepting, believing are not enough. They are incomplete until that which they imply is translated into the dynamic action of daily living. This, then, is the finest source of personal testimony. One knows because he has experienced. He does not have to say, "Brother Jones says it is true, and I believe him." He can say, "I have lived this principle in my own life, and I know through personal experience that it works. I have felt its influence, tested its practical usefulness, and know that it is good. I can testify of my own knowledge that it is a true principle." (67–02, p. 102)

Many fail to recognize a testimony. Many people carry . . . a testimony in their own lives and do not recognize its worth. Recently a young lady said, "I do not have a testimony of the gospel. I wish I did. I accept its teachings. I know they work in my life. I see them working in the lives of others. If only the Lord would answer my prayers and give me a testimony, I would be one of the happiest persons alive!" What this young lady wanted was a miraculous intervention; yet she had already seen the miracle of the gospel enlarging and uplifting her own life. The Lord *had* answered her prayers. She did have a testimony, but she did not recognize it for what it was. Of such Jesus said, "They seeing see not;

and hearing they hear not, neither do they understand" (Matthew 13:13). (67–02, p. 102)

How does a testimony come? There comes a time when we understand the principles of our creation and who we are. Suddenly these things are illuminated to us and the cords of our hearts do vibrate. This is the time when testimony enters into our very souls and we know beyond a question of a doubt that God is our father—that he lives, that he is a reality, that we are literally his children. (79–11)

By experimenting with gospel principles we will find the truth. Students spend hours in scientific laboratories experimenting to find the truth. If they will do the same thing with faith, prayer, forgiveness, humility and love, they will find a testimony of Jesus Christ, the giver of these principles. (85–02)

Steadfastness and Diligence

Setting our hand to the plow involves hard work and determination. We have in Church leadership great plowmen with firm hands and stout hearts—stake presidents and mission presidents— determined men who work in the fields. Bishops, branch presidents, heads of priesthood quorums and auxiliary organizations are toiling in their assigned fields. Missionaries have been called and have put their hands to the plow. Nearly 15,000 stake and full-time missionaries are now in the fields. Furrows are being cut and seeds planted and every day we see the results of the harvest. Close at home and in distant countries new lands are being broken up by these plowmen, and the subsurface exposed to the light of the gospel of Jesus Christ.

Is it hard work? Of course, but that which is worthwhile is seldom easy. As individuals we have a responsibility to plow. Some accept the opportunity, but some shrink from the responsibility. Some of those who commence cut only a short furrow and then leave the field for what appears to be escape from the toil to follow the false illusion of the ease which they had left behind. Their plowshares are left to rust in the furrow.

Whatever the past may have been in our individual lives, it is gone. The future lies ahead, and we must face it with resolution. There is always a point from which we can begin. Even though we may have been faithful in the past, if we turn away, that faithfulness will profit us nothing. "No man, having put his hand to the plough, and looking back, is fit for the kingdom of God" (Luke 9:62).

There is danger in looking backward. One must keep his eyes ahead in order to cut a straight furrow. When the plowman commences to look backward, he cuts a crooked furrow, and his work is spoiled. We cannot continue to walk forward when at the same time we are looking backward. It makes no difference what object or occasion causes us to look backward, the backward glance commences the backward turning, and may be the beginning of our disendowment in the kingdom of God.

As plowing requires an eye intent on the furrow to be made and is marred when one looks backward, so will they come short of exaltation who prosecute the work of God with a distracted attention or a divided heart. We may not see clearly the end of the furrow, but we dare not look back. Eternity stretches on ahead, challenging us to be faithful. (61–01, p. 399)

Developing spirituality requires sincere effort. There may be so very much our Father in Heaven would like to give us—young, old, or middle-aged—if we would but seek his presence regularly through such avenues as scripture study and earnest prayer. Of course, developing spirituality and attuning ourselves to the highest influences of godliness is not an easy matter. It takes time and frequently involves a struggle. (88–06, p. 61)

5

THE
SCRIPTURES

We must measure every decision by the scriptures and the prophets. I commend to you the revelations of God as the standard by which we must live our lives and by which we must measure every decision and every deed. Accordingly, when you have worries and challenges, face them by turning to the scriptures and the prophets. (89–03, p. 112)

Scripture Study

God speaks to mankind through the scriptures. Central to all truth is the testimony that Jesus of Nazareth is the Christ, the Great Jehovah, the Savior of the World, and the Only Begotten Son of the Living God. This is the message of the scriptures. Throughout each of these holy books there is an appeal to believe and have faith in God the Eternal Father and in his son, Jesus Christ; and from the first to the last of these books of scripture is the call to do the will of God and keep his commandments.

Scriptures contain the record of the self-revelation of God, and through them God speaks to man. Where could there be more profitable use of time than reading from the scriptural library, the literature that teaches us to know God and understand our relationship to him? . . . Time is always precious; but . . . study of the scriptures is absolutely essential. (84–04)

The scriptures teach us to know God and understand him. We hope that you are studying the gospel regularly. Read from the scriptures, especially the Book of Mormon, each day as individuals and as families. Study the word of the Lord, and your faith and testimony will increase. What could be a more profitable use of discretionary time than reading from the scriptural library, the literature that teaches us to know God and understand our relationship to him? (94–22)

Church members ought to know the scriptures thoroughly. We ought to have a Church full of women and men who know the scriptures thoroughly, who cross-reference and mark them, who develop lessons and talks from the Topical Guide, and who have mastered the maps, the Bible Dictionary, and the other helps that are contained in this wonderful set of standard works. There is obviously more there than we can master quickly. Certainly the scriptural field is "white already to harvest." (89–01)

We will be held accountable if we do not read the scriptures. Not in this dispensation, surely not in any dispensation, have the scriptures—the enduring, enlightening word of God—been so readily available and so helpfully structured for the use of every man, woman, and child who will search them. The written word of God is in the most readable and accessible form ever provided to lay members in the history of the world. Surely we will be held accountable if we do not read them. (89–01)

Scripture study brings an outpouring of the Spirit. Brothers and sisters, we urge each of you to carefully consider how much time you are currently giving to prayerful pondering of the scriptures.

As one of the Lord's servants, I challenge you to do the following:

1. Read, ponder and pray over the scriptures daily as individual members of the Church.

2. Hold family scripture reading on a regular basis. We commend those of you who are already doing this and urge those of you who have not yet started to begin doing so without delay.

3. Seek the Spirit to know better how to learn and teach by the Spirit. The Lord has said, "The Spirit shall be given unto you by the prayer of faith" (D&C 42:14). As you continually have a prayer in your heart for those who are teaching you, and pray for a receptive and understanding heart for yourselves, you will open

the windows of heaven to an outpouring of God's Spirit. . . .

May each of us go forth with a firm resolve to be more prayerful; to seek to live more fully by the Spirit; and to draw closer to our Father in Heaven and his Beloved Son through consistent study of the holy scriptures. (88–09)

Through searching the scriptures we come to know the will of the Lord. Our Church leaders have laid great stress on the matter of reading the scriptures and the words of the prophets, ancient and modern. Fathers and mothers have been asked to read the scriptures so that they may properly teach their children. Our children are reading the scriptures as the result of the example being set by parents. We are studying the scriptures at our family home evenings, and some families are reading scriptures together at an early morning hour.

Young people are learning to know the scriptures in seminary and institute classes. Missionaries are studying, becoming familiar with, and memorizing the scriptures so that they can better teach the gospel. This is the way we learn to know the will of the Lord, that we might be obedient. (78–02)

The most profitable of all study is scripture study. When we follow the counsel of our leaders to read and study the scriptures, benefits and blessings of many kinds come to us. This is the most profitable of all study in which we could engage. (79–05, p. 64)

Scriptural understanding requires concentrated study on a regular basis. Those who delve into the scriptural library . . . find that to understand requires more than casual reading or perusal— there must be concentrated study. It is certain that one who studies the scriptures every day accomplishes far more than one who devotes considerable time one day and then lets days go by before continuing. Not only should we study each day, but there should be a regular time set aside when we can concentrate without interference. . . .

It would be ideal if an hour could be spent each day; but if that much cannot be had, a half hour on a regular basis would result in substantial accomplishment. A quarter of an hour is little time, but it is surprising how much enlightenment and knowledge can be acquired in a subject so meaningful. The important thing is to allow nothing else to ever interfere with our study. (79–05, p. 64)

Prayer will enhance our understanding of the scriptures. There is nothing more helpful than prayer to open our understanding of the scriptures. Through prayer we can attune our minds to seek the answers to our searchings. The Lord said: "Ask, and it shall be given you; seek, and ye shall find; knock, and it shall be opened unto you" (Luke 11:9). Herein is Christ's reassurance that if we will ask, seek, and knock, the Holy Spirit will guide our understanding if we are ready and eager to receive. (79–05, p. 64)

Family scripture study brings great blessings. Families are greatly blessed when wise fathers and mothers bring their children about them, read from the pages of the scriptural library together, and then discuss freely the beautiful stories and thoughts according to the understanding of all. Often youth and little ones have amazing insight into and appreciation for the basic literature of religion. (79–05, p. 64)

It is better to have a set amount of time rather than chapters to read. We should not be haphazard in our reading but rather develop a systematic plan for study. There are some who read to a schedule of a number of pages or a set number of chapters each day or week. This may be perfectly justifiable and may be enjoyable if one is reading for pleasure, but it does not constitute meaningful study. It is better to have a set amount of time to give scriptural study each day than to have a set amount of chapters to read. Sometimes we find that the study of a single verse will occupy the whole time.

The life, acts, and teachings of Jesus can be read rapidly. . . . Sometimes, however, many hours might be spent in contemplation of profound thoughts expressed in a few simple words. (79–05, pp. 64–65)

Read the scriptures and conference reports on a regular basis. We hope you are reading and studying the scriptures on a daily basis as individuals and as families. We should not take lightly the command of the Lord, "Search the scriptures; for in them ye think ye have eternal life: and they are they which testify of me" (John 5:39). The Spirit will come into your homes and your lives as you read the revealed word. President John Taylor has wisely taught, "I would not only search the scriptures that we now have, but I would search also every revelation that God has given, does give, or will give for the guidance and direction of his people, . . . and I would seek to be governed by the principles that are contained in that sacred word." *(The Gospel Kingdom*, pp. 35–36.) We hope, therefore, that you will also make a study of the conference reports part of your scripture study. (94–11)

The Book of Mormon and Latter-day Scripture

The Book of Mormon helps us accomplish the work of the Lord. One of the most significant resources the Lord has provided to assist us in accomplishing this divine work is the Book of Mormon, subtitled "Another Testament of Jesus Christ." . . . We hope you brothers and sisters are feeding your spirits by regularly reading the Book of Mormon and the other scriptures and using them in your ministries. (90–02)

The Book of Mormon is the most remarkable book. The Book of Mormon is the word of God.

We invite you to read this wonderful record. It is the most remarkable volume in existence today. Read it carefully and prayerfully, and as you do, God will give you a testimony of its truthfulness as promised by Moroni (see Moroni 10:4). (62–07)

Reading the Book of Mormon will have a profound effect on your life. To those who may not be familiar with the Book of Mormon but are sincerely seeking truth, reading it will have a profound effect on your life. It will expand your knowledge of the way God deals with man and will give you a greater desire to live in harmony with his gospel teachings. It will also provide for you a powerful testimony of Jesus. (83–01, p. 16)

The teachings of the Doctrine and Covenants point the way to eternal life. I add my apostolic witness . . . that the commandments, covenants, truths, doctrines, and principles taught in the

Doctrine and Covenants are from God. They are intended for our salvation. They point the way to eternal life, "which gift is the greatest of all the gifts of God" (D&C 14:7). (88–09)

The Doctrine and Covenants contains the word of the Lord for our day. As one of our standard works, the Doctrine and Covenants is studied on a rotating basis with other scripture volumes in the Gospel Doctrine course in Sunday School. Church members are, of course, urged to continually study the revelations found in the Doctrine and Covenants on a regular basis just as we have been asked to study all books of scripture. It is a treasure trove of doctrines, covenants, and commandments that can bless our lives immeasurably, and if we will follow the command to "search" the revelations we will be blessed.

The Doctrine and Covenants is a unique book. It is the only book on the face of the entire earth with a preface composed by the Creator himself. Furthermore, this book of scripture contains more direct quotations from the Lord than any other existing book of scripture.

It is not a translation of an ancient document, but is of modern origin. It is a book of revelation for our day. It is a unique and divinely inspired selection of revelations that came through prophets of God in our day in answer to questions, concerns, and challenges they and others faced. It contains divine answers to real-life problems involving real people.

The Doctrine and Covenants contains the word and will of the Lord as revealed to men and women in this dispensation of time. It is a book of scripture specifically for our day. It is a book for the entire world. (88–08)

By reading the Doctrine and Covenants we can hear the voice of the Lord. Did you realize that by reading the Doctrine and Covenants you can hear the voice of the Lord through scripture? Consider these words spoken by the Lord in 1829, found in section 18 of the Doctrine and Covenants:

"And I, Jesus Christ, your Lord and your God, have spoken it.

"These words are not of men nor of man, but of me; wherefore, you shall testify they are of me and not of man;

"For it is my voice which speaketh them unto you; for they are given by my Spirit unto you, and by my power you can read them one to another; and save it were by my power you could not have them;

"Wherefore, you can testify that you have heard my voice, and know my words." (D&C 18:33–36.)

Think of that: By the power of his Spirit you may hear the voice of the Lord Jesus Christ to you by reading the Doctrine and Covenants. That voice of enlightenment will usually come into your mind as "thoughts" and into your heart as "feelings" (see D&C 8:1–3). The promise of that witness is not limited to the Brethren or a select few, but is a promise available to every worthy man, woman, and child who prayerfully seeks for such a witness. Should not each of us resolve to read, study, ponder, and pray over these sacred revelations? (88–08)

There are benefits to reading the Doctrine and Covenants regularly. Consider [the following] reasons why we should regularly read the Doctrine and Covenants and inspired writings of God's servants:

1. This telestial earth is but a temporary place for us to live—a home away from our real home. Our purpose in life is to find and follow the path that will lead *us back to our heavenly home* in the presence of the Father of us all. The Doctrine and Covenants represents *divine instructions* in our day showing us this fact and how this might be accomplished.

2. The Doctrine and Covenants not only tells us what we need to *know*, but also what *we need to do in order to be saved* in the Kingdom of God. It tells of commandments to be kept, ordinances to be done and preparations to be made before the Second Coming.

3. In a world filled with fear and conflict, the Doctrine and Covenants is a source *of peace and tranquility.* When the Savior promised peace to his ancient disciples, he was not promising a world free from war and contention, for we await the Millennium for such a wonderful day. James said: "Peace I leave with you, my peace I give unto you: Not as the world giveth, give I unto you. Let not your heart be troubled, neither let it be afraid." (John 14:27.) The Doctrine and Covenants further states, he who walks "in the meekness of my Spirit . . . shall have peace in me" (D&C 19:23).

4. Those who regularly read the Doctrine and Covenants will find themselves *spiritually strengthened* and better able to handle the constant challenges of living in this world. In moments of discouragement or despair, we are reminded that he who descended below all things and suffered in our behalf is aware of us and our needs and can provide hope and comfort.

5. Through the Doctrine and Covenants we receive an *assurance of the reality of God.* He is our Father and Jesus is his Son. They live! In a day when the existence of God and the divine nature of Jesus Christ is questioned and even ridiculed, we stand firm in such witnesses as the following from the Doctrine and Covenants:

"And now, after the many testimonies which have been given of him, this is the testimony, last of all, which we give of him: That he lives!" (D&C 76:22.)

To that witness I add my own. I know Jesus Christ to be the Son of God. I know that he lives. I know that the Doctrine and Covenants is an inspired book of scripture that will bless your lives as you prayerfully study its contents and seek to live its teachings. (88–08)

Many Polynesians originally came from the Americas. We know that the Lord inspired a valiant group of his children to leave America to travel to Tahiti and from there populate other areas, including this beautiful land [New Zealand]. . . . They followed true principles, had faith in themselves and trusted completely in the Lord. They were successful in what was an extraordinarily difficult mission. Many here today are the benefactors of their courage and conviction, their determination and obedience. (90–09)

It has been the position of the Church that Polynesians are related to the American Indians as descendants of Father Lehi, having migrated to the Pacific from America. Elder Mark E. Petersen, speaking on this subject in General Conference, said:

"As Latter-day Saints we have always believed that the Polynesians are descendants of Lehi and blood relatives of the American Indians, despite the contrary theories of other men" (in Conference Report, April 1962, p. 112).

Our belief in this regard is scriptural (see Alma 63:4–10). (84–03)

The Bible

The Bible is a great literary and spiritual book. One who is interested in fine literature and the learning of great men and is seeking to learn the will of God should turn to the Bible. No greater literary work was ever compiled. To understand the books of the men of old, so that they yield up their secrets in rich measure, is indeed an object worthy of effort. The book recalls history and contains biographies, sociology, philosophy, poetry, and the meaning of life itself. (51–01)

No man shall add to or take away from the book of Revelation. A young friend in the mission field wrote a letter to me regarding a question that had been asked of him concerning the concluding verses of the Bible and how they apply to the Book of Mormon. We remember that at the end of the book of Revelation, the last book of the Bible, the author, John, issues a warning and a curse upon any man who adds to or takes away from the book. Specifically, these are the words he wrote:

"For I testify unto every man that heareth the words of the prophecy of this book, If any man shall add unto these things, God shall add unto him the plagues that are written in this book:

"And if any man shall take away from the words of the book of this prophecy, God shall take away his part out of the book of life, and out of the holy city, and from the things which are written in this book" (Revelation 22:18–19).

These verses of scripture have been cited repeatedly by those attempting to discredit the Book of Mormon, claiming that God's revelation to man is closed. Nothing more is to be added and nothing is to be taken away. They assert that the Book of Mormon is an attempt to add to the words of the Bible. These claims were made when the Book of Mormon was first published and have continued to be made, and are made today. Is there any validity to such assertions?

The answer to this query is really very simple. A careful reading of the words makes it clear that the warning against adding to or taking away does not refer to the whole Bible or even to the New Testament, but to use John's words, only to the words of "the book of this prophecy." That is, the prophecy contained in the book of Revelation. This is substantiated by the fact that some of the books of the New Testament had not yet been written when John wrote the book of Revelation, and even those that had been written and were in existence at that time had not yet been gathered into one compilation.

The collection of writings consisting of the sixty-six books we know as the Bible were brought together and compiled into one volume long after John wrote the prophetic book that has been placed at the end of the collection. It is clear, therefore, that the terrible judgments pronounced upon those who add to the book could not possibly apply to the whole of the Bible or even to the New Testament, but only to the book of Revelation. . . .

It is also interesting to note that John himself added to scripture after writing the book of Revelation, which is generally conceded to have been written while he was on the Isle of Patmos. It was long after John left Patmos that he wrote his first epistle. This fact standing alone would be sufficient to defeat the claim that revelation was closed and that man was enjoined from adding to scripture. This adds cumulative evidence that John had reference to the book of Revelation only. (81–01, p. 64)

6

RIGHTEOUSNESS, PERFECTION, AND TRIALS

Striving for Perfection

We must strive all our lives to attain exaltation. "Strive to enter in at the strait gate: for many, I say unto you, will seek to enter in, and shall not be able" (Luke 13:24).

"Strive to enter in," he said. Striving is the thing which prepares us to be worthy. The mere fact that we receive salvation by grace, that is, that we will live again because of the atoning sacrifice of our Lord and Savior, does not make us worthy to be saved in the highest degree of glory. He has said that every man will be judged according to his works.

Thus it requires earnest striving all of our lives and the doing of good works—those things which he has commanded us to do in order to be worthy for that exaltation whereby we shall live again in his presence.

In this day of moral confusion may we so live and conduct our lives that when we see him face to face he will say, "Well done thou good and faithful servant." (60–09)

There is a need for spiritual maturity. Just because we have become of age, or entered into marriage, or have acquired gray in our hair, does not mean that we have attained spiritual maturity.

Among our acquaintances we know people who are adults, but have not matured beyond the age of childhood. Children cry and create a disturbance when they don't get what they want. We know of adults who do the same thing. Some persons find it difficult to work with others because they want their own way in everything that is done. There are some who do not go to church for the childish reason that someone has offended them. We have many people who have been members of the Church since childhood and yet are so immature spiritually that they do not live the Word of Wisdom, pay their tithing, hold family evening, or comply with the simple things the Lord has asked us to do. Paul must have been thinking of these things when he wrote to the Corinthians to build up their faith. He said, "When I was a child, I spake as a child, I understood as a child, I thought as a child: but when I became a man, I put away childish things" (1 Corinthians 13:11). . . .

Can we say as Paul said that we have put away childish things and so developed ourselves by conscious effort that we are demonstrating the attributes the Lord would have us acquire? How much maturity will be required of us to live in exaltation in the celestial kingdom of the Lord? The Master made a very significant statement when he said: "Not every one that saith unto me, Lord, Lord, shall enter into the kingdom of heaven; but he that doeth the will of my Father which is in heaven" (Matthew 7:21).

Spiritual maturity is a process that continues through life if we consciously seek this maturity. This becomes imperative if we are to be successful leaders in teaching spirituality to others. (68–02)

Excellence requires strict discipline. Excellence comes because it is achieved, and it cannot be achieved except by strict discipline and definiteness of purpose. (71–04)

The Lord requires us to be willing and obedient. Part of our difficulty as we strive to acquire spirituality is the feeling that there is much to do and that we are falling far short. Perfection is something yet ahead for every one of us; but we can capitalize on our strengths, begin where we are, and seek after the happiness that can be found in pursuing the things of God. We should remember the Lord's counsel:

"Wherefore, be not weary in well-doing, for ye are laying the foundation of a great work. And out of small things proceedeth that which is great.

"Behold, the Lord requireth the heart and a willing mind; and the willing and obedient shall eat the good of the land of Zion in these last days." (D&C 64:33–34.)

It has always been encouraging to me that the Lord said it is the "willing and obedient [who] shall eat the good of the land of

Zion in these last days." All of us can be willing and obedient. If the Lord had said the perfect shall eat the good of the land of Zion in these last days, I suppose some of us would be discouraged and give up. (79–02, pp. 25–26)

Inflated expectations can distort our view of greatness. I am concerned that some among us today are undoubtedly unhappy. Some of us feel we are falling short of our expected ideals. I have particular concern for those who have lived righteously, but think—because they haven't achieved in the world or in the Church what others have achieved—that they have failed. Each of us desires to achieve a measure of greatness in this life. And why shouldn't we? As someone once noted, there is within each of us a giant struggling with celestial homesickness.

Realizing who we are and what we may become assures us that with God nothing really is impossible. From the time we learn that Jesus wants us for a Sunbeam until we learn more fully the basic principles of the gospel, we are taught to strive for perfection. It is not new to us then to talk of the importance of achievement. The difficulty arises when inflated expectations of the world alter our definition of greatness. (87–01, p. 111)

In our spiritual progression we must be careful not to compare ourselves to others. While true godly sorrow leads to repentance of sins, our reflections on the past should not be self-debasing nor generate self-doubt. Indeed, one of the signs of mature Latter-day Saint life is the ability to see a limitation in ourselves without letting it cast a shadow over all the many other good things we do and say. We read of, and sometimes know, individuals who are so self-critical that their attitude leads to extremes—even destructive behavior. It is almost as if they are compelled to belittle themselves.

I suppose it is inevitable that we will compare ourselves to others, but that is an unfortunate mortal tendency in us and seldom leads to anything very constructive. Usually we just get depressed, thinking everyone else is doing so well while we are not or has this or that quality we don't have. Why are we so hard on ourselves, knowing full well that everyone has problems and limitations, as well as strengths and talents? We would never let others be so hard on themselves, but we are certainly inclined to be hard on ourselves.

Let me use an example close at hand. I think of two young men who are both fine BYU basketball players. More important they are both fine young men. But they are not alike in physical makeup or personal interests or academic majors or a hundred and one other differences that one person has from another. But we applaud that and understand it. Wouldn't it be foolish, even destructive, if these two men spent a lot of time wishing they were the other person? It would not help our basketball fortunes to have a nearly seven-foot man bringing the ball down the court nor one slightly over six feet playing the post position. Obviously, each of these young men has a task of his own, best suited to himself, and individual talents to develop.

If that is so obvious on the basketball court, why can't it be a little more obvious in life? Why do we allow ourselves to waste such energy and emotion comparing ourselves to others when our real task is to develop what we are and what we have, to be all that we can be?

This is especially true in matters of the spirit and salvation. (92–01, pp. 40–41)

Thoughtfully pursued resolutions can bless our lives. The practice of reviewing the past and setting new directions for the future is a very healthy one, a scripturally encouraging one, in which we can beneficially alter our lives. I commend the practice to you, especially if it is thoughtfully pursued and the resolutions made are made in righteousness, bringing behaviors and attitudes that truly bless your lives and the lives of others. . . .

Sometimes our resolutions are a part of the process of repentance from past sins—actual transgressions for which we need forgiveness. Sometimes our goals focus on less serious matters, such as errors of judgment or flaws in our personality that may not be sins as such but that we nevertheless desire to change. Yes, life offers a multitude of lessons and plenty of things to improve. It is wonderful to believe in the gospel of Jesus Christ, which encourages such lofty views and gives us every avenue to achieve them. (92–01, p. 40)

The gospel is the divine plan for spiritual growth. None of us has attained perfection or the zenith of spiritual growth that is possible in mortality. Every person can and must make spiritual progress. The gospel of Jesus Christ is the divine plan for that spiritual growth eternally. It is more than a code of ethics. It is more than an ideal social order. It is more than positive thinking about self-improvement and determination. The gospel is the saving power of the Lord Jesus Christ with his priesthood and sustenance and with the Holy Spirit. With faith in the Lord Jesus Christ and obedience to his gospel, a step at a time improving as we go, pleading for strength, improving our attitudes and our ambitions, we will find ourselves successfully in the fold of the Good Shepherd. (79–02, p. 26)

Progressing towards perfection is a long-term commitment. As I understand it, in this mortal life the direction we are moving is more important than a particular degree of perfection. We all experience cycles of progression and times when we fight against these inevitable challenges of regression. Great blessings from the Lord attend our efforts to progress. And progression is certainly more effective if it is a process, a long-term commitment, rather than just a series of isolated and irregular events. (92–01, pp. 41–42)

What does the word "saint" mean? The word *saint* does not mean that any of us is perfect. What it does mean is that we are all trying, all serving, and all vowing to stand firm in the faith. (87–03, p. 17)

Maintaining Our Standards

The gospel must become the motivating influence in all we do. Righteousness must start in our own individual lives. It must be incorporated into family living. Parents have the responsibility to follow the principles of the gospel of Jesus Christ and teach them to their children. Religion must be part of our living. The gospel of Jesus Christ must become the motivating influence in all that we do. There must be more striving within in order to follow the great example set by the Savior if we are to become more like him. This becomes our great challenge. (94–08, pp. 2, 4)

The ability to stand by our principles is what matters. The ability to stand by one's principles, to live with integrity and faith according to one's belief—that is what matters, that is the difference between a contribution and a commitment. That devotion to true principle—in our individual lives, in our homes and families, and in all places that we meet and influence other people—that devotion is what God is ultimately requesting of us. (90–03, p. 61)

Our Father in Heaven requires a total commitment. As I think of the blessings God has given us and the many beauties of the gospel of Jesus Christ, I am aware that along the way we are asked to make certain contributions in return, contributions of time or of money or of other resources. These are all valued and all necessary, but they do not constitute our full offering to God. Ultimately, what our Father in Heaven will require of us is more than a contribution; it is a total commitment, a complete devotion, all that we are and all that we can be.

Please understand that I do not speak only of a commitment to the Church and its activities, although that always needs to be strengthened. No, I speak more specifically of a commitment that is shown in our individual behavior, in our personal integrity, in our loyalty to home and family and community, as well as to the Church. (90–03, p. 60)

The principles of Christianity will survive. It is claimed by some prominent authorities that Christianity is on the wane, but the principles of Christianity will never be defeated. Man may hate man, and nation rise against nation, and there may be dark periods when it would seem that God has forsaken; but in the end, right will win, and the principles of Christianity survive. (41–01)

By obeying God's laws we can make the world a better place. The world would be a better place to live if we would think and act as God would have us do. . . .

They are the most happy whose lives have been dedicated to the endeavor of making the world a better place to live by raising the standards of thought and action. This can only be done by strict observance to the laws which God has laid down for the conduct of man in this mortal existence. (60–04, p. 126)

We should measure everything against the teachings of the Savior. Measure whatever anyone else asks you to do, whether it be from your family, loved ones, your cultural heritage, or traditions you have inherited—measure everything against the teachings of the Savior. Where you find a variance from those teachings, set that matter aside and do not pursue it. It will not bring you happiness. (90–09)

Fix your attention on your goals and don't look back. [Quotes Luke 9:61–62] To dig a straight furrow, the plowman needs to keep his eyes on a fixed point ahead of him. That keeps him on a true course. If, however, he happens to look back to see where he has been, his chances of straying are increased. The results are crooked and irregular furrows. . . . Fix your attention on your . . . goal[s] and never look back on your earlier problems. . . . If our energies are focused not behind us but ahead of us—on eternal life and the joy of salvation—we assuredly will obtain it. (87–03, p. 17)

Sacrifice, Service, and Unselfishness

Beware of the spiritual danger of the spotlight. I think we should be aware that there can be a spiritual danger to those who misunderstand the singularity of always being in the spotlight. They may come to covet the notoriety and thus forget the significance of the service being rendered. . . . You must not allow yourselves to focus on the fleeting light of popularity or substitute that attractive glow for the substance of true, but often anonymous labor that brings the attention of God even if it does not get coverage on the six o'clock news. In fact, applause and attention can become the spiritual Achilles' heel of even the most gifted among us. . . .

At times of attention and visibility it might also be profitable for us to answer the question, Why do we serve? When we understand why, we won't be concerned about where we serve. (90–06, p. 5)

We should be willing to serve and grow quietly. If you feel that much of what you do this year or in the years to come does not make you very famous, take heart. Most of the best people who ever lived weren't very famous either. Serve and grow, faithfully and quietly. Be on guard regarding the praise of men. (90–06, p. 6)

The Savior's life was a life of service. As the trials of Gethsemane and Calvary fast approached, with much weighing heavily upon his mind, the Savior took time to notice the widow casting in her mite (see Mark 12:41–44). Similarly his gaze took in the small-statured Zacchaeus who, unable to see because of the size of those congregating around the Savior, had climbed a sycamore tree for a view of the Son of God (see Luke 19:1–5). While hanging in agony upon the cross, he overlooked his own suffering and reached out in caring concern to the weeping woman who had given him life (see John 19:25–27).

What a marvelous example for us to follow! Even in the midst of great personal sorrow and pain, our Exemplar reached out to bless others. This was typical of one whose mortal life had known few comforts and who had said, "The foxes have holes, and the birds of the air have nests; but the Son of man hath not where to lay his head" (Matthew 8:20). His was not a life focused on the things he did not have. It was a life of reaching out in service to others. (89–02, p. 77)

Serving brings happiness. Let us look backward for just a moment to our childhood and analyze that which gave us the greatest happiness when we were children. I am inclined to believe that the things we enjoyed most and those that gave us the greatest happiness when we were children were the things that were given to us. When our parents went away and returned, we always looked for some little token they would bring back to us. We looked forward to Christmas because of the things we were going to receive. Our whole life was built around receiving. At that time we did not understand the other side of giving. Sometime during our progress through this life, we came to that point when we suddenly realized it was not receiving that brings us happiness. To some this comes early in life; to others it comes later; and I am inclined to believe that there are some who never have this awakening during the daytime of their lives. They miss one of the great principles that brings happiness to us.

When the time comes that we learn to share and do things for other people, life takes on a new vision for us. This has come to the lives of most of you. To some it comes when a young man goes on a mission and he suddenly discovers that he is giving of himself, his time, his energy and his means for the benefit of others. To some, this awakening comes at marriage. Suddenly one discovers that happiness does not come from receiving, but from that which one gives to another. (61–02, pp. 2–3)

The true gift is a portion of ourselves. Giving does not always consist of material things. Ralph Waldo Emerson wrote: "Rings and jewels are not gifts, but apologies for gifts; the only gift is a portion of thyself." In this sense we have unlimited resources. (61–02, p. 3)

There are gifts that money cannot buy. The gifts money cannot buy are those which bring happiness to us in life. These are the gifts we pass on to others from the attributes we acquire as we go through life. First is the attribute of thoughtfulness to others, and second, its close cousin, consideration for others. Third, we must have courage—courage to do the right thing always. Fourth, those who have a good nature enjoy life. A pleasant smile begets smiles; smiles beget friends; friends are better than fortunes. Fifth is the attribute of tolerance. I think of an old Indian prayer: "Great spirit, help me never to judge another until I have walked two weeks in his moccasins." Sixth, we must have appreciation for those things that come to us or we never find happiness. Seventh, we enjoy life when we have the ability to praise others for their good works. George Matthew Adams said: "He who praises another, enriches himself more than he does the one praised. To praise is an investment in happiness. The poorest human being has something to give that the richest cannot buy."

David Dunn told the story of a man sitting on the doorstep of his house when a little girl walked by looking very dejected. He said to her, "That is a pretty red dress you have." She looked up at him and smiled and said, "Thank you," and went skipping off down the street. Later when he passed her house she came out to the sidewalk and waving to him said, "Hello man." He had found a friend. It is easy to find friends as we pass this way if we acquire the attributes that attract friends; they are some of our most priceless possessions. Robert Louis Stevenson said, "A friend is a present you give yourself."

Eighth, to find happiness we must help others as we go through life. Elihu Root wrote: "I observe that there are two entirely different theories according to which individual men seek to get on in the world. One theory leads a man to pull down everybody around him in order to climb up on them to a higher place. The other leads a man to help everybody around him in order that he may go up with them."

If we rise to success in life, it is because we have lifted others up with us. I like to think of success as a journey, not as a destination. Happiness is found along the way of this journey, not at the end of the road. The time for happiness is today, not tomorrow. A century ago Stephen Grellet wrote: "I expect to pass through this world but once. Any good therefore that I can do, or any kindness that I can show to any fellow creature, let me do it now. Let me not defer or neglect it, for I shall not pass this way again." (61–02, pp. 3–4)

When we give we are blessed. "It is more blessed to give than to receive."

When we learn this lesson of giving, we are on the high road. Our lives change, our attitudes change, maturity develops, and we are ready to face life. If each day we could be kind and courteous and thoughtful, our circle of friends would increase. If we could forget the grumbling and all the other things that are negative, how bright our lives would become. We can do it if we will merely follow the counsel of the Savior, think of him and his life, and lift ourselves by living close to the Spirit and that inspiration. He will bless us, walk with us, and extend his hand to us, and life will become what we would like it to be—high, noble, and elevating. (61–02, pp. 5–6)

Strive to do something worthwhile for others. If it is your aim to do something worthwhile, something beneficial to others, your endeavor can be accomplished in any field. It isn't necessary to seek the unusual or the extraordinary to achieve that which will enhance men's lives by making them happier or better. This more commonly comes about through the endeavor one sets upon in making his daily living. Men who are sincere in their work will have the opportunity to do something worthwhile for the benefit of others, in whatever field they are striving, whether it be in the arts or sciences, in business or the professions, or in any other chosen field. Great is the man who so conducts himself and his affairs that if others follow his example, the world would live on a higher plain. This becomes your challenge.

Every human being has the natural instinct to seek and acquire food for himself. When he comes to the point where he earnestly and sincerely desires that there shall be food for others, his life has been enriched by what might be termed a "moral or spiritual consciousness." I would have called this "religion" except for the fact that many people are still thinking of religion as a list of things not to do. The development of moral or spiritual consciousness, or "real religion," is, of course, the ultimate enrichment of life. It transforms human life from the earth to the skies, from the clod to the cloud, from the beast to the god. (63–04, p. 17)

The Lord expects us to use our talents in his service. Those who use their talents find they will grow. One who exercises his strength finds it will increase. If we sow a seed, it will grow; if we fail to plant, it will be lost. One who possesses some insight and is attentive to his teacher will gain more knowledge and insight and will have growth in mind and spiritual understanding. Understanding increases as it is used. As we learn, we acquire greater capacity to learn. As we use our opportunities for knowledge, more opportunities come to us. How sad it is when the opposite course is followed, and talent and capacity are wasted and not used. "From him that hath not shall be taken away even that which he hath" (Matthew 25:29).

Talents are not given to us to be put on display or to be hidden away, but to be used. The Master expects us to make use of them. He expects us to venture forth and increase what we have been given according to our capacities and abilities (see Matthew 25:26–30). As servants of the Lord, we should use every opportunity to employ our talents in his service. To fail to do so means to lose them. If we do not increase, we decrease. Our quest is to seek out the talents the Lord has given us and to develop and multiply them, whether they be five, two, or one. We need not attempt to imitate the talents given to other persons. . . .

May the Lord give us the desire to be faithful servants and to make gain for him so that he might say to us, also, "Well done, thou good and faithful servant: thou hast been faithful over a few things, I will make thee ruler over many things: enter thou into the joy of thy lord" (Matthew 25:21). (71–07, p. 172)

The greatest gift of all is the gift of ourselves. If I were giving an assignment to the young people, it would be to give something to someone tomorrow—to make a gift. I don't mean a gift that we would go to the store to buy and have wrapped in colorful paper and ribbon, I am thinking of the gift we make when we give of ourselves—the greatest gift of all.

If today's spirituality has meant anything to you, find someone tomorrow and do something for that person. It may be someone at home or it may be a friend. It's an interesting experience to find someone who has wronged us or who has been anything but friendly, and see the change that comes about when you give him a gift.

The Lord said it is more blessed to give than to receive. We understand that principle. As little children we looked for the thing we were going to receive at Christmas time, but then came the time in our lives when we found more pleasure in giving to someone else. That was when maturity came into our lives and we stepped aside from being self-centered and found it was more blessed to do things for others as the Lord had indicated. (79–14)

What is true greatness? In a short editorial written by President Joseph F. Smith in 1905, he made this most profound statement about what true greatness really is:

"Those things which we call extraordinary, remarkable, or unusual may make history, but they do not make real life.

"After all, to do well those things which God ordained to be the common lot of all mankind, is the truest greatness. To be a successful father or a successful mother is greater than to be a successful general or a successful statesman." (*Juvenile Instructor*, 15 December 1905, p. 752.)

This statement raises a query as to what are the things God has ordained to be the common lot of all mankind. Surely they include the things that must be done in order to be a good father or a good mother, but, to generalize, they are also the thousands of little deeds and tasks of service and sacrifice that constitute the giving or losing of one's life for others and for the Lord. They include gaining a knowledge of our Father in Heaven and his gospel. They include bringing others into the faith and fellowship of his kingdom. These things do not usually receive the attention or the adulation of the world.

To extend the statement of President Smith and to be more specific, we could say: To be a successful Primary president or den mother or Spiritual Living teacher or loving neighbor or listening friend is much of what true greatness is all about. To do one's best in the face of the commonplace struggles of life, and possibly in the face of failures, and to continue to endure and persevere with the ongoing difficulties of life—when those struggles and tasks contribute to the progress and happiness of others and the eternal salvation of one's self—this is true greatness. (82–02, p. 19)

Simple service and sacrifice can bring true greatness. Frequently it is the commonplace tasks that have the greatest positive effect on the lives of others, as compared with the things that the world so often relates to greatness.

It appears to me that the kind of greatness that our Father in Heaven would have us pursue is within the grasp of all who are within the gospel net. We have an unlimited number of opportunities to do the many simple and minor things that will ultimately make us great. To those who have devoted their lives to service and sacrifice for others and for the Lord, the best counsel is simply to do more of the same.

To those who are doing the commonplace work of the world but are wondering about the value of their accomplishments; to those who are the workhorses of this Church, who are furthering the work of the Lord in so many quiet but significant ways; to those who are the salt of the earth and the strength of the world and the backbone of each nation—to you we would simply express our admiration. If you endure to the end, and if you are valiant in the testimony of Jesus, you will achieve true greatness and will live in the presence of our Father in Heaven.

As President Joseph F. Smith has said, "Let us not be trying to substitute an artificial life for the true one" (*Juvenile Instructor*, p. 753). Let us remember that "out of small things proceedeth that which is great" (D&C 64:33). (82–02, p. 20)

The Lord measures our devotion by how we love and serve our fellowmen. In ancient times, one test of the purity of gold was performed with a smooth, black, siliceous stone called a touchstone. When rubbed across the touchstone, the gold produced a streak or mark on its surface. The goldsmith matched this mark to a color on his chart of graded colors. The mark was redder as the amount of copper or alloy increased or yellower as the percentage of gold increased. This process showed quite accurately the purity of the gold.

The touchstone method of testing the purity of gold was quick and was satisfactory for most practical purposes. But the goldsmith who still questioned the purity completed a more accurate test by using a process that involved fire.

I suggest to you that the Lord has prepared a touchstone for you and me, an outward measurement of inward discipleship that marks our faithfulness and will survive the fires yet to come. . . .

He will measure our devotion to him by how we love and serve our fellowmen. What kind of mark are we leaving on the Lord's touchstone? Are we truly good neighbors? Does the test show us to be 24-karat gold, or can the trace of fool's gold be detected? (86–03, p. 34)

Self-Mastery and Thoughts

To have peace we must not harbor evil thoughts. To have peace, we must banish enmity for others. Having an evil thought is far more injurious to the person who harbors it than it is to the one against whom he harbors the evil thought. The Lord taught that peace comes from within, not from outward circumstances. (45–01)

Living the law of the harvest brings peace and prosperity. If you are dishonest in your dealings, if you cheat in your examinations, you are sowing the seeds of slavery and you will reap that harvest even though you might rationalize to yourself, "I am free." If you are involved in necking and petting and immoral practices, you are becoming enslaved to your own passions and appetites, even though in your self-justifying pride you may say, "I am free." If you, yourself, resist these satanic temptations and determine to pay the daily price, to live the Law of the Harvest by clean, moral thoughts and practices, by upright, honest dealings, by integrity and conscientiousness in your studies, by fasting, prayer and worship, you will reap the harvest of freedom and inner peace and prosperity. (66–01, pp. 10–11)

Noble character is the result of right thinking. A man's mind might be likened to a flower garden. It may be a thing of beauty or it may be filled with weeds and the potential beauty hidden.

As a plant springs from a seed, so every act of man springs from the hidden seed of thought. This applies equally to those acts that are described as spontaneous and unpremeditated as well as to those which are deliberately conceived. It has been said that our actions are the blossoms of thought, and joy and suffering are its fruits. Therefore, a man reaps the fruit of his own husbandry.

A noble character is not a thing of chance, but is the result of continued effort in right thinking. Man is made or unmade by himself. He fashions the tools with which he builds mansions of joy and happiness for himself, or he forges the weapons by which he destroys himself.

As a being of power, intelligence, and the master of his own thoughts, a man holds the key to every situation, to make his life what he chooses it to be. When he discovers the divine power within his soul, he can lead his life to a God-like nature. If one dreams lofty dreams, so shall he become. There is magic in the way one thinks. If we expect the worst, we will get the worst. If we expect the best, we will receive the best. If we train our minds to have faith in God and ourselves, we are using one of the great laws of life. If we think and live righteously, happiness will find its place in our lives. It is amazing when we expect the best how forces are set in motion which cause the best to materialize. (83–02)

Our thoughts more than circumstances determine the course of our lives. Outward circumstances do not determine the course of our lives as much as the thoughts that habitually occupy our minds. These thoughts carve their impression on our faces, in our hearts, and on the tablet of our eternal souls. (83–02)

The gospel teaches us to avoid negative thinking. The news media, radio, television, newspapers, national magazines, and many other things we hear and read, bring to us depressing, negative thoughts. We are constantly reminded of crime, war, riots, divorce, theft, murder, death, disease, vulgarity, pornography, strikes, short skirts and long hair, marijuana, hunger, birth control, LSD, corruption in government, and even questionable politics. A few days ago, I examined every article on the first few pages of the newspaper. Every article I read expressed a negative thought or a depressing situation. There was nothing to add a cheerful note, a positive or uplifting thought, or a hope for the future. . . .

Stepping out of a negative world into such an atmosphere of love and a positive hope for the future, not only in mortality but exaltation in eternity, is known only by a small minority. How blessed we are for an understanding of the gospel of Jesus Christ. His gospel of love encourages us to look upward and not down, to look for the good in life and not the bad, to seek the positive and not the negative.

Negative thinking has ruined many lives. Persons who might otherwise have been successful have been defeated because their thinking was negative. (68–02)

Personal purity is a requirement of those who serve the Lord. We must strive to be pure in thought and action.

It is impressive to me that the primary requirement of the Lord for the work of his ministry is personal purity. To the first elders of the Church, the Lord said:

"Sanctify yourselves; yea, purify your hearts, and cleanse your hands and your feet before me, that I may make you clean" (D&C 88:74).

This implies more than just a chaste life. To those ordained to the ministry, the Lord said, "Strip yourselves from jealousies and fears, and humble yourselves before me" (D&C 67:10). We are further told that we cannot be pure in heart until we have acquired the pure love of Christ, which is charity, "that we may be purified even as he is pure" (Moroni 7:48).

Purity of thought and action therefore requires us to take on the mind of Christ! As we ponder on the meaning of this thought, it is evident that spiritual promptings do not come to one who is covetous in heart, nor will they come to one who has an irritable disposition, one who is jealous, one who doubts, or one who constantly worries.

Faith in God is essential to be a vessel through whom the Lord can work. (83–06)

Agency

Free agency is an eternal principle. Man's free agency and individual freedom is God-given and is an eternal principle. Any nation or any form of government which takes away the free agency of an individual and makes the individual subservient to the state is basically wrong. One of our great leaders has said, "Individual freedom is innate in the human soul. God has given us our free agency, and next to life itself that is our greatest gift from heaven." (David O. McKay, *Church News*, April 30, 1952, p. 1.)

As Christians and as liberty-loving people we should band together in opposition to any system or political theory that deprives men of their agency and takes from them the light that was brought into the world by the Son of man. (59–04)

All of us have been free moral agents from the beginning. Since the beginning, men have been born free moral agents with the freedom to choose between good or evil. Even in the preexistence the spirit children of the Father had their choice. "For, behold, the devil was before Adam, for he rebelled against me, saying, Give me thine honor, which is my power; and also a third part of the hosts of heaven turned he away from me because of their agency" (D&C 29:36).

This same choice was given to the first man placed upon the earth, for after he was formed and placed amid the abundance that had been created the Lord said: "Of every tree of the garden thou mayest freely eat, [b]ut of the tree of the knowledge of good and evil, thou shalt not eat of it, nevertheless, thou mayest choose for thyself" (Moses 3:16–17). . . .

There has never been a time when man has been forced to do good or forced to obey the commandments of God. He has always been given his free choice—his free moral agency. If one looks back through the events of history, there come into view the results of the greatness of men who kept the commandments of the Lord and made the choice on his side. One also sees strewn along the wayside the ruins that stand as silent reminders of those who chose otherwise. Both had their free moral agency. (66–03, pp. 515, 516)

There is a difference between free agency and freedom. It would be impossible for us to achieve our destiny without having free agency. God intended for man to be free and to exercise his choice. He may choose the right or the wrong, he may walk in darkness or in light, but he has the right of election to shape his own destiny. One of the principle purposes of mortality is for man to have the opportunity to learn the difference between right and wrong and between good and evil. This knowledge is necessary to gain the spiritual maturity to make righteous choices.

Sometimes the term "free agency" is confused with the word "freedom," and the two are often used as though they meant the same thing. Even though they are similar there is a difference in meaning. To have free agency means that we have unrestrained or unrestricted privilege and opportunity of exercising the right of choice if there is an alternative. Freedom, on the other hand, is the privilege to act upon choices after they are made. As individuals we want to be free from oppression; free from discrimination; free from laws, restraints, or restrictions that limit our exercise of agency or choice. In short, we may say free agency is the right, ability, and opportunity to choose between possible alternatives, while freedom is the right, ability, and opportunity to do things that have been chosen.

A few years ago you [graduates] were faced with the choice of going on to the university or not going forward with your education. If you had chosen not to continue, that would have concluded the matter. Choices made in the negative have this effect, but if made in the positive, positive action becomes necessary. Your decision at that time was to continue with your education; thus you gained a new freedom. Choices made in the negative usually terminate our progression, whereas if made in the positive, a new course of action is opened up to us. The choice opens the way; action carries it forward. Choice, then, is a matter of free agency, and freedom is realized in the performance of the action. (79–03)

We are free to follow or oppose the Lord's direction. We came to mortal life to encounter resistance. It was part of the plan for our eternal progress. Without temptation, sickness, pain, and sorrow, there could be no goodness, virtue, appreciation for well-being, or joy. The law of opposition makes freedom of choice possible; therefore, our Heavenly Father has commanded his children, "Choose ye this day, to serve the Lord God who made you" (Moses 6:33). He has counseled us to yield to his spirit and resist temptation. Free agency, of course, permits us to oppose his directions; thus, we see many who resist the truth and yield to temptation. (80–01, p. 25)

Measure all your decisions against the teachings of the Savior. I would like to say something to you that I consider to be very important. Throughout your life, you will be faced with many choices. How well you select among the alternatives will determine your success and happiness in life. Some of the decisions you will make will be absolutely critical and can affect the entire course of your life. Please measure those alternatives against the teachings of Jesus Christ.

To be able to do that you must know and understand his teachings. As you exercise faith and live worthy of inspiration, you will be directed in the important choices you make. The very wise know and obey the will of our Father in Heaven. (90–09)

Our future is fashioned by the choices we make. "Behold, I set before you this day a blessing and a curse;

"A blessing, if ye obey the commandments of the Lord your God, which I command you this day:

"And a curse, if ye will not obey the commandments of the Lord your God" (Deuteronomy 11:26–28).

That is the choice the Lord puts before us as we face our own promised lands and our own bright futures. We are given the knowledge, the help, the enticement, and the freedom to choose the path of eternal safety and salvation. The choice to do so is ours. By divine decree before this world was, the actual choice is and always has been our own.

Let us be conscious of the fact that our future is being fashioned by the decisions we make. May we exercise our faith and our agency in choosing the blessings God has set before us in the great gospel plan of our Savior. (89–06, p. 18)

God will not violate our agency. To fully understand this gift of agency and its inestimable worth, it is imperative that we understand that God's chief way of acting is by persuasion and patience and long-suffering, not by coercion and stark confrontation. He acts by gentle solicitation and by sweet enticement. He always acts with unfailing respect for the freedom and independence that we possess. He wants to help us and pleads for the chance to assist us, but he will not do so in violation of our agency. He loves us too much to do that, and doing so would run counter to his divine character.

Brigham Young once said, "The volition of [man] is free; this is a law of their existence, and the Lord cannot violate his own law; were he to do that, he would cease to be God. . . . This is a law which has always existed from all eternity, and will continue to exist throughout all the eternities to come. Every intelligent being must have the power of choice." (*Journal of Discourses* 11:272.)

To countermand and ultimately forbid our choices was Satan's way, not God's, and the Father of us all simply never will do that. He will, however, stand by us forever to help us see the right path, find the right choice, respond to the true voice, and feel the influence of his undeniable Spirit. His gentle, peaceful, powerful persuasion to do right and find joy will be with us "so long as time shall last, or the earth shall stand, or there shall be one man upon the face thereof to be saved" (Moroni 7:36). (89–06, p. 18)

God gave man the power to choose what he will be. Since the beginning God has given to every man the power to control his thoughts. He has also given man the freedom to select the course in life he wishes to pursue. . . .

Scriptures are replete with God's promised blessings to us if we will keep his commandments and comply with his laws, but it is a fundamental principle that we are never compelled to do his will. . . .

Marcus Aurelius once said, "A man's life is what his thoughts make of it." Emerson said, "A man is what he thinks about all day long." Man's mind may be likened unto a flower garden. It can be a thing of beauty and inspiration to the gardener and all who may gaze upon it, or it may be ill kept and overrun with weeds. As the plant which produces the beautiful flower grows from a seed, so every act of man springs from the hidden seed of thought. As a being of power and intelligence, and master of his own thoughts, man has the divinely given ability to make of himself what he chooses to be. (60–04, p. 124)

We must open the door to our heart. The well-known painting of Holman Hunt, which he titled "The Light of the World," has been the subject of much discussion for many years. It portrays the scripture in which Jesus said:

"Behold, I stand at the door, and knock: if any man hear my voice, and open the door, I will come in to him, and will sup with him, and he with me" (Revelation 3:20).

In the painting, Jesus is standing outside of a closed door with one of his hands on the door knocker. A crown of thorns is on his head, and he is standing in the weeds that have grown up in front of the door, indicating that it has not been opened for a long time. He is standing quietly and patiently. In his other hand he holds a lantern that casts a light on the door and the weeds and also on the nail prints in his hands.

The comments we have repeatedly heard from the critics is to the effect that the painter was careless—he put the knocker on the door, but failed to paint a doorknob or handle on the outside to open the door. Mr. Hunt answered his critics by saying that a knock would only indicate a desire for entry, but the door would need to be opened from inside.

Doors are not different today. We knock on the outside, but the door is unlocked and opened from the inside. This simple portrayal demonstrates a great principle. Isn't it true that the door to one's heart is opened from within? No one forces his way into the affections or love of another person. God does not force us to do right, and Satan does not have the power to force us to do wrong. They may stand at the door and knock, but we have the power to open it to whomsoever we wish. (81–04)

Afflictions, Suffering, and Trials

Disease and illness test our faith. We all struggle with health problems occasionally—others do so constantly. Illness and disease are part of the burden of mortality. Have faith and be positive. The power of the priesthood is real, and there is so much that is good in life, even if we struggle physically. It is a joy to know that there will be no injury or disease in the resurrection. (89–03, p. 115)

Life is not an easy journey. Life is certainly no straight and easy corridor along which we travel free and unhampered. Many times, it is a maze of passages through which we must find our way. If we have true faith, our Father in Heaven will open a door for us. Perhaps not the one which we ourselves would have thought of, but one that will ultimately prove good for us. Success does not come from following the easy course in life, but from hard work and effort.

An unknown author wrote a poem entitled "Adversity" that portrays this very thought:

> The tree that never had to fight
> For sun and sky and air and light;
> That stood out in the open plain,
> And always got its share of rain,
> Never became a forest king.
>
> The man who never had to toil,
> Who never had to win his share,
> Of sun and sky and light and air,
> Never became a manly man,
> But lived and died as he began.
>
> Good timber does not grow in ease;
> The stronger wind, the tougher trees;
> The more the storm, the more the strength;
> By sun and cold, by rain and snow,
> In tree or man, good timber grows.
>
> Where thickest stands the forest growth,
> We find the patriarchs of both,
> And they hold converse with the stars,
> Whose broken branches show the scars
> Of many winds and much of strife;
> This is the common law of life. (74–02)

We must emphasize our blessings and minimize our disappointments. My message to you today is to "fear not, little flock." It is to encourage you to rejoice in the great blessings of life. It is to invite you to feel the great thrill of gospel living and our Father in Heaven's love. Life is wonderful, even in the hard times, and there is happiness, joy, and peace at stops all along the way, and endless portions of them at the end of the road.

Sure, there are plenty of things to worry about—some of them very serious things—but that is why we speak in gospel terms of faith, and hope, and charity. As Latter-day Saints, ours is "the abundant life," and we try to emphasize our blessings and opportunities while we minimize our disappointments and worries. (89–03, p. 111)

If we suffer, it does not necessarily mean we have sinned. The lesson [the book of Job] portrays of a righteous man who remains faithful despite adversities stays with us. It is a lesson to those who are prone to criticize, who feel their lot is hard, or who are envious of their neighbor. Because hardship or misery comes to us does not necessarily mean that we have sinned—our faith is tested in many ways. (51–01)

The greatest growth occurs when the opposition is greatest. One hundred fifty years of Church history provide us with a lesson that when resistance and opposition are greatest, our faith, commitment, and growth have the greatest opportunity for advancement; when opposition is least, the tendency is to be complacent and lose faith. President Brigham Young said: "Let any people enjoy peace and quietness, unmolested, undisturbed,—never be persecuted for their religion, and they are very likely to neglect their duty, to become cold and indifferent, and lose their faith" (*Journal of Discourses* 7:42). This lesson, which applies to the Church collectively, also applies to individuals. (80–01, p. 25)

God will have a tried people. Today other biographies of faith are being written—Saints who, like Job, suffer physical pain, emotional sorrow, and even disloyalty from friends—yet remain faithful; Saints who, like Jacob, see sons and daughters not so valiant as they should be, but who bless them for their potential; Saints who, like Paul, endure great ridicule and endure to the end; Saints who, like Nephi, must separate themselves from family because of their commitment to the gospel. There are those who know pain and sorrow because of loss of loved ones; who know spiritual sorrow because children go astray; who experience loss of health, financial reverses, and emotional distress, and yet, like Job, resolve, "When he hath tried me, I shall come forth as gold" (Job 23:10). . . .

We stand on the summit of 150 years of Church history; yet there are other summits to climb before the work of God is crowned with victory. There will be tribulations collectively and hardships personally—that resistance so essential to the eternal plan.

What makes us imagine that we may be immune from the same experiences that refined the lives of former-day Saints? We must remember that the same forces of resistance which prevent our progress afford us also opportunities to overcome. God will have a tried people! (80–01, p. 26)

Fear is a principal weapon of Satan. Fear, which can come upon people in difficult days, is a principal weapon in the arsenal that Satan uses to make mankind unhappy. He who fears loses strength for the combat of life in the fight against evil. Therefore, the power of the evil one always tries to generate fear in human hearts. In every age and in every era fear has faced mankind. (93–01, p. 72)

We all must face adversity in our lives. We will all have some adversity in our lives. I think we can be reasonably sure of that. Some of it will have the potential to be violent and damaging and destructive. Some of it may even strain our faith in a loving God who has the power to administer relief in our behalf.

To those anxieties I think the Father of us all would say, "Why are ye so fearful? How is it that ye have no faith?" And of course that has to be faith for the whole journey, the entire experience, the fullness of our life, not simply around the bits and pieces and tempestuous moments. . . .

Jesus was not spared grief and pain and anguish and buffeting. No tongue can speak the unutterable burden he carried, nor have we the wisdom to understand the prophet Isaiah's description of him as "a man of sorrows" (Isaiah 53:3). His ship was tossed most of his life, and, at least to mortal eyes, it crashed fatally on the rocky coast of Calvary. We are asked not to look on life with mortal eyes; with spiritual vision we know something quite different was happening upon the cross.

Peace was on the lips and in the heart of the Savior no matter how fiercely the tempest was raging. May it so be with us—in our own hearts, in our own homes, in our nations of the world, and even in the buffetings faced from time to time by the Church. We should not expect to get through life individually or collectively without some opposition. (84–05, pp. 34–35)

Adversity and suffering are required even of the faithful. Doors close regularly in our lives, and some of those closings cause genuine pain and heartache. But I *do* believe that where one such door closes, another opens (and perhaps more than one), with hope and blessings in other areas of our lives that we might not have discovered otherwise.

President Marion G. Romney had some doors swing closed for him even in the work of his ministry. He knew considerable pain and discouragement and saw his plans changed during the last few years of his life. But it was he who said that all men and women, including the most faithful and loyal, would find adversity and affliction in their lives because, in the words of Joseph Smith, "Men have to suffer that they may come upon Mount Zion and be exalted above the heavens" (*History of the Church*, 5:556; see Conference Report, October 1969, p. 57). (87–04, p. 10)

Adversity is within the Lord's purposes. Adversity touches many, many lives. What makes the difference is how we accept it. It's important to know it's all within the purposes of the Lord, whatever they are for us. If we can submit ourselves to that, we can go forward in faith and understanding. (*Church News*, March 11, 1995, p. 13)

God knows more than we do concerning our trials. At various times in our lives, probably at repeated times in our lives, we do have to acknowledge that God knows what we do not know and sees what we do not see. "For my thoughts are not your thoughts, neither are your ways my ways, saith the Lord" (Isaiah 55:8).

If you have troubles at home with children who stray, if you suffer financial reverses and emotional strain that threaten your homes and your happiness, if you must face the loss of life or health, may peace be unto your soul. We will not be tempted beyond our ability to withstand. Our detours and disappointments are the straight and narrow path to him, as we sing in one of our favorite hymns:

When through fiery trials thy pathway shall lie,
My grace, all sufficient, shall be thy supply.
The flame shall not hurt thee; I only design
Thy dross to consume and thy gold to refine.
("How Firm a Foundation," *Hymns*, 1985, no. 85.)

May God bless us in the ups and downs of life, in the opening and closing of doors. (87–04, p. 56)

We have a promise of divine assistance in times of need. All of us face times in our lives when we need heavenly help in a special and urgent way. We all have moments when we are overwhelmed by circumstances or confused by the counsel we get from others, and we feel a great need to receive spiritual guidance, a great need to find the right path and do the right thing. In the scriptural preface to this latter-day dispensation, the Lord promised that if we would be humble in such times of need and turn to him for aid, we would "be made strong, and [be] blessed from on high, and receive knowledge from time to time" (D&C 1:28). That help is ours if we will but seek it, trust in it, and follow what King Benjamin, in the Book of Mormon, called "the enticings of the Holy Spirit" (Mosiah 3:19).

Perhaps no promise in life is more reassuring than that promise of divine assistance and spiritual guidance in times of need. It is a gift freely given from heaven, a gift that we need from our earliest youth through the very latest days of our lives. (88–06, p. 59)

Our Heavenly Father wants to help us in our times of trial. Sometimes we may feel that our spiritual edge has grown dull. On some very trying days, we may even feel that God has forgotten us, has left us alone in our confusion and concern. But that feeling is no more justified for the older ones among us than it is for the younger and less experienced. God knows and loves us all. We are, every one of us, his daughters and his sons, and whatever life's lessons may have brought us, the promise is still true: "If any of you lack wisdom, let him ask of God, that giveth to all men liberally, and upbraideth not; and it shall be given him" (James 1:5). (88–06, p. 60)

The Lord uses our weaknesses or infirmities to help us see him more clearly. Listen to these lines written by Elizabeth Lloyd Howell when she considered how the majestic poet John Milton must have felt when he went blind late in life.

> I am old and blind!
> Men point at me as smitten by God's frown:
> Afflicted and deserted of my kind,
> Yet am I not cast down.
>
> I am weak, yet strong;
> I murmur not that I no longer see;
> Poor, old, and helpless, I the more belong,
> Father supreme, to thee! . . .
>
> Thy glorious face
> Is leaning toward me; and its holy light
> Shines in upon my lonely dwelling place,—
> And there is no more night.
>
> On my bended knee
> I recognize thy purpose clearly shown:
> My vision thou hast dimmed, that I may see
> Thyself, thyself alone.
> ("Milton's Prayer for Patience," in *The World's Great Religious Poetry*, ed. Caroline Miles Hill [New York: MacMillan, 1954], p. 19.)

"My vision thou hast dimmed, that I may see / Thyself, thyself alone." That is a wonderfully comforting thought to young and old alike who must look inward and upward when the external world around us is so confusing and unstable and grim. Joseph Smith's view of what to do was certainly a dim one until he found the illumination of the scriptures and the searchlight of prayer.

Obviously, it was important to God's purposes that young Joseph was not able to see too clearly amidst the confusion caused by men, lest that half-light keep him from seeking and beholding the source of all light and all truth. Like Mrs. Howell's reference to Milton, the blind poet, "on bended knee" we can all recognize God's "purpose clearly shown" if we will rely on spiritual resources, letting our age and experience—yes, and even our infirmities—turn us yet closer to God. (88–06, pp. 60–61)

7

HONESTY, GRATITUDE, AND RESPECT FOR OTHERS

Honesty and Integrity

Suppressing the truth is a form of dishonesty. "Thou shalt not bear false witness against thy neighbour." (Exodus 20:16). Primarily this commandment has reference to false testimony in judicial proceedings, but it is extended to cover all statements which are false in fact. Any untruth which tends to injure another in his goods, person, or character is against the spirit and letter of this law. Suppression of the truth which results in the same injury is also a violation of this commandment. (65–02, p. 511)

It is important to be honest. School work is training for the future. When we cheat in school we cheat our own future. When you have a toothache, how would you like to be treated by a dentist who cheated his way through dental school?

If you need an operation, how would you like to be under the knife of a surgeon who cheated his way through college?

If you need the help of an attorney, how would you like to be defended by a man who cheated his way through law school?

If you were to ride in an airplane, how would you like to be piloted by an aviator who cheated his way through his training?

Would you want to place your life in the hands of a cheat?

Of a person whose failure should have eliminated him as a doctor or a lawyer or a pilot, but who was on the job because he lied his way through?

Let us stop and ask ourselves about dishonest people and what they have done. Let us ask ourselves if we want to place ourselves in their class. . . .

We are Latter-day Saints. We believe in God and in the gospel. We cannot allow ourselves to join the ranks of the dishonest, whether at school or in a store or on the athletic field. Why?

Because—we believe in being honest, even if it hurts. (62–09)

Honesty helps us maintain our self-respect. The Lord knows our innermost thoughts. He knows each deed we do. We will meet him someday, and we will look him in the face. Will we be proud of our life's record?

We make that record every day. Each act, each thought is a part of it. Will we be proud of it? We will if we have done our best—if we have been honest with ourselves, with our loved ones, with our friends, with all mankind.

Blessed are they which do hunger and thirst after righteousness.

Blessed are they who are honest.

Blessed are they who are clean.

Blessed are they who avoid evil people.

Blessed are they who choose good friends.

Blessed are they who are obedient to the Lord.

They are they who are free—who are happy—who can walk with their heads high. They have their self-respect. They have the respect of those who know them best.

And above all, they have the respect and blessing of our Father in Heaven. Jesus invites us to follow him. His paths are straight and clean and upright and honest. Let us follow him into the abundant life of happiness. It is the only way. (62–09)

Are there degrees of honesty? Why is it so many believe in the high and lofty principles of honesty, yet so few are willing to be strictly honest? . . .

There are some who will admit it is morally wrong to be dishonest in big things yet believe it is excusable if they are of lesser importance. Is there really any difference between dishonesty involving a thousand dollars or that which involves only a dime? Is there any difference in principle between a little white lie and the perjury of a witness in a court of law or in a congressional investigation committee under oath? Are there really degrees of dishonesty, depending upon whether or not the subject is great or small?

I know our criminal codes distinguish between petty theft and grand theft. The penalty attached to grand theft is much more severe than in the case of petty theft. Consider for a moment, is there really any difference between the two, in basic principle?

Scripture is replete with admonitions to be honest, and commandments are myriad to the effect that we should be honest. We think of them in bold type: THOU SHALT NOT—thou shalt not steal; thou shalt not bear false witness; thou shalt not covet. . . .

Some of the more common examples of dishonesty are these:

(1) *Stealing.* I seldom read a newspaper that I do not find a number of reports of burglary, robbery, purse-snatching, shoplifting, car theft, stolen hubcaps, tires, clothes from a clothesline, and a thousand other things. Even on the campus there are reports of petty theft.

(2) *Cheating.* Newspapers carry similar accounts of fraudulent transactions in security dealings, in business transactions, cheating in investments, and other things which are called to public attention. There are some who would cheat their way through school, and some who would cheat in examinations.

(3) *Violations of Word of Wisdom Standards.* These are Church standards. . . . They are not violations of the standards of the world. But you have been given the word of the Lord on this subject.

(4) *Violation of Traffic Ordinances.* One cannot be basically honest and violate laws formulated by society and government for the welfare of other persons.

(5) *Not Making the Best Use of Time.* The more I think about this, the more impressed I become with this concept of dishonesty. (62–13, pp. 2–4)

When we are honest we experience joy. We often speak of that scriptural reference, "Man is that he might have joy" (2 Nephi 2:25). There is a joy which comes to one from being honest. Let me tell you how. By this means you can have the companionship of the Master and you can have the spirit of the Holy Ghost. Violations of the code of honesty will deprive you of these two great blessings. Could you believe that one who would lie or cheat or violate the Word of Wisdom could have the companionship of the Master or have the spirit of the Holy Ghost? (62–13, p. 4)

No dishonest act will go unobserved. If we are sensitive to our relationship to the Savior, we must be honest in little things as well as the big. We should always remember that we are never alone. There is no act which is not observed; there is no word spoken which is not heard; there is no thought conceived in the mind of man which is not known to God. There is no way we can get beyond the point where we are not noticed. There is no darkness which can conceal the things which we do. We must think before we act.

Do you think you can be alone when you commit a dishonest act? Do you think you can be unobserved when you cheat in an examination, even though you are the only person in the room? We must be honest with ourselves. If we would have the companionship of the Master and the spirit of the Holy Ghost, we must be honest with ourselves, honest with God and with our fellowmen. This results in true joy. (62–13, p. 4)

We should think about the results of dishonesty. Think of what an act of dishonesty will do to you. It does not make any difference whether it is great or small. First, it will affect your whole life. We never live it down. We never forget about it because it is engraved upon our conscience, never to be forgotten. Secondly, it will affect others in many ways. The injury is far-reaching. Its malignancy extends to our friends, our relatives, our loved ones, and persons we may never see. Thirdly, it affects our relationship to the Savior. It closes the channel of communication and shuts out light from our life.

How enjoyable it would be to live in a world of strict honesty. (62–13, pp. 4–5)

There is a real need for honesty. Moral qualities must be added to knowledge. I refer now to principles of right and wrong in a man's behavior—just common, everyday honesty. A man must be honest with himself and with every person with whom he comes in contact. What a great change would come over the world if we could all rely upon others as far as honesty is concerned. Men would have perfect confidence in each other in personal and business dealings. There would not be the present distrust between labor and management. There would be integrity in public office and in government affairs, and nations would exist in peace rather than the turmoil we presently know in the world. . . .

In business dealings there are some who will take a dishonest advantage if it is placed before them. They rationalize and justify their position by saying that in business one is expected to take every offered advantage. Such transactions can amount to large sums of money, but in principle are no different than the failure to return a penny that has been overpaid by the cashier to one who notices the error. It is a form of cheating. Fraudulent transactions are not altogether unknown in business dealings, security transactions, and the sale of commodities or property. I think of a hand-lettered parchment I once saw which read: "Every man takes care that his neighbor does not cheat him. But a day comes when he begins to care that he does not cheat his neighbor. Then all goes well. He has changed his market-cart into a chariot of the sun." (63–04, p. 17)

We believe in being honest. I would like to [tell] a little story which I heard on a recent trip to California. It is about a milk truck and its two drivers.

The driver of this truck quit his job, after having worked for the company for a number of months. He then moved from the community.

A young Latter-day Saint with a small family needed a job and applied for work at the dairy on the same day the truck driver quit. He was hired. His work was to deliver milk from door to door, collect the money due to the company, and turn it in at the office.

Hardly had the Latter-day Saint begun work than the dairy owner noticed that he was turning in more money for the same volume of milk than the other driver had done. By the end of the month, the dairy's profit had almost doubled from the very same route.

It was then discovered that the other driver had been keeping a part of the dairy's money for himself.

The owner of the dairy was so impressed with the honesty of the young Latter-day Saint that he came to the stake president in that city and asked if he would find three more drivers for him as honest as the one he now had.

It was a great tribute to the Church, but it was even more a tribute to the people who are willing to live up to their own Article of Faith which says—"We believe in being honest." (62–09)

Integrity will make us successful now and in eternity. We hear an endless list of complaints about how hard it is to live our religion in these days. The temptations of evil surround us on every side. Without the protection of integrity, we are at the mercy of all kinds of sin and wrongdoings.

Job had no difficulty with these problems. He was protected by his own integrity. This is how he felt:

"All the while my breath is in me, and the spirit of God is in my nostrils;

"My lips shall not speak wickedness, nor my tongue utter deceit. . . .

"My righteousness I hold fast, and will not let it go: my heart shall not reproach me so long as I live." (Job 27:3–4, 6.)

How inspiring. Because of his strength, he had no concerns for the trivial temptations before which most people fall. Job had built into his own life a strength and satisfaction that Satan himself could not crash. It is also interesting to see how God was delighted with him: "There is none like him in the earth, a perfect and an upright man, one that feareth God, and escheweth evil[,] and still he holdeth fast his integrity" (Job 2:3).

This great quality of integrity is fully available to us. If effectively used, it will solve all of our problems in government, religion, industry, and our individual lives. It would wipe out the awful scourge of crime, divorce, poverty, and misery. It would make us successful here and save our souls hereafter. (88–01)

Integrity is the golden key to the door of success. One of the greatest accomplishments of our lives is to promote an honest, earnest integrity within ourselves. This means that we become spiritually sound, intellectually sincere, morally honest, and always personally responsible to God. Integrity is that golden key which will unlock the door to almost any success. (88–01)

Gratitude

Gratitude is a spiritual attribute. One of the most esteemed spiritual attributes we can acquire in life is sincere gratitude. It enriches our lives as we, through this attribute, enrich the lives of others. If we have a thankful heart we will have the blessings that come from constant appreciation for the things done for us and the Lord's goodness. (74–03, p. 28)

How can we pay the debt of gratitude? How can we really pay the debt of gratitude we owe to our parents, brothers and sisters, teachers, and those who have served us in so many ways? How can we show appreciation for good homes, husbands and wives who are true and faithful, children who have the desire to live righteously and serve the Lord? How do we express thankfulness for our baptisms, for the privilege of partaking of the sacrament and renewing our covenants, for the priesthood we bear, for the light of the restored gospel, for the program of the Church devised to help us make progress toward exaltation and eternal life?

We pay our debt of gratitude by living in such a way as to bring credit to our parents and the name we bear, by doing good to others, by being of service, by being willing to share the light and knowledge we have received so that others will also have joy and happiness, by living the principles of the gospel in their fulness. Paul told us we should be filled with the Spirit, "giving thanks always for all things unto God and the Father in the name of our Lord Jesus Christ" (Ephesians 5:20). (74–03, p. 28)

Happiness is not complete unless accompanied by gratitude. The ten men were healed of [their] dreaded disease because of their faith in the Master; they did as he directed [see Luke 17:15–19]. . . .

Of the ten men who were healed, only one returned to express appreciation. This must have been a disappointment to the Master, but there are many who receive blessings, many who are endowed with good things in life, yet never take the time or go to the effort to show gratitude to the benefactor or express appreciation to God. Happiness and joy from blessings are never complete until there is a deep feeling of gratitude within oneself which moves an expression of appreciation. (74–03, p. 27)

Thanksgiving is a time to reflect on the real reason we are thankful. When we celebrate Thanksgiving Day after the pattern of our Pilgrim Fathers, our thoughts should turn to the real reason why they were thankful. If we would make God first in our lives, freedom and prosperity would be added and Thanksgiving would become more than a day, or a season, but always. (92–06)

Every day should be a day of thanksgiving. As we approach this Thanksgiving, we should be grateful for the goodness of the Lord to us. It's a fine thing to have friends come in. It's a fine thing to have the family home. It's a good thing to sit around the board where we have the bounties of life to partake of, but every day should be a day of thanksgiving. (57–02)

We should never delay expressing appreciation. Some time ago I had a lesson of gratitude taught to me. I was in the mission home in San Francisco when the mission president received a telephone call and said, "I must cross the bay and take a message to an elder that his father has just passed away." I went with him. We crossed over the Bay Bridge, up to Berkeley, and stopped at an apartment building. A fine-looking elder came to the door. He was excited to see his mission president and said, "Oh, president, come in; we want to tell you what happened this morning." The president said, "Elder, sit down with us for a moment; we have a sad message to deliver to you."

I will never forget that occasion as the young man's head fell into his arms and he commenced to sob. After we had comforted him he said, "My father was the greatest man I have ever known. I have never told him that. I don't believe I realized it in my years of growing up, but since I have come into the mission field a maturity has come to me to make me appreciate my father and my mother. I decided last week I was going to sit down and write my father a letter and tell him how much I loved him and how much he has meant to me, but now it is too late." He commenced to sob again.

My heart went out to that young man, but I thought how typical that is of many of us. The letter we intended to write, the word of appreciation we intended to express, the prayers we intended to offer when we had more time to express to the Lord our appreciation for his goodness. We are grateful for all of these things that are done for us, of course, but in our busy life we don't always express appreciation for what others do for us. (79–08)

We need to express gratitude. We need to be expressive of appreciation for the good things that come to us, both from the Lord who has blessed us abundantly and also from those who do things for us.

A few years ago, the teacher of a seminary class gave each of the pupils several sheets of paper and asked them to write the names of all the people to whom they owed a debt of gratitude. This was an interesting experiment. They wrote feverishly for the first part of the hour and then commenced to gaze off into space, not because they had run out of names, but because they concluded that the task was insurmountable. There are thousands and hundreds of thousands of people to whom we owe debts of gratitude. Isn't that true? People we have never seen. People we have never heard of but who have made contributions to our lives. (79–12)

Love and Respect for Others

Love should have no boundary. An old axiom states that a man "all wrapped up in himself makes a small bundle." Love has a certain way of making a small bundle large. The key is to love our neighbor, including the neighbor that is difficult to love. We need to remember that though we make our friends, God has made our neighbors—everywhere. Love should have no boundary; we should have no narrow loyalties. Christ said, "For if ye love them which love you, what reward have ye? do not even the publicans the same?" (Matthew 5:46). (86–03, p. 35)

Love could cure the ills of the world. To love one's neighbor is noble and inspiring, whether the neighbor is one who lives close by, or in a broader sense, a fellow being of the human race. It stimulates the desire to promote happiness, comfort, interest, and the welfare of others. It creates understanding. The ills of the world would be cured by understanding. Wars would cease and crime disappear. The scientific knowledge now being wasted in the world because of the distrust of men and nations could be diverted to bless mankind. (62–01, pp. 75–76)

We should love others, even our enemies. As a young man, Brother Vern Crowley said he learned something of the crucial lesson the Prophet Joseph had taught the early Saints in Nauvoo when he told them to "love others, even our enemies as well as friends." This is a good lesson for each of us.

After his father became ill, Vern Crowley took responsibility for running the family wrecking yard although he was only fifteen years of age. Some customers occasionally took unfair advantage of the young man, and parts were disappearing from the lot overnight. Vern was angry and vowed to catch someone and make an example of him. Vengeance would be his.

Just after his father had started to recover from his illness, Vern was making his rounds of the yard one night at closing time. It was nearly dark. In a distant corner of the property, he caught sight of someone carrying a large piece of machinery toward the back fence. He ran like a champion athlete and caught the young thief. His first thought was to take out his frustrations with his fists, and then drag the boy to the front office and call the police. His heart was full of anger and vengeance. He had caught his thief, and he intended to get his just dues.

Out of nowhere, Vern's father came along, put his weak and infirm hand on his son's shoulder, and said, "I see you're a bit upset, Vern. Can I handle this?" He then walked over to the young would-be thief and put his arm around his shoulder, looked him in the eye for a moment, and said, "Son, tell me, why are you doing this? Why were you trying to steal that transmission?" Then Mr. Crowley started walking toward the office with his arm around the boy, asking questions about the young man's car problems as they walked. By the time they had arrived at the office, the father said, "Well, I think your clutch is gone and that's causing your problem."

In the meantime, Vern was fuming. "Who cares about his clutch?" he thought. "Let's call the police and get this over with." But his father just kept talking. "Vern, get him a clutch. Get him a throwout bearing, too. And get him a pressure plate. That should take care of it." The father handed all of the parts to the young man who had attempted robbery and said, "Take these. And here's the transmission, too. You don't have to steal, young man. Just ask for it. There's a way out of every problem. People are willing to help."

Brother Vern Crowley said he learned an everlasting lesson in love that day. The young man came back to the lot often. Voluntarily, month by month, he paid for all of the parts Vic Crowley had given him, including the transmission. During those visits, he asked Vern why his dad was the way he was and why he did what he did.

Vern told him something of their Latter-day Saint beliefs and how much his father loved the Lord and loved people. Eventually the would-be thief was baptized. Vern later said, "It's hard now to describe the feelings I had and what I went through in that experience. I, too, was young. I had caught my crook. I was going to extract the utmost penalty. But my father taught me a different way."

A different way? A better way? A higher way? A more excellent way? Oh, how the world could benefit from such a magnificent lesson. As Moroni declares:

"Wherefore, whoso believeth in God might with surety hope for a better world. . . .

"In the gift of his Son hath God prepared a more excellent way." (Ether 12:4, 11.) (92–02, p. 62)

We are all children of God. In the eyes of the Church and in the followers of Christ there are no differences. Color makes no difference. Language makes no difference. Nationality makes no difference. We are all children of God, and we are brothers and sisters. (90–04)

Our Heavenly Father loves all his children and so should we. It should be manifestly evident to members of the Church that our Father loves all of his children. He desires all of them to embrace the gospel and come unto him. Only those are favored who obey him and keep his commandments.

As members of the Lord's church, we need to lift our vision beyond personal prejudices. We need to discover the supreme truth that indeed our Father is no respecter of persons. Sometimes we unduly offend brothers and sisters of other nations by assigning exclusiveness to one nationality of people over another. . . .

We have members of the Church in the Muslim world. These are wonderful Saints, good members of the Church. They live in Iran, Egypt, Lebanon, Saudi Arabia, and other countries. Sometimes they are offended by members of the Church who give the impression that we favor only the aims of the Jews. The Church has an interest in all of Abraham's descendants, and we should remember that the history of the Arabs goes back to Abraham through his son Ishmael.

Imagine a father with many sons, each having different temperaments, aptitudes, and spiritual traits. Does he love one son less than another? Perhaps the son who is least spiritually inclined has the father's attention, prayers, and pleadings more than the others. Does that mean he loves the others less? Do you imagine our Heavenly Father loving one nationality of his offspring more exclusively than others? As members of the Church, we need to be reminded of Nephi's challenging question: "Know ye not that there are more nations than one?" (2 Nephi 29:7). (79–01, p. 35)

Love is the highest reason for shunning evil and pursuing righteousness. What causes some men in a declining morality to shun evil and wrongdoing and to follow the course of righteousness in their temporal, moral, and spiritual lives? In my mind, there are three reasons for this phenomenon, and it is to these three points I would like to address my remarks.

The first is fear. . . .

There are many people who live the so-called good life because of fear, but as Christians we must not serve for this reason. Fear must be banished from our hearts. In one of the epistles of John he wrote: "There is no fear in love; but perfect love casteth out fear: because fear hath torment. He that feareth is not made perfect in love." (1 John 4:18.)

The second reason for men to shun evil, pursue righteousness, and serve their fellowmen is duty. Often we hear men say they do certain things because it is their duty. . . .

Men who only carry out that which is within their duty and go no further have no claim to any reward beyond the scope of that duty and are unprofitable servants (see Luke 17:7–10).

The Lord requires obedience not because it is our duty nor because we fear him (quotes D&C 58:26–30). . . .

Now I come to the third reason, which in my opinion ought to be the objective of all men everywhere. The greatest motivating influence for righteousness and for service to one's fellowmen is the divine principle of love. . . .

We must strive to obtain this virtue if we are to serve the Lord without faltering or growing weary in our pursuit of eternal life. We will do this not because of fear, nor merely because it is our duty, but because we have sought for and obtained the greatest of all virtues, love. (66–03, pp. 516, 517)

Pure love is the highest pinnacle the human soul can reach. "A new commandment I give unto you," he said, "That ye love one another; . . . By this shall all men know that ye are my disciples, if ye have love one to another" (John 13:34–35). This love that we should have for our brothers and sisters in the human family, and that Christ has for every one of us, is called charity or "the pure love of Christ" (Moroni 7:47). It is the love that prompted the suffering and sacrifice of Christ's atonement. It is the highest pinnacle the human soul can reach and the deepest expression of the human heart. . . .

Charity encompasses all other godly virtues. It distinguishes both the beginning and the end of the plan of salvation. When all else fails, charity—Christ's love—will *not* fail. It is the greatest of all divine attributes. (92–02, p. 61)

True disciples of Christ exercise charity. The world in which we live would benefit greatly if men and women everywhere would exercise the pure love of Christ, which is kind, meek, and lowly. It is without envy or pride. It is selfless because it seeks nothing in return. It does not countenance evil or ill will, nor rejoice in iniquity; it has no place for bigotry, hatred, or violence. It refuses to condone ridicule, vulgarity, abuse, or ostracism. It encourages diverse people to live together in Christian love regardless of religious belief, race, nationality, financial standing, education, or culture.

The Savior has commanded us to love one another as he has loved us; to clothe ourselves "with the bond of charity" (D&C 88:125), as he so clothed himself. We are called upon to purify our inner feelings, to change our hearts, to make our outward actions and appearance conform to what we say we believe and feel inside. We are to be true disciples of Christ. (92–02, pp. 61–62)

We should strive to emulate the love and compassion of the Savior. I would invite all members of the Church to live with ever-more attention to the life and example of the Lord Jesus Christ, especially the love and hope and compassion he displayed.

I pray that we might treat each other with more kindness, more courtesy, more humility and patience and forgiveness. (94–03, p. 4)

Love of God and man is the fundamental commandment of Christians. "And thou shalt love the Lord thy God with all thy heart, and with all thy soul, and with all thy mind, and with all thy strength: this is the first commandment.

"And the second is like, namely this, Thou shalt love thy neighbour as thyself. There is none other commandment greater than these." (Mark 12:30–31.) . . .

The logic of this is simple, clear, and unequivocal: the proof of love of God is love of one's brother. This becomes the fundamental commandment of Christianity. This was the religion taught by the Master. How happy would society be were these two plain, rational precepts properly observed: Love me, and love thy fellows.

The living of this commandment by all men would restore peace to the earth. It would cause them to love the Lord and thereby keep his commandments; thus the troubles of our age would vanish, and man's happiness in a moral world would result. (66–03, p. 517)

A cabinet minister of Egypt once told me that if a bridge is ever built between Christianity and Islam, it must be built by the Mormon Church. In making inquiry as to the reason for his statement, I was impressed by his recitation of the similarities and the common bonds of brotherhood.

Both the Jews and the Arabs are children of our Father. They are both children of promise, and as a church we do not take sides. We have love for and an interest in each. The purpose of the gospel of Jesus Christ is to bring about love, unity, and brotherhood of the highest order. Like Nephi of old, may we be able to say, "I have charity for the Jew. . . . I also have charity for the Gentiles." (2 Nephi 33:8, 9.) (79–01, p. 36)

The purpose of the gospel is to bring about unity and brotherhood. The purpose of the gospel of Jesus Christ is to bring about love, unity and brotherhood of the highest order . . .

As our Father loves all his children, we must love all people of every race, culture, and nationality, and teach them the principles of the gospel, that they might embrace it and come to a knowledge of the divinity of the Savior. (83–04)

Knowing that we are all of the family of God should affect our relationships with each other. In the message of the gospel, the entire human race is one family descended from a single God. All men and women have not only a physical lineage leading back to Adam and Eve, their first earthly parents, but also a spiritual heritage leading back to God the Eternal Father. Thus, all persons on earth are literally brothers and sisters in the family of God.

It is in understanding and accepting this universal fatherhood of God that all human beings can best appreciate God's concern for them and their relationship to each other. This is a message of life and love that strikes squarely against all stifling traditions based on race, language, economic or political standing, educational rank, or cultural background, for we are all of the same spiritual descent. We have a divine pedigree; every person is a spiritual child of God.

In this gospel view there is no room for a contracted, narrow, or prejudicial view. (91–04, p. 18)

All of mankind share an inheritance of divine light. We believe there is a spiritual influence that emanates from the presence of God to fill the immensity of space (see D&C 88:12). All men share an inheritance of divine light. God operates among his children in all nations, and those who seek God are entitled to further light and knowledge, regardless of their race, nationality, or cultural traditions.

Elder Orson F. Whitney, in a conference address, explained that many great religious leaders were inspired. He said: "[God] is using not only his covenant people, but other peoples as well, to consummate a work, stupendous, magnificent, and altogether too arduous for this little handful of Saints to accomplish by and of themselves. . . .

"All down the ages men bearing the authority of the Holy Priesthood—patriarchs, prophets, apostles and others, have officiated in the name of the Lord, doing the things that he required of them; and outside the pale of their activities other good and great men, not bearing the Priesthood, but possessing profundity of thought, great wisdom, and a desire to uplift their fellows, have been sent by the Almighty into many nations, to give them, not the fulness of the Gospel, but that portion of truth that they were able to receive and wisely use." (In Conference Report, April 1921, pp. 32–33.) (91–04, p. 19)

Love of God and love of our fellowman are inseparable. Eternal life, God's life, the life we are seeking, is rooted in two commandments. The scriptures say that "on these two commandments hang all the law and the prophets" (Matthew 22:40). Love God and love your neighbor. The two work together; they are inseparable. In the highest sense they may be considered as synonymous. And they are commandments that each of us can live. (86–03, p. 34)

Most man-made laws fall under the command to love our neighbor. Hundreds of thousands of laws, statutes, and codifications of laws have been written by man in an effort to spell out man's rights and duties in society, most of which fall within the meaning of the simple statement of the Lord, "Thou shalt love thy neighbor." (65–02, p. 58)

To love God we must love his children. We cannot love God unless we love his children also. These are our neighbors, and true love of them knows no class or culture, race, color, or creed. (70–02, p. 117)

8

MEASURABLE PRINCIPLES

Reverence

Reverence disappears when morals decline. In the process of moral decline, reverence is one of the first virtues to disappear, and there should be serious concern about that loss in our times. (77–04, pp. 52–53)

Reverence is the atmosphere of heaven. There are wide areas of our society from which the spirit of prayer and reverence and worship has vanished. Men and women in many circles are clever, interesting or brilliant, but they lack one crucial element in a complete life. They do not look up. They do not offer up vows in righteousness (see D&C 59:11). . . . Their conversation sparkles, but it is not sacred. Their talk is witty, but it is not wise. Whether it be in the office, the locker room, or the laboratory, they have come too far down the scale of dignity who display their own limited powers and then find it necessary to blaspheme those unlimited powers that come from above.

Unfortunately we sometimes find this lack of reverence even within the Church. Occasionally we visit too loudly, enter and leave meetings too disrespectfully in what should be an hour of prayer and purifying worship. Reverence is the atmosphere of heaven. (77–04, p. 53)

Spiritual matters must be practiced or they will be lost. Prayer, reverence, worship, devotion, respect for the holy—these are basic exercises of our spirit and must be actively practiced in our lives or they will be lost. (77–04, p. 54)

We must avoid irreverent statements about God. "Thou shalt not take the name of the Lord thy God in vain; for the Lord will not hold him guiltless that taketh his name in vain" (Exodus 20:7).

By this we are commanded not to engage in false oaths or any irreverent statement pertaining to God or any of his attributes or common swearing where his name is used. Swearing or cursing is usually the result of an effort of one who is inarticulate to impress others. Blasphemy is a disgusting habit which commands no respect. (65–02, p. 511)

The Word of Wisdom

Live the Word of Wisdom. We encourage you to live the Word of Wisdom. The Apostle Peter challenged the Saints of his day to be "a peculiar people" (1 Peter 2:9). One of the unique characteristics of the Latter-day Saints is obedience to this law which encourages us to avoid that which is damaging to our body. The prophets have taught that we should not partake of tea, coffee, tobacco, alcohol, or any substance that contains illegal drugs or harmful or habit-forming ingredients. In a world where so much of this is both acceptable and accessible, we encourage you to walk squarely on the Lord's side of the line. Do not tamper with any of these substances, nor similar products which give the "appearance of evil" (1 Thessalonians 5:22). (94–11)

Avoid the problem of drinking. One of the great problems that has become so common with young people is social drinking. They soon learn that the way to avoid the problem of drinking is to associate with people who do not drink. Nearly every young person, however, is at some time faced with this problem, and when it comes, the boy or girl must make a choice. Those who do not want to drink must learn how to refuse. . . . It is not hard to refuse a drink if you have made up your mind not to drink. The important thing to do is to make this decision ahead of time, then the answer of "No, thank you" comes easy. (60–03, p. 3)

Live the spirit of the Word of Wisdom. We complicate the simplicity of the Word of Wisdom. The Lord said don't drink tea, coffee, or use tobacco or liquor and that admonition is simple. But we confuse it by asking if cola drinks are against the Word of Wisdom. The 89th Section of the Doctrine and Covenants doesn't say anything about cola drinks, but we ask questions that go beyond the simplicity of the lesson that has been taught. We know that caffeine is taken out of coffee and used as an ingredient of cola drinks. It seems to me that if we really want to live the spirit of the law we probably wouldn't partake of that which had been taken from what we were told not to drink. (79–09)

Tithing and Fast Offerings

Tithing is clearly defined. The law [of tithing] is simply stated as "one-tenth of all their interest" (D&C 119:4). Interest means profit, compensation, increase. It is the wage of one employed, the profit from the operation of a business, the increase of one who grows or produces, or the income to a person from any other source. The Lord said it is a standing law "forever" as it has been in the past. (64–01, p. 476)

The law of tithing is simple. The Lord gave the law [of tithing]. If we follow his law, we prosper, but when we find what we think is a better way, we meet failure.

As I travel about the Church and see the results of the payment of tithes, I come to the conclusion that it is not a burden, but a great blessing. Like all of the Lord's commandments and laws, it is simple if we have a little faith. The Lord said in effect, "Take out the decimal point and move it over one place." That is the law of tithing. It's just that simple. (70–03)

Pay an honest tithing. Pay an honest tithing. This eternal law, revealed by the Lord and practiced by the faithful from the ancient prophets down to the present, teaches us to put the Lord first in our lives. We may not be asked to sacrifice our homes or our lives, as was the case with the early Saints. We are challenged today to overcome our selfishness. We pay tithing because we love the Lord, not because we have the means to do so. We can expect that the Lord will open "the windows of heaven" (Malachi 3:10) and shower down blessings upon the faithful. I hope each of the children who are present today will remember that which I was taught as a boy:

What is tithing? I will tell you every time.

Ten cents from a dollar, and a penny from a dime. (94–11)

The value of the cost of tithing. In 2 Samuel 24:18–25 we read that David would not make an offering unto the Lord of that which cost him nothing. He no doubt reasoned that unless the gift cost the giver something of value, it was not fit or appropriate to be an offering for the Lord. Christ said it is more blessed to give than to receive, yet there are some who will give only if it costs them nothing. This is not according to the teachings of the Master who said: "If any man will come after me, let him deny himself" (Matthew 16:24).

There are some who will not live the law of tithing because of the cost. This is in contrast to the reasoning of David who would not make an offering unto the Lord unless it cost him something. The great moral principles encompassed in the law of tithing are overlooked by those who are not tithe payers, and they lack the understanding of the law and the reasons for it.

The word "tithe" is derived from the Anglo-Saxon, meaning "a tenth." It may be defined as a tenth of property or income which is paid over or dedicated for sacred uses or purposes. (64–01, p. 475)

Tithing has existed from the beginning. There are some who take the position that the law of the tithe was only a Levitical institution, but history confirms the fact that it has been and is a universal law. It was basic in the Mosaic law. It had existed from the beginning and is found in the ancient Egyptian law, in Babylonia, and can be traced throughout biblical history. It was mentioned by the Prophet Amos and by Nehemiah who was charged with the rebuilding of the walls of Jerusalem. Shortly thereafter Malachi began an even greater task of rebuilding the faith and the morale of a nation. In his supreme effort to strike out against the covetousness of those who were religious only in name, he lashed them with the accusation of a crime against God.

"Will a man rob God? Yet ye have robbed me. But ye say, Wherein have we robbed thee? In tithes and offerings.

"Ye are cursed with a curse: for ye have robbed me, even this whole nation.

"Bring ye all the tithes into the storehouse, that there may be meat in mine house, and prove me now herewith, saith the Lord of hosts, if I will not open you the windows of heaven and pour you out a blessing, that there shall not be room enough to receive it" (Malachi 3:8–10). . . .

The words of Malachi close the Old Testament with a reiteration of the law of tithing, indicating there had been no abrogation of this law which had existed from the beginning. (64–01, p. 476)

Beware of a mechanical compliance to the law of tithing. There are some who make the assertion that Jesus denounced tithing in his last public discourse in the temple court when he struck out against the practices and teachings of the Pharisees. He said:

"Woe unto you, scribes and Pharisees, hypocrites! for ye pay tithe of mint and anise and cummin, and have omitted the weightier matters of the law, judgment, mercy, and faith: these ought ye to have done, and not to leave the other undone" (Matthew 23:23).

This is not a denunciation of tithing but a rebuke of the Pharisees and their legalisms. They were paying a tithing of their herbs and vegetables, while overlooking the great gospel principles of judgment, mercy, and faith. . . .

The principle of tithing should be more than a mathematical, mechanical compliance with the law. The Lord condemned the Pharisees for mechanically tithing herbs without coming into the circumference of spirituality. If we pay our tithes because of our love for the Lord, in complete freedom and faith, we narrow our distance from him and our relationship to him becomes intimate. We are released from the bondage of legalism, and we are touched by the Spirit and feel a oneness with God. (64–01, p. 476)

Tithing is a voluntary obligation. The tithe is God's law for his children, yet the payment is entirely voluntary. In this respect it does not differ from the law of the Sabbath or from any other of his laws. We may refuse to obey any or all of them. Our obedience is voluntary, but our refusal to pay does not abrogate or repeal the law.

If tithing is a voluntary matter, is it a gift or a payment of an obligation? There is a substantial difference between the two. A gift is a voluntary transfer of money or property without consideration. It is gratuitous. No one owes the obligation to make a gift. If tithing is a gift, we could give whatever we please, when we please, or make no gift at all. It would place our Heavenly Father in the very same category as the street beggar to whom we might toss a coin in passing.

The Lord has established the law of tithing, and because it is his law, it becomes our obligation to observe it if we love him and have a desire to keep his commandments and receive his blessings. In this way it becomes a debt. The man who doesn't pay his tithing because he is in debt should ask himself if he is not also in debt to the Lord. The Master said: "But seek ye first the kingdom of God, and his righteousness; and all these things shall be added unto you" (Matthew 6:33).

We can't walk east and west at the same time. We can't serve both God and mammon. The man who rejects the law of the tithe is the man who has not given it a fair try. Of course it costs something. It takes work and thought and effort to live any of the laws of the gospel or any of its principles. (64–01, p. 476)

We cannot afford to not pay tithing. The payment of tithing strengthens faith, increases spirituality and spiritual capacity, and solidifies testimony. It gives the satisfaction of knowing one is complying with the will of the Lord. It brings the blessings that come from sharing with others through the purposes for which tithing is used. We cannot afford to deny ourselves these blessings. We cannot afford not to pay our tithing. We have a definite relationship to the future as well as to the present. What we give, and how we give, and the way we meet our obligations to the Lord has eternal significance.

A testimony of the law of tithing comes from living it. Like all other of God's laws, when we live them we receive the blessings. (64–01, pp. 476–77)

Blessings come from tithe paying. We follow the principle of returning to the Lord a portion of his goodness to us, and this portion we refer to as tithing. Tithing is an interesting principle and it is entirely voluntary. We can pay tithing, or not pay tithing.

Those who do, receive blessings that are not known to others. . . .

Those who pay tithing are a different kind of people. They have a different look in their faces. Their families are different.

We have thousands of tithe payers in the world, and out of their giving has come a great central fund in the Church. Out of this fund comes the help that builds buildings, educates children, and does many good things. It perpetuates the great missionary system. It finances the Church. (67–04)

All of us should attend tithing settlement. Each of us should sit in conference with the bishop when he announces tithing settlement, and go over our record for the past year. Every person should attend tithing settlement and declare whether he is a full tithe payer, . . . or making only a partial contribution. These are the things the bishop needs to know from us. We [should] not fail to meet with him and make a declaration of our standing in this regard. (56–03)

The construction of buildings is one purpose of tithing. Buildings are now being constructed in the Church at the rate of just a little more than one each day [1970]. The sun doesn't rise in the morning that a building isn't commenced somewhere in the world, and the sun doesn't set at night that a building hasn't been completed somewhere in the world and is ready for dedication. You know a little about costs, and it doesn't require much arithmetic to know that this amounts to millions and millions of dollars. Through the principle [of tithing], this beautiful building and hundreds of others are being built in the world to accomplish the work of the Lord. (70–03)

Multiple blessings result when we pay a generous fast offering. The payment of a generous fast offering, which will bless the lives of the poor and needy, will also make our prayers more meaningful and bring additional spiritual and temporal blessings into our lives (see Isaiah 59:5–11). (94–22)

The history of fast day is one of faithful observance. From the early period when the Saints came to the valleys of the mountains to 1896, a regular fast day was held on the first Thursday of each month, and offerings were brought and given largely in kind.

In the early days when the membership of the Church was small, the holding of fast day on Thursday was not a problem, but as time went on it caused employees to take time from their work to attend fast meeting, merchants had to close their businesses, and many other difficulties resulted from weekday observance. A decision was made by the First Presidency and the Twelve that the monthly fast meeting should be held on the first Sunday of each month. The first Sunday of December, 1896, was the date set for the change. From that time to the present—nearly a century—the fast day has been observed, in most instances, on the first Sunday of the month as a religious practice. (85–03, pp. 73–74)

The Sacrament

It is significant that Christ instituted the sacrament during the Passover. From the time the firstborn of the faithful children of Israel had been "passed over" in the destruction brought on Egypt by Pharaoh's intransigence, the Passover meal, with all its symbolic emblems and gestures, had been faithfully observed by Israel's families. How fitting it was during the observance of this ancient covenant of protection that Jesus should institute the emblems of the new covenant of safety—the emblems of his own body and blood. As he took the bread and broke it, and took the cup and blessed it, he was presenting himself as *the* Lamb of God who would provide spiritual nourishment and eternal salvation. (74–01, p. 18)

The sacrament is a time for self-examination. I asked myself this question: "Do I place God above all other things and keep all of his commandments?" Then came reflection and resolution. To make a covenant with the Lord to always keep his commandments is a serious obligation, and to renew that covenant by partaking of the sacrament is equally serious. The solemn moments of thought while the sacrament is being served have great significance. They are moments of self-examination, introspection, self-discernment—a time to reflect and to resolve. (77–03, p. 25)

During the sacrament we covenant to stand as a witness of God. We are "to stand as witnesses of God at all times . . . in all places . . . even until death" [Mosiah 18:9]. We renew that covenant during the sacrament when we covenant to take the name of Christ upon us. (88–04)

The Sabbath Day

The Sabbath has been desecrated. A father and a mother who take their children to a movie on the Sabbath day will pay dearly for that failure to follow advice and counsel. . . . There was a time when the Sabbath was not violated among God-fearing people. We live in a [time] where those things are much forgotten. Stores are open. Things go along as usual except that employees, in most instances, have a day off for recreation.

The Sabbath day has been desecrated from the day of rest to a day of sports and recreation. We must look to the proper definition of the word "rest." It is a day when there is cessation from labor and we give thought to those things which pertain to God. (57–01)

Religion is more than Sunday worship. There is a growing concept among men of the world that religion is something reserved for the Sabbath day, or for the hour spent in places of worship or in prayer. Men distinguish between the everyday affairs that occupy their minds and direct their activities in the busy business world, and those things within the realm of theology. "Don't mix religion with business," some say. Can religion be eliminated from the affairs of everyday living? . . .

James said, "Pure religion and undefiled before God and the Father is this, To visit the fatherless and widows in their affliction, and to keep himself unspotted from the world" (James 1:27).

In other words, religion is more than a knowledge of God or a confession of faith, and it is more than theology. Religion is the doing of the word of God. It is being our brother's keeper, among other things. To keep unspotted from the world does not mean that one must withdraw from all association with the world, but rather to keep away from the evils of the world; or as more beautifully put in one of our hymns, "freedom from earth stains."

We can be religious in worship on the Sabbath day, and we can be religious in our duties on the other six days of the week. The

Apostle Paul, writing to those called to be "saints" at Corinth, stated:

"Whether therefore ye eat, or drink, or whatsoever ye do, do all to the glory of God" (1 Corinthians 10:31).

If such little things as eating and drinking are to be done to the glory of God, how much more important it must be that all of our thoughts, the words we speak, our acts, conduct, dealings with neighbors, business transactions, and all of our everyday affairs be in harmony with our religious beliefs. In the words of Paul, "Whatsoever ye do, do all to the glory of God" (1 Corinthians 10:31). Can we therefore eliminate religion from our weekday affairs and relegate it to the Sabbath day only? Surely not, if we follow Paul's admonition.

Religion can be part of our daily work, our business, our buying and selling, building, transportation, manufacturing, our trade or profession, or of anything we do. We can serve God by honesty and fair dealing in our business transactions in the same way we do in Sunday worship. The true principles of Christianity cannot be separate and apart from business and our everyday affairs. (61–07, p. 962)

The Sabbath should be like a secondary Christmas. One of the greatest needs of our personal lives is to get closer to the Savior of the World, and this is one of the primary reasons we commemorate Christmas. This is also why we set apart one day out of each seven as the Sabbath—a holy day—a day which becomes like a secondary Christmas in which our thoughts should turn to the Master, and his Spirit be invited into our lives. (81–04)

We should avoid Sunday employment. Choose employment which will be uplifting. You will spend at least a third of your time at your work. It will influence your thinking and your habits, it will largely shape your life. Choose an occupation which will help you fill your destiny with God. Choose clean work. Choose work which will not involve you in compromises with your faith or standards. Plan to avoid Sunday employment. Six days shalt thou labor—but the seventh is the Sabbath of the Lord your God. Keep it holy. (62–06)

The meaning of the Sabbath was defined by God when he created the earth. Throughout recorded history, repeated reference is made to the day of rest ordained of God (see, for example, Genesis 2:1–3 and Exodus 16:23–30). It is known in scripture as the Sabbath, from the Hebrew word meaning to cease, to desist, to bring to rest a thing in action. The Sabbath, then, refers to a day of rest from labor. So it was that after the six days of creation, God rested from his work on the seventh day and blessed and sanctified it. . . .

The Israelites were admonished to observe it strictly in these words:

"Remember the sabbath day, to keep it holy. Six days shalt thou labour, and do all thy work: But the seventh day is the Sabbath of the Lord thy God: in it thou shalt not do any work, thou nor thy son, nor thy daughter, thy manservant, nor thy maidservant, nor thy cattle, nor thy stranger that is within thy gates: For in six days the Lord made heaven and earth, the sea, and all that in them is, and rested the seventh day: wherefore the Lord blessed the sabbath day, and hallowed it." (Exodus 20:8–11.)

This, however, was not the institution of the Sabbath day. It had been known to the Babylonians before this time, and reference had previously been made to it when manna was prepared for the Israelites. Unquestionably its observance had come down from Eden following the pattern set by God when he rested on the seventh day after the six days of creation. Hence the wording used in the commandment "Remember the sabbath day, to keep it holy."

The commandment is addressed to the heads of families, for it referred to sons and daughters. It mentions manservants and maidservants, and is therefore a directive to employers of labor requiring that they must themselves rest from labor and allow those in their employment to rest also.

Although the fundamental concept is the cessation from labor, this alone does not exhaust the idea of the Sabbath. It is not to serve solely as a convenience for man by which he might rest from the labors of the days which precede; there is a religious aspect as well. The Lord blessed the Sabbath Day and hallowed it, thus making it a holy day, a day of worship, a day of devotion, a day to contemplate those things that pertain to God and man's relationship to him. (63–05)

The Lord commands us to keep the Sabbath day holy. What respect is paid today to the commandment to keep the Sabbath day holy? Of recent years there has been a growing trend toward using the Sabbath as a holiday, a day for sporting events, pleasure, travel, and play. This tempo of activity seems to be increasing. The admonition "Remember the sabbath day to keep it holy" would appear to be largely ignored. The word of God spoken to the Israelites and graven in stone tablets has never been rescinded or modified. The teachings of Jesus have never been retracted.

In this latter dispensation the Lord has said:

"And that thou mayest more fully keep thyself unspotted from the world, thou shalt go to the house of prayer and offer up thy sacraments upon my holy day;

"For verily this is a day appointed unto you to rest from your labors, and to pay your devotions unto the Most High" (D&C 59:9–10).

Are we entitled to the blessings of the Lord as a nation, communities, families, or individuals if we fail to keep his commandments? To know God, one must know his laws. To receive the blessings of God, one must keep his laws. I pray we may come to observe the Sabbath day and to keep it holy. (63–05)

Church meetings should assist us to live better lives. If our meetings are to be impressively meaningful in assisting those assembled to better live the Lord's law and commandments, meetings should be:

1. Well planned.

2. Conducted with reverence and dignity by one "led by the Holy Ghost." "The elders are to conduct the meetings as they are led by the Holy Ghost, according to the commandments and revelations of God" (D&C 20:45).

Our Church meetings should therefore be both instructional and inspirational. People should leave our meetings lifted up, motivated to walk more uprightly before the Lord and to feel more of the joy which comes through better living his commandments. (67–09)

Miracles

Great miracles are all around us. Should we not stand in awe of the blessing of hearing and give glory to God for that miracle, even as we do when hearing is restored after it has been lost?

Is it not the same for the return of one's sight or the utterance of our speech, or even that greatest miracle of all—the restoration of life? The original creations of the Father constitute a truly wonder-filled world. Are not the greatest *miracles* the fact that we have life and limb and sight and speech in the first place? Yes, there will always be plenty of miracles if we have eyes to see and ears to hear. (89–05, p. 16)

Faith should both precede and follow the miracle. President Spencer W. Kimball taught us with a book by the title *Faith Precedes the Miracle* (Salt Lake City: Deseret Book Co., 1972). But there is, of course, an increase of faith that should *follow* the miracle as well. As a result of the many miracles in our lives, we should be more humble and more grateful, more kind and more believing. When we are personal witnesses to these wonders which God performs, it should increase our respect and love for him; it should improve the way we behave. We will live better and love more if we will remember that. We are miracles in our own right, every one of us, and the resurrected Son of God is the greatest miracle of all. He is, indeed, the miracle of miracles, and every day of his life he gave evidence of it. We should try to follow after him in that example. (89–05, p. 17)

9

TO THE YOUTH
OF THE CHURCH

Counsel for Youth

The Lord has provided wise counsel for youth. Let us grow up the way the Lord planned it.

He provided four stages: Infancy, childhood, adolescence, and adulthood. It was not his plan that we should skip any of them. But we do skip adolescence when we date and marry too young.

The Lord gave us parents to help us through at least three of those stages—in infancy to care for our babyhood needs; in childhood to provide us with direction, food, clothing, and a home; in adolescence to counsel us and prepare us for adulthood.

The Lord is all-wise. It was he who gave us parents. It was he who made them our guardians. He is our parent himself—our Father in Heaven. Should we pit our wisdom against his? Then let us fit into his plan of salvation:

His way of life provides for happy home life, for loving care from parents, for a willingness on the part of young people to be taught, and for a partnership of parent and child leading to the eventual success of the child.

So let us delay any dating until our mid-teens. Let us avoid serious dating before twenty. Let every boy go on a mission. Let every girl encourage boyfriends to fill missions and not prevent it by early marriage or sin.

Let every boy and every girl plan for a temple marriage.

Plan for a good education. Plan for the abundant life. Crowding too much adulthood into a teenager's life can only impoverish him. (62–02)

The world needs more faith in youth. The world has need for more faith in the young people of our generation. I believe the Church has this confidence as I see its program reach out to them with an invitation to do good and refrain from evil—to follow the path upward to happiness in life rather than the decline which carries the minority to destruction and unhappiness. I am grateful for my membership in a church which has an interest in youth and gives them a spiritual education, mutual improvement, and a real purpose in life. I am grateful for the response of young people to that program. It places them in the vanguard of youth in the world which are giving leadership in righteous endeavors. (67–03)

The majority of our youth are spiritually strong. I have faith in modern youth. I believe there is a great good in the young people of today. . . .

We rely upon the newspaper, the radio and television, or the national news periodicals to bring us the happenings in the world. Today's news consists of the unusual, the sensational. Headlines of crime and corruption are far more conspicuous than the reports of those who do good. I, for one, would like to see equal time given to the majority of youth who are making marvelous contributions to the moral fabric of our society, who are doing great things in service to their fellowmen, and who are setting marks in the world not known to any former generation.

There has been no generation in the past which has had the promise we have today in the age group between 15 and 25 years. This is the group that is being distinguished in education. These young people are the ones who are giving promise to the future of modern business and industry. They are the ones who are defending our way of life on the battlefields. In the Church it is they who are spreading the principles of the gospel in the world and are largely responsible for the growth of the Church. Some persons have the idea that talent, creativity, moral stability, or greatness are not in the realm of youth, but are reserved to those who are older. This is not so. (67–03)

Youth must learn obedience to achieve. [Young people], it is important for you to understand that you have three creators: God, your parents, and yourself. God furnished the raw materials and the law. Your parents were instrumental in molding the materials. What you do with the mold and how you obey the law depends altogether on you. You can be anything you want to be. You can have anything you want to have. You can do anything you want to do, but you must be obedient to the laws of the land and the eternal laws of God. You must have a desire followed by a firm faith and be willing to put forth the work and effort to achieve. (74–02)

The world needs youth who are prepared to meet today's challenges. My young brothers and sisters, there is room, adequate room, in every area of human endeavor for the person who, in addition to a worldly knowledge, is armed and fortified with virtue, temperance, a sense of justice, wisdom, benevolence, and self-control. The world will step aside for a young man or a young woman who is so equipped and prepared to meet the challenges of today's world. (74–02)

Youth must be taught and prepared. The burden cast upon youth today in this upset world is greater than it has ever been before. Population has shifted from the rural districts to the metropolitan cities where the family no longer works as a unit. The family is divided because of the diversity of employment and individual interests. In many instances the mother works and children are left without a guide. The family unit becomes unstable. Divorces result. . . . Where is youth to get its guide? . . .

As to members of The Church of Jesus Christ of Latter-day Saints, this problem facing youth has been anticipated. Young people in our Church are taught from childhood the principles of Christianity and the problems they will meet in life as members of society. They are taught the rewards of virtue, the necessity of marriage, and the sacredness of marriage ties. The Mutual Improvement Association was purposely created to help equip young people for life and proper living.

The conclusion is this: Youth may be guided in this world of unrest and confusion by strict adherence and obedience to the principles of Christianity. It is youth that must survive the unrest of the present day and the apparent breaking down of morals and democratic principles. They will be the leaders of tomorrow, and upon them will rest the burden of rebuilding a better world. (41–01)

The youth of the Church are strong. [A Protestant minister once said to me], "You have something that is greater than you realize in the youth of your Church."

I love the young people. I love to hear them bear their testimonies. I like their attitude and outlook on life. They reach for things eternal. I, too, am sure that we have something greater than we realize. . . .

Our young people are solid and substantial. We are grateful for the leaders who help them, and the good homes from which they come. We hope it is the resolution of every young person here today to enter into the sealing that is performed in the House of the Lord when they marry. I have no fear of the future or fear of the future leadership of the Church, because these faithful young people will soon take our places when we turn the reins over to them. I know they will remain strong and pay to the Church great dividends in leadership in the years to come. (58–04)

Who among you will be the greatest? As you prepare to leave these portals [Brigham Young University] we do not point out to you the false illusions of honor, of being elevated to high places, or the amassing of wealth. We point out to you a greater mission, of ministering to the highest good of men. Who among you will be the greatest? He or she who best serves others. There are great goals to be obtained in many fields—in education, science, industry, and the professions. There are papers to be edited, judges' benches to be filled, factories to be built and operated, schools to be taught, homes to be established, and we expect you to be leaders in these pursuits. But in all of these we want you to stand forth with the vision of today in mind and say, as did Paul to the Romans: "For I am not ashamed of the gospel of Jesus Christ: for it is the power of God unto salvation to every one that believeth" (Romans 1:16). (60–07, p. 7)

Youth, confide in your parents. Your parents know that the friends you choose play a great part in your development as you grow up, and for that reason have an interest in your dating. They want you to be happy. They love you and want you to be successful and have the good things of life. Your parents will understand you, and you will better understand your parents when you can confide in them and talk things over. Young people sometimes feel they are not understood by their parents. This can often be overcome by the boy or girl trying to understand the parents' viewpoint. When young people learn that it is fun to share their experiences with their parents, they will find that their parents will understand them, and this will help solve dating problems. (60–02, p. 3)

There are some important rules for youth. Here are some good rules to follow:

(1) Make the Church standards of conduct your standards.

(2) Make the decision not to violate these standards.

(3) Decide now that your answer will be "No" to an invitation which will lower these standards.

(4) Stand firmly on your decision.

After a young man or a young woman has made a decision and choice concerning the course he or she will follow in life, and the occasion arises for an answer to a question of conduct, the answer will come easily and quickly because the choice has already been made. (60–03, pp. 3, 17)

Don't set religion to one side. Roger W. Babson, an economist, said:

"Try as you will you cannot separate the factor of religion from economic development. . . . A nation can prosper only as its citizens are religious, intelligent, capable of service and eager to render it. . . .

"Most of the prosperity of this nation is due to the family prayers which were held daily in the homes of our fathers."

Young people, if you wish to succeed in life, stay close to the Church, keep the commandments of the Lord, pray, be clean, be active in your ward and stake.

Don't be so concerned about your daily living that you will set your religion to one side. If you are faithful, the Lord will guide and help you. The Lord is a mighty factor in the economic progress of both individuals and of nations. (62–03)

The youth of the Church are a people of destiny. It is indeed a pleasure to address you [young people] this evening. It is more than a pleasure. I feel it is a distinct privilege because I realize that you are one of the most remarkable generations of youth that has ever been born.

You are a people of destiny. What awaits you is almost beyond our comprehension. If you remain faithful to the Church, God will use your talents to guide his work through one of the most important periods of the world's history, leading toward the Second Coming of our Lord and Savior, Jesus Christ.

Are you ready for that destiny? Are you getting ready?

Do not suppose that your destiny is limited to your neighborhood, or to your city, or even to your state. Yours is a world destiny.

Why is it worldwide?

Many years ago, the Prophet Daniel saw that the work of God would come forth in the latter days. He likened it to a stone cut out of a mountain without hands. It had a small and very humble beginning.

But Daniel saw that the little stone rolled on despite all obstacles, and eventually it filled the whole earth. That stone is the work of the Lord in our day. Mormonism is that work. It is destined to fill the whole earth (see Daniel 2:35). You are called to help to roll it forth.

But as in everything else, it takes preparation.

As young people you are now being prepared for that work. Your loyalty to the Church will determine the extent of your preparation. As in the parable of the sower—

Some will fall by the wayside, and be consumed.

Some will catch but a shallow root and grow for a short time only, and then will be overcome by the influences of the world.

But many will be sturdy and loyal and true—they will carry forward their great destiny. They will be true to the faith!

Most of our young people are exceptional. Most of them—nearly all of them—want to do right, they want to succeed, they want to do their part. (62–06)

Youth need to be prepared. May I say once more to the youth of the Church—prepare, believe, be ready, have faith. Do not say or do or be that which would limit your service or render you ineffective in the kingdom of God. Be ready when your call comes, for surely it will come. (78–01, p. 35)

Youth, in all you do, live the gospel. In all that you do, live the principles of the gospel of Jesus Christ that have been taught to you. This will become the guiding influence and the element that will make your lives happy and give you hope for the future. (79–03)

We need youth with great faith. As the Church moves into the challenges of the last decades of this century, the need for leadership through the wards and stakes of Zion will increase dramatically. What is needed is not just young people of training and skill, but rather we will need a generation of great faith, those who have learned discipline and discipleship. What will be needed is a generation who understand not only how to organize a ward but also how to build faith, how to sustain the weak and faltering, and how to defend the truth. What is needed is a generation whose glory comes from their capacity to comprehend light and truth, who can with that light and truth then enlarge their capacity to love and to serve. (84–04)

Youth should consider four steps in choosing employment. May I offer to the youth—these young people we want to help—for their consideration, four steps which are important in obtaining the right employment. They are: first, to invite the Lord's help in this important search; second, to plan ahead carefully; third, to gather all possible necessary information; and fourth, [to make] proper vocation or education preparation. (75–02, p. 123)

Morality and Modesty

Moral cleanliness is basic to success. Cleanliness is basic to success in any endeavor. Could an unclean doctor with unclean instruments defeat disease? Could a hospital with unclean operating rooms cure a patient? Can an unclean mind produce anything but filth? Can unclean habits build strength? Isn't filth always a sign of weakness?

Weakness never succeeds. The battle is to the strong. To be strong—be clean. (62–06)

The girl who chooses to be modest chooses to be respected. A boy who is honest with himself will admit that he likes a girl who is modest in speech, conduct, and dress. Modesty is one of the great virtues he looks for in the girl he hopes to marry. Most of us know what is modest, and most of us know when modesty ends and immodesty commences. We know that nothing detracts from the loveliness of a young lady more than immodesty in speech or immodesty in conduct. A girl fools only herself if she thinks she is impressing a boy by immodest conduct. The young lady who dresses in an immodest manner ceases to be attractive and embarrasses the young man. She has called his attention to the person rather than the personality. The girl who chooses to be modest, chooses to be respected. (60–03, p. 3)

Youth are on safer grounds when they set standards. Consider the young lady who adopts the Church standards of modesty in speech, action, and dress, who refuses to smoke and drink and go to questionable places, and who abstains from promiscuous kissing and petting. Is she on safer ground in her relations with the young men than one who does not adopt such standards? . . . It is extremely important that we make decisions as to our course and conduct, and after making these decisions we must give an uncompromising answer when the occasion arises. (60–03, p. 3)

Young people, prepare to enter the temple. I encourage the young people . . . to prepare diligently for the day when you can enter the holy temple to receive your own blessings and, most particularly, a temple marriage. Do not be satisfied with anything less than a marriage in the house of the Lord. The protecting hand of the Lord will be evident in your personal lives as you strive to live worthy of the privilege of entering the temple. (94–22)

Proper Dating Patterns

Freedom of choice in dating places a great responsibility on young people. Freedom of choice places a great responsibility on young people. Each year that we live, as we are growing up, we find that our ideas change. What we like today may not be the thing that we will like tomorrow. Haven't you found this true in studies at school, in sports, in clothes, or in the things you do or places you go? Haven't you also found this to be true in persons you have known? Our ideas change as we have more experience.

This is really the process we go through in finding a mate in life rather than by having someone else make the selection for us.

Dating has become the accepted form of social recreation for the purpose of getting acquainted before young people can safely have a serious interest in each other. Because the selection of a mate in life is so extremely important, we should intelligently seek the experiences which will help us to make that great decision. (60–02, p. 3)

Youth should seek the counsel of their parents on dating. Parents have a deep interest in seeing that their young people have the opportunities that come from good, wholesome dating experiences. Your parents are interested in your dating. As young people you may feel that they are too interested, but there is good reason why they should be. . . . If you will carefully study your parents you will discover that what your parents really want you to have is what they themselves would want if they were young again. . . . It is a wise boy or girl who understands that parents have had many more years of experience and can give good counsel and advice concerning dating problems. (60–02, p. 3)

Youth are cautioned against steady dating. Steady dating presents a real problem to most young men and women. The same question arises with respect to age. When should a young man or a young woman commence steady dating? I am sure you will agree that it is not a good idea for a young man and a young woman to begin steady dating until they have arrived at the marriageable age. . . . There is plenty of time after high school to go steady. (60–02, p. 3)

Youth should date only those with high standards. Many young people are faced with such problems as smoking, drinking, kissing, and petting at some time in their dating experiences. These problems will never appear if we choose our friends from among those who have the same high standards in these things as have been set for us by the Church. . . .

If we adopt the standards of the Church as our standards, date only those who share the same interests and spiritual aspirations, and look to temple marriage as the great achievement, we have learned a great lesson in successful dating. (60–02, p. 3)

Greater freedom brings need for greater care. A major change has taken place within recent years. Today each of you young people has greater freedom of thought and action than has ever been enjoyed by any previous generation. The opportunity to enjoy and participate in many good and fine things has increased, but in sharp contrast, this change has brought about the problem of a great many temptations to you young people. The automobile takes you away from your home and sometimes from your community. Leisure time has been increased. There are many opportunities for entertainment both good and bad. Modern advertising glamorizes to youth numerous things which creates false illusions. Never before has there been such freedom of uncontrolled dating. These things make it necessary that you choose between that which is good and that which is not good. (60–03, p. 3)

We should marry within our faith. Young people—we do marry our "dates." If our religion means anything to us, we will not be happy without a Mormon marriage, a Mormon family, prayer and harmony in the home. When the romance wears off, the unbelievers may become distasteful. Many have found this to be so.

So date seriously only with Latter-day Saint young men and women. Let the others be friends, in their own place, but when it comes to serious dating, let us date Latter-day Saints.

A marriage in the temple is one of the principal goals of our entire lives, or should be if we understand the facts.

To miss out on temple marriage is to miss out on one of the main reasons for our existence in mortality.

God's whole purpose—his work and his glory—is to bring to pass the immortality and eternal life of man (see Moses 1:39).

Eternal life with God comes to us as couples, married in the temple, not as single individuals.

So you must plan now for this great goal. The planning must begin with your first dates—and all those that follow. Make certain that your serious dates are with people you can take to the temple.

If you do this, my young friends, I promise that your lives and the lives of your future children will be more assured of the happiness you desire in this life. (62–08)

There is danger in early dating. Early dating leads to early marriage.

When it does not bring marriage, it often ends in sin. Familiarity leads to necking and petting, and that to loss of virtue.

Many think that since they have gone together a long time, they have certain rights, which is a great mistake. But they think so, and take liberties which lead to sin.

The difficulty is that too many want to grow up too fast. They lack sound judgment, which only years and experience can bring. They are immature.

They have no way to earn a living, they haven't finished their schooling, they haven't gone on their missions, and yet in spite of all of that unreadiness, they still want the social privileges of grown-ups. (62–02)

Early marriage is seldom successful. Girls—do not rush yourselves and your boyfriends into early marriage. Early marriage is seldom successful. It often prevents completing one's education. It usually condemns a couple to a low income and low standard of living. It prevents the boy from going on a mission. Every girl should plan to encourage her boyfriend to enter the mission field. (62–06)

Drinking and dating don't mix. Everyone will agree that drinking and driving do not mix, but I assure you that an even more deadly combination is drinking and dating.

Liquor makes those who drive lose their control.

In exactly the same way, liquor makes people who date lose *their* control. To lose one's balance mentally is worse than to lose one's balance physically.

To lose our good judgment by allowing liquor to make our minds abnormal leads to all manner of dreadful consequences which may ruin our lives.

Young people who lose control of themselves may indulge in behavior which they will regret for the rest of their lives. Human passions are strong, and must be kept under control by stability and good judgment. . . .

If our judgment is thrown off balance the controls are gone. Tragedy enters our lives. Remorse will follow us for years afterward. The price we pay for a supposed thrill is far too high! . . .

Bad as liquor may be in driving a car or in injuring our health, its worst effect is in the field of spirituality. Spirituality is priceless.

Each of us loves the Lord:

We follow him. We seek to become like him. It was he who gave us the Word of Wisdom.

It was he who said: "Inasmuch as any man drinketh wine or strong drink among you, behold, it is not good, neither meet in the sight of your Father" (D&C 89:5). . . .

It is the *Lord* who calls to us in this matter. The warning against liquor comes from our Father in Heaven. Let us listen to what he says, and obey him. He warns us against conspiring men who have made both liquor and cigarettes popular, to the detriment of mankind. He gives us a wonderful promise if we will but keep faithful (quotes D&C 89:18–21). (62–05)

There are some good rules about dating and automobiles. When you are in your car on a date—will you especially remember to be good Latter-day Saints? Our conduct should be no different in our cars than it would be in our homes.

As there should be no smoking in our homes, there should be no smoking in our cars.

As there should be no drinking in our homes, there should be no drinking in our cars.

As there should be no necking or petting in our homes, there should be no necking or petting in our cars.

It is always safer to have a crowd in the car than just one couple, but when there is a crowd, don't allow any fooling or interference with the driver which would cause an accident.

It is safe to stay where other people are. Avoid dark and lonely streets and lanes. Avoid stopping in the dark. Drive home after your date and go into your well-lighted house for further visiting rather than to sit in the car in the dark.

Do not allow anyone to use your car for unclean purposes, and never use it that way yourself.

Cleanliness is next to Godliness.

Godliness is required of Latter-day Saints, wherever they are.

Some people love darkness because their deeds are evil.

The Lord and his righteous people work in the light. Their deeds are open for all to see. (62–04)

10

MARRIAGE

Building a Strong Marriage

There is danger in teenage marriage. We have already mentioned one of the difficult facts about early marriage. That is, that the youngsters are usually sorry very soon afterward.

Why are they sorry? Because the newness wears off their romance very fast when they begin to face the hard facts of living together as they must.

When the romance fades away, love cools.

When love cools, divorce comes.

Why does love cool?

For one thing, teenagers are not yet ready to settle down to the ways of older married folks. Many of them have not fully grown up yet—in other words, they are still immature.

Often the boys get tired of this one steady "date" whom they have married and want a change of scenery, so they begin to date other girls, even though married, and some girls are foolish enough to date with them.

The young wives often do the same thing, unless a new baby ties them down. Sometimes the baby is abandoned, or left with grandmother to rear.

One bad "out of marriage date" leads to another. Often there is sin in this as well as heartbreak.

When you remember that mother and dad love you, and want to protect you, can you see how they would like to prevent trouble like we have described from coming into your lives?

Teenagers wanting an early marriage seldom think of that.

They see their parents merely in the role of objectors, almost as enemies to their supposed happiness.

But how wrong! Parents want only the best for their children and when they advise against trouble like this, it is to avoid breaking your hearts and theirs too. Actually, they will be more heartbroken than you if that is possible, since they love you so much. (62–02)

Husbands and wives need to listen to each other. Many problems could be quickly answered, and many difficult situations resolved, if we could understand that there are times when we need to listen. In school we learned the lesson when we listened, but failed when we refused to give attention. In marriage there is a complete lack of understanding unless we are willing to listen. In business we are headed for failure unless we listen to the lesson that will help us succeed, or the advice of persons that might give us the key to turn a collision course with failure into success. Of course, we need to talk, but we must listen to the other view in order to increase our understanding sufficiently to make an intelligent decision. A listening ear can oftentimes make the difference. (73–03)

Marriages must have more than physical attraction to endure. [Quotes Luke 6:46–49—the parable of two houses, one built on sand, the other built on rock.] Friendships cannot endure if they are based on the sands of selfishness. Marriages do not endure when they have no ground except in physical attraction, and do not have the foundation of a deeper love and loyalty. (67–07, p. 46)

Successful marriage is more a matter of being the right person than marrying the right person. [Marriage] is a learned behavior. Our conscious effort, not instinct, determines the success. The motivating force stems from kindness, true affection, and consideration for each other's happiness and welfare.

Prior to marriage we looked at life from our own point of view, but after stepping over that threshold, we began to consider it from another's viewpoint also. There is a necessity to make sacrifices and adjustments as manifestations of reassurance and love.

It is often said that being happily and successfully married is generally not so much a matter of marrying the right person as it *is being the right person*. Statistics showing the high rate of divorce might indicate unwise choices of partners. If they had married other persons, the particular problem might have been eliminated, but surely another problem would have been in its place. A wise choice of a partner is a large contribution to a successful marriage, yet the conscious effort to do one's part fully is the greatest element contributing to success. (78–03)

Marriage is a partnership with God. Marriage is often referred to as a partnership with God. This is not just a figure of speech. If this partnership remains strong and active, the man and woman will love each other as they love God, and there will come into their home a sweetness and affection that will bring eternal success. In order to keep our lives and marriages beautiful there needs to be a balance between business affairs and day to day living, with goals and aspirations for the eternities. (78–03)

Marriage insurance is available to those who live righteously. Marriage insurance is available also to those who live righteous lives, love the Lord, keep his commandments, and strive to be worthy co-creators with God. (78–03)

Marriage is life's greatest partnership. Life's greatest partnership is in marriage—that relationship which has lasting and eternal significance. (94–07)

The Importance of Temple Marriage

Settle for nothing less than a temple marriage. In the temple we receive the highest ordinance available to men and women, the sealing of husbands and wives together for eternity. We hope our young people will settle for nothing less than a temple marriage. We hope you who are married will remember the feelings of love which led you to the altar in the house of the Lord. Our hearts are saddened as we learn of many whose love has grown cold or who through reasons of selfishness or transgression forget or treat lightly the marriage covenants they made in the temple. We plead with husbands and wives to have love and respect for each other. Indeed, it would be our fondest hope that each family would be blessed with a mother and father who express love for each other, who are deferential to each other, and who work together to strengthen the bonds of marriage. (94–11)

Eternal marriage is the most powerful principle in promoting stable homes. There is no more powerful principle of life to promote love, forbearance, and devotion in the home than that of eternal marriage. Good adjustment and performance in adult life depend largely on the quality of home life. The principle of eternal marriage is a most powerful stabilizing influence in promoting the kind of home needed to rear children who are happy and well adjusted. (72–03, p. 65)

The Church stands alone in teaching eternal marriage. Among other things, temples are established for the purpose of eternal marriage. The Lord intended that the marriage covenant should be for time and for all eternity; therefore, those who are worthy may come to the House of the Lord to be united in this eternal covenant. "Neither is the man without the woman, neither the woman without the man, in the Lord." (1 Corinthians 11:11). Thus The Church of Jesus Christ of Latter-day Saints stands alone in teaching the doctrine of the eternal duration of the marriage covenant and the family unit. What could eternity offer to interest one unless he could enjoy it with those with whom he has lived in mortality? In the temple the marriage covenant is made eternal, and in this relationship the family becomes an eternal unit. As one of our great Church leaders has said: "The chairs of the eternal tables are not left vacant by death in the Gospel of Jesus Christ." (56–01)

We cannot fulfill our ultimate aims without temple marriage. Just as baptism is a commandment of the Lord, so is temple marriage. As baptism is essential to admittance to the Church, so temple marriage is essential to our exaltation in the presence of God. It is part of our destiny. We cannot fulfill our ultimate aims without it.

Do not be satisfied with anything less.

You wouldn't accept a worldly form of baptism, would you?

God has his mode of baptism—by immersion by one who holds the authority.

Then would you accept a worldly form of marriage?

He has his mode of marriage also: It is temple marriage. (62–06)

Young people should resolve to marry in the temple. We would like to tell the young people . . . that when they contemplate a marriage which is contrary to the advice and the counsel of the leadership of the Church, they tread upon dangerous ground. There are exceptions to most rules, but when we follow the exception hoping it may prove successful, we are taking chances that we cannot afford to take in such important decisions.

I wish we could influence every young person . . . in making a strong resolution, perhaps something to this effect: "As far as I am concerned, I will follow the teachings of the leadership of the Church, knowing that from their great experience and the divine inspiration that comes from them, I will be led in the path which will lead to happiness and joy as I approach marriage." There is nothing more pleasing to us than these young people who look toward the temple as they approach marriage. (57–01)

Celestial marriage is the crowning ordinance. Celestial marriage is the crowning gospel ordinance, and if men and women obey this commandment "they shall be gods," in the words of the revelation (see D&C 132:19–20). How high, how noble, how lofty is this concept of marriage—marriage ordained of God. (58–01)

Marriage is intended to be eternal. Let me call your attention to the fact that the first marriage was performed by the Lord. It was an eternal marriage because there was no such thing as time when that ceremony took place. The ceremony was performed for a couple not then subject to death; thus, under the circumstances the relationship would never be terminated. After the fall, our first parents were driven from the Garden. They were then subject to death, but resurrection was promised to them. At no time was it said that their eternal marriage should come to an end. . . .

When man and wife become no more twain but one flesh, that relationship survives the resurrection if we believe what the Lord has said. In the temple a woman is sealed to a man for eternity, and children who are born in that covenant are sealed to their parents for eternity. The family relationship will never come to an end. If persons will not enter into this relationship or follow the divine commandment which has been given to them, it will not exist in the hereafter because hereafter they neither marry nor are given in marriage (see Matthew 22:30).

God does not perform marriages for time only. He didn't say to the Pharisees that marriage does not continue, that there is no marriage in the hereafter; he did say what God joins remains joined and will endure forever (see Matthew 19:3–6). (79–09)

Marriage is a sacred privilege and obligation. With a knowledge of the plan of salvation as a foundation, a man who holds the priesthood looks upon marriage as a sacred privilege and obligation. It is not good for man nor for woman to be alone. Man is not complete without woman. Neither can fill the measure of their creation without the other (see 1 Corinthians 11:11; Moses 3:18). Marriage between a man and a woman is ordained of God (see D&C 49:15–17). Only through the new and everlasting covenant of marriage can they realize the fullness of eternal blessings (see D&C 131:1–4; 132:15–19). (94–15, p. 49)

In the temple the foundations of the eternal family are sealed in place. Another temple ordinance is that of celestial marriage, where wife is sealed to husband and husband sealed to wife for eternity. We know, of course, that civil marriages end at death; but eternal marriages performed in the temple may exist forever. Children born to a husband and wife after an eternal marriage are automatically sealed to their parents for eternity. If children are born before the wife is sealed to her husband, there is a temple sealing ordinance that can seal these children to their parents for eternity, and so it is that children can be sealed vicariously to parents who have passed away.

In the ordinances of the temple, the foundations of the eternal family are sealed in place. The Church has the responsibility—and the authority—to preserve and protect the family as the foundation of society. (95–01, p. 2)

Only marriage for eternity has lasting value. When I think of marriage I'm only speaking of one kind, and that's a marriage for eternity. For a marriage that isn't for eternity is hardly much more than just a compliance with the law of the land, for there is no lasting value to it. (62–60)

Dealing with Marital Problems

A husband should avoid any domineering or unworthy behavior in intimate relationships with his wife. Keep yourselves above any domineering or unworthy behavior in the tender, intimate relationship between husband and wife. Because marriage is ordained of God, the intimate relationship between husbands and wives is good and honorable in the eyes of God. He has commanded that they be one flesh and that they multiply and replenish the earth (see Moses 2:28; 3:24). You are to love your wife as Christ loved the Church and gave himself for it (see Ephesians 5:25–31).

Tenderness and respect—never selfishness—must be the guiding principles in the intimate relationship between husband and wife. Each partner must be considerate and sensitive to the other's needs and desires. Any domineering, indecent, or uncontrolled behavior in the intimate relationship between husband and wife is condemned by the Lord.

Any man who abuses or demeans his wife physically or spiritually is guilty of grievous sin and in need of sincere and serious repentance. Differences should be worked out in love and kindness and with a spirit of mutual reconciliation. A man should always speak to his wife lovingly and kindly, treating her with the utmost respect. Marriage is like a tender flower, brethren, and must be nourished constantly with expressions of love and affection. (94–15, p. 51)

In marriage we learn to live with imperfection. You will remember the story of Thomas Moore, the famous nineteenth century Irish poet who was called away on a business trip. Upon his return he was met at the door not by his beautiful bride, but by someone who gave him the message that his wife was upstairs and had asked that he not come up. Then the poet learned the terrible truth. His wife had contracted smallpox during his absence and the disease had left her once flawless and beautiful face scarred and pocked with the disease. She had taken one look at her reflection in the mirror and commanded that the shutters be drawn and that her husband never see her again.

Thomas Moore would not listen. He ran upstairs and threw open the door of his wife's room, but the room was dark and she made no sound. As he went to turn on the lamp she cried out, "No, don't light the lamps. Please go, this is the greatest gift I can give you. Go now." He left the room and went downstairs to his study and sat up all night prayerfully thinking and composing not a poem, as he had before, but his first song. He not only wrote the words but he wrote the music.

The next morning, as soon as the sun was up, he returned to his wife's room and called out, "Are you awake?" She answered, "I am, but do not come in." He sang to his wife that song that we hear today on occasions:

> Believe me if all these endearing young charms,
> Which I gaze on so fondly today,
> Were to change by tomorrow and flee in my arms
> Like fairy gifts fading away,
> Thou would still be adored
> As this moment thou art
> Let thy loveliness fade as it will.

And then he heard a movement from the corner of the room where his wife lay in her loneliness, and he finished the song:

> Let thy loveliness fade as it will
> And around the dear ruin
> Each wish of my heart
> Would entwine itself verdantly still.

The song ended. She arose from her bed, crossed the room, and they fell into each other's arms.

Your marriage partner probably doesn't have scars from small-pox, or any other things that would make him ugly in appearance, but most partners have imperfections, imperfections that may not make them as desirable as they might otherwise be. Wives some-times pick at their husbands behind their backs, and husbands talk about their wives, not understanding them because of petty little things.

Richard L. Evans once said, "Perhaps any of us could get along with perfect people, but our task is to get along with imperfect people." We understand in marriage that we are not dealing with perfect people; we are seeking perfection and we are traveling the course in which we hope to find perfection, but we must have understanding, give our best, and make life beautiful. William Cooper said it this way:

> The kindest and the happiest pair
> Will find occasion to forebear.
> Find something every day they live
> To pity and perhaps forgive.

Maybe what we need in marriage is not a new partner, but a little more good-natured tolerance. The Song of Love in the Bible tells us: "Charity suffereth long, and is kind" (see 1 Corinthians 13:4). That kind of love, the kind that is not taken lightly, not terminated at pleasure and thrown away like disposable plastic, but which faces all of life's little difficulties hand in hand entwining the souls, is the ultimate expression of human happiness. (79–08)

The tragedy of divorce is increasing. What has happened to the marriage institution ordained of God? [In 1957] the national average . . . [was] one divorce for every three marriages. We speak of marriage as embarking upon the sea of matrimony. What if one of every three ships that embarked upon the sea failed to return or crashed upon the rocks? It would be a national catastrophe if every third aircraft leaving the ground was wrecked, but every third home in the United States has been wrecked by this enemy from within and we pay very little attention. (58–01)

Marriages are not intended to be disposable. It seems to me that we live in somewhat of a plastic world—a kind of a throw-away society. Many things we hold in our hands are not permanent, but used only for the occasion and then thrown into the trash. If the little girl of yesterday had broken her doll, she would have nursed it back to health with love and tenderness, using a needle and thread and perhaps some glue. But in today's world when the little girl breaks her plastic doll, it goes into the trash and she is on her way back to the store to get a new one. For better or for worse, that's the way it is.

I have wondered if restlessness and the endless searching for something new, something shinier, is the reason for the rate of divorce that seems to be spiraling in our societies. There is one chance in five [1979] that the one who courts and marries a girl will soon be in a different court—a court of divorce—and that seems to be the throw-away world in which we live.

The Lord has defined marriage for us. He said, "For this cause shall a man leave father and mother, and shall cleave to his wife: and they twain shall be one flesh" (Matthew 19:5). Surely the happiest marriages are those where your hurt is my hurt, my pain is your pain, my victory, your victory, my concerns, your concerns. The oneness of heart, of soul, of flesh seems to be more of a challenge than ever before in the world in which the question seems to be: "What is there in this for me?" Far too many marriage partners have become merely an ornament on the sleeve rather than a part of the heart. (79–08)

Divorce often results from failure to live the gospel. Many questions are asked by conscientious people in the Church regarding the effect of divorce. The Church, of course, frowns upon divorce, but we learn many things from it to help us understand that living the principles of the gospel makes a happy marriage. The causes of divorce are usually from such things as liquor, unfaithfulness, financial problems, abuse, selfishness, and simple incompatibility. In most instances the cause is from failure to live the principles of the gospel. When two people can live the principles of the gospel, marriage can be sweet and it can be happy. We need to have patience and understanding, and to carry out in its fullest the admonition given by the Lord that we have love for one another. (79–09)

The Church discourages divorce. The Church, of course, frowns upon divorce, realizing that in most instances, many instances at least, a divorce can be avoided if two people are willing to live the gospel. The causes of divorce are many—liquor, infidelity, and many other things with which we are familiar. Sometimes it is on the part of both persons, sometimes it is only on the part of one; and although the Church abhors divorce, it recognizes that there are instances in which it is justified. Divorce is increasing, as we know, and every year the statistics are higher. We need the spirit of the gospel in our homes. Marriages that are performed for eternity where there is love and respect and all of the other things that the gospel implies, brings a solidarity to marriage that we each seek. (79–13)

If you are divorced, don't lose faith in marriage. To you who have experienced divorce: Don't let disappointment or a sense of failure color your perception of marriage or of life. Do not lose faith in marriage or allow bitterness to canker your soul and destroy you or those you love or have loved. (89–02, p. 77)

Responsibilities of Husbands and Wives

Husband and wife relationships are based on principles of righteousness. In giving instructions to the Ephesians that husbands and wives should love each other, [Paul] said:

"Wives, submit yourselves unto your own husbands, as unto the Lord. . . .

"Husbands, love your wives even as Christ also loved the church, and gave himself for it." (Ephesians 5:22, 25.)

This requirement that wives submit to their husbands, of course, is predicated upon and presupposes the principles of righteousness on the part of husbands. (58–01)

In their roles husbands and wives should keep an eternal perspective. Perhaps it is just a man's viewpoint, but it seems to me that sweetness and spirituality in the home are often brought about by the conduct of the woman. Husbands and wives have a great responsibility in raising children. They have the responsibility of looking far beyond mortality regarding many things that become of prime importance as we walk this way through mortality. Eternity is so long, mortality is so short, that it would seem reasonable we would give attention to those things which are of such great importance that they will last without ever coming to an end. (79–13)

Women should maintain their spiritual superiority in marriage. I suppose you would say it is a man's viewpoint to throw a burden upon a woman to maintain the stability and the sweetness of marriage, but this seems to be her divine nature. She has a superior spirituality in the marriage relationship, and the opportunity to encourage, uplift, teach, and be the one who sets the example in the family for righteous living. When women come to the point of realizing that it is more important to be superior than to be equal, they will find the real joy in living those principles that the Lord set out in his divine plan. (79–09)

A man should show perfect moral fidelity to his wife. A man who holds the priesthood shows perfect moral fidelity to his wife and gives her no reason to doubt his faithfulness. A husband is to love his wife with all his heart and cleave unto her and none else (see D&C 42:22–26). President Spencer W. Kimball explained:

"The words *none else* eliminate everyone and everything. The spouse then becomes pre-eminent in the life of the husband or wife and neither social life nor occupational life nor political life nor any other interest nor person nor thing shall ever take precedence over the companion spouse." (*The Miracle of Forgiveness* [Salt Lake City: Bookcraft, 1969], p. 250.)

The Lord forbids and his church condemns any and every intimate relationship outside of marriage. Infidelity on the part of a man breaks the heart of his wife and loses her confidence and the confidence of his children (see Jacob 2:35).

Be faithful in your marriage covenants in thought, word, and deed. Pornography, flirtations, and unwholesome fantasies erode one's character and strike at the foundation of a happy marriage. Unity and trust within a marriage are thereby destroyed. One who does not control his thoughts and thus commits adultery in his heart, if he does not repent, shall not have the Spirit, but shall deny the faith and shall fear (see D&C 42:23; 63:16). (94–15, p. 50)

Advice to the Unmarried

No eternal blessings will be denied to worthy individuals. May I hasten to add that no blessing, including that of eternal marriage and an eternal family, will be denied to any worthy individual. While it may take somewhat longer—perhaps even beyond this mortal life—for some to achieve this blessing, it will not be denied. (89–02, p. 76)

Unmarried men have the responsibility to take the lead in seeking eternal companionship. To you who are unmarried men: Don't put off marriage because you are not in a perfect career and financial position. Do not, however, rush into a relationship without proper forethought and inspiration. Prayerfully seek the Lord's guidance on this matter. Stay worthy of receiving that divine assistance. Remember that as a priesthood bearer you have the obligation to take the lead in seeking eternal companionship. (89–02, p. 77)

If you are faithful, all blessings will be yours. To you unmarried women: The promises of the prophets of God have always been that the Lord is mindful of you; if you are faithful, all blessings will be yours. To be without marriage and a family in this life is but a temporary condition, and eternity is a long time. President Benson has reminded us that "time is numbered only to man. God has your eternal perspective in mind" *(Ensign,* November 1988, p. 97.) Fill your lives with worthwhile, meaningful activities. (89–02, p. 77)

Do not postpone marriage. As a matter of priesthood responsibility, a man, under normal circumstances, should not unduly postpone marriage. Brethren, the Lord has spoken plainly on this matter. It is your sacred and solemn responsibility to follow his counsel and the words of his prophets. (94–15, p. 49)

Don't worry unduly about marriage. Unless I'm seriously mistaken, many of you also worry about courtship, marriage, and starting a family. You probably will not find the name of your future spouse in Nephi's vision or the book of Revelation; you probably will not be told it by an angel or even by your bishop. Some things you must work out for yourself. Have faith and be obedient, and blessings will come. Try to be patient. Try not to let what you don't have blind you to that which you do have. If you worry too much about marriage, it can canker the very possibility of it.

Live fully and faithfully as one person before having undue anxiety about living as two. (89–03, p. 114)

You who are widowed, continue to grow. To you who are widowed: The most important part of your life is not over. For some, there will be appropriate opportunity for further companionship and remarriage. But for those who, for whatever reason, do not choose this path, there can still be marvelous opportunities in life for personal growth and service to others. (89–02, p. 77)

Priesthood and auxiliary leaders should take an interest in those who are single. To you priesthood and auxiliary leaders: Follow the scriptural counsel to look after the widows and the fatherless (see D&C 83:6). Take a prayerful interest in those who are single or in single-parent homes. Help them feel wanted, but not uncomfortably singled out. Remember: the Church is for *all* members. (89–02, p. 77)

Do not lose promised blessings by wandering in self-pity. This is the church of Jesus Christ, not the church of marrieds or singles or any other group or individual. The gospel we preach is the gospel of Jesus Christ, which encompasses all the saving ordinances and covenants necessary to save and exalt every individual who is willing to accept Christ and keep the commandments that he and our Father in Heaven have given. . . .

How foolish we would be to fail to enjoy the rich gifts of God to us! We could well miss opportunities for providing needed blessings to others because we felt personally deprived of some hoped-for blessing and were blinded by our own self-pity.

Not only should we be careful not to deprive others of blessings because of our wanderings in the wastelands of self-pity or self-recrimination, but we should be careful not to deprive ourselves of other blessings that could be ours.

While waiting for promised blessings, one should not mark time, for to fail to move forward is to some degree a retrogression. Be anxiously engaged in good causes, including your own development. (89–02, pp. 76, 77)

Marriage is the most important decision after a mission. I think the greatest decision you must make when you come [home from this mission] is the decision that's going to shape your life for eternity, and that is your marriage. I'm sure that you would agree with me that this is going to be far more important than anything else you do in life, because your work and your profession or whatever you're going to do is not nearly as important as eternal values, and you have a decision yet lying ahead of you that's going to affect you through eternity; it's going to affect you while you live here upon the earth too, . . . you can't [afford to] make a mistake, nor can you postpone this decision indefinitely.

I'm always disturbed when a young man says to me, "I don't have time to think of marriage now because I've got the service ahead of me and then I've got the rest of my schooling, and I don't want to get married until I can provide for a family the way they should be provided for." Now this is . . . just poor thinking when you think that way. (62–00)

Marriage is not a detriment to our progress. Marriage is never a detriment to getting where you want to go. As a matter of fact I think it could be said that it's a benefit rather than a detriment. You've seen young married men in school with children coming along, and they're usually the ones that get the best grades and get along the best. It will help you rather than be a detriment to you. (62–06)

11

FAMILY RELATIONSHIPS

Church Programs and the Family

Every family is encouraged to hold family home evening. We encourage you to make family life a preeminent focus. In the Church, families will never be "out of style" or "out of date." One of the keys to strong family life is family home evening. The First Presidency has recently issued a letter regarding this inspired program. In part it states, "If the Saints obey this counsel to hold family home evenings, we promise that great blessings will result. Love at home and obedience to parents will increase. Faith will be developed in the hearts of the youth of Israel, and they will gain power to combat the evil influence and temptations which beset them." (First Presidency letter, August 30, 1994.) We hope every family will follow this counsel. (94–11)

Hold family home evening every Monday. We encourage [Monday] to be the evening for the family hour so we can be at home with our families—no meetings to distract our attention, no business, but a time when we can devote ourselves to our families and grow close together. Under the influence of prayer in our homes, we can learn the lessons we should learn. Those of us who are parents have learned great and valuable lessons from the little ones on these occasions.

We hope that your family hour will be a period of ritual when the family joins together, plays together, prays together, and enjoys the association of each other. We are a family church. (57–02)

In strengthening individuals and families, none should be neglected. In seeking after the welfare of individuals and families, it is important to remember that the basic unit of the Church is the family. However, in focusing on the family we should remember that in the world in which we live families are not restricted to the traditional grouping of father, mother, and children. Families in the Church today also consist of couples without children, single parents with children, and single individuals living alone or with roommates. Each of these families must receive priesthood watch care. Often those which may need the most careful watch care are those families of the non-traditional structure. Caring and committed home teachers are needed in each home. None should be neglected. (91–01)

The Church has the responsibility to help preserve the family. The Church has the responsibility—and the authority—to preserve and protect the family as the foundation of society. The pattern for family life, instituted from before the foundation of the world, provides for children to be born to and nurtured by a father and mother who are husband and wife, lawfully married. Parenthood is a sacred obligation and privilege, with children welcomed as a "heritage of the Lord" (Psalm 127:3).

A worried society now begins to see that the disintegration of the family brings upon the world the calamities foretold by the prophets. The world's councils and deliberations will succeed only when they define the family as the Lord has revealed it to be. "Except the Lord build the house, they labour in vain that build it" (Psalm 127:1). (94–14, p. 9)

Parents' Obligation Toward Children

Great blessings come through family prayer. Pray as families both night and morning. Great blessings will come into the lives of children who hear their parents petition the Lord in their behalf. (94–22)

Parents' responsibility to children involves more than providing food and raiment. As summer draws to a close, fathers and mothers are busy in stores and shops selecting clothing, shoes, and other things necessary for the return of our children to school, and preparation is being made for the departure of the older youth to college. This season should remind us that children require more than food and raiment. They need proper instruction from their parents to prepare them for the temptations and problems that will arise while they are away from the home. We look to our schools to provide a liberal education for our children, but the school cannot replace the parents' duty to teach them the principles of being honest, true, chaste, benevolent, virtuous, and in doing good. The Lord has said: "But I have commanded you to bring up your children in light and truth" (D&C 93:40). This is the great responsibility of parents which is often overlooked.

I am reminded of an experience in the life of one of my close associates. While yet a young boy his parents removed to a logging community, taking with them their four small children. His father, having fear of the consequence of his children wandering into the dangerous and uninhabited mountain area, proceeded to build a high board fence to protect the little family, taking pride in his accomplishment and the offered security. The very day following the completion of the enclosure, the boy found a way to surmount the fence. Over he went into the wilds of the pine forest. Searching parties combed the adjacent mountains and canyons for many anxious hours, and at last the boy was returned to his home by a trapper who had picked up his trail and located him. The father learned a great lesson when the trapper said: "You can't fence in children. You must teach them of the dangers of the forest and the peril of wandering away into unknown regions, and instruct them to look for the landmarks that will guide them back to safety in the event they become lost." Our duty as parents is to prepare our youth for the great decisions they must make in order that they will not depart from the light and truth and become lost. (52–01)

Children must be cultivated by careful attention. A tender sapling can be cultivated by careful attention and training to grow straight and upright. So it can be with the children that God has placed in our care. They should be impressed from the cradle to the time they leave the parental roof to make homes and assume the duties of life for themselves; that there is a seedtime and harvest, and as a man sows, so shall he reap. The sowing of bad habits in youth will bring forth nothing better than vice, and the sowing of seeds of indolence will result invariably in poverty and lack of stability in old age. Evil begets evil, and good will bring forth good.

We should be good examples to our children, for the greatest teaching is done by way of example. We must never teach our children one thing and then practice another, but rather always be the example of our teaching. This is the great challenge of parenthood. (52–01)

Family prayer ties families together. Our class leaders say it is easy to tell whether family prayers are held in the home by the conduct and the attitude of the children. Parents who kneel with their little ones and teach them the lessons that come from family prayer tie their families closely together. When we talk to young people facing marriage, we tell them of the great value that will come to their lives if, as husband and wife, they will kneel and pray together. When little ones join them in family prayer and take their turn as they grow old enough to speak, they will learn lessons that will stay with them all of their lives. What a great blessing we are passing by if we do not take the time to kneel with our families in family prayer. (57–02)

Example is the best teacher. Fathers and mothers have a great responsibility with respect to the children which are entrusted to their care. . . . In the book of Proverbs we find this admonition to parents:

"Train up a child in the way he should go: and when he is old, he will not depart from it" (Proverbs 22:6).

The greatest training that can be given to a child is that which comes from the example of parents. Parents need to set the example for young people to follow. Great strength comes from the home where righteous principles are taught, where there is love and respect for each other, where prayer has been an influence in the family life, and where there is respect for those things that pertain to God. (60–04, p. 125)

Parents of wayward children should remember eight helpful thoughts. If a parent has made what could be considered an error—or, on the other hand, has never made a mistake, but still the lamb has wandered from the fold—in either case there are several thoughts I would like to share with you.

First, such a father or mother is not alone. Our first parents knew the pain and suffering of seeing some of their children reject the teachings of eternal life (see Moses 5:27). Centuries later Jacob came to know of the jealousy and ill feelings of his older sons toward his beloved Joseph (see Genesis 37:1–8). The great prophet Alma, who had a son named Alma, prayed at length to the Lord regarding the rebellious attitude of his son, and no doubt was overwhelmed with concern and worry about the dissension and the wickedness his son was causing among those who were within the Church (see Mosiah 27:14). Our Father in Heaven has also lost many of his spirit children to the world; he knows the feelings of your heart.

Second, we should remember that errors of judgment are generally less serious than errors of intent.

Third, even if there was a mistake made with full knowledge and understanding, there is the principle of repentance for release and comfort. Rather than constantly dwelling on what we perceive as a mistake or a sin or a failure to the detriment of our progress in the gospel or our association with family and friends, it would be better for us to turn away from it. As with any mistake, we may repent by being sorrowful and by attempting to correct or rectify the consequences, to whatever extent possible. We should look forward with renewed faith.

Fourth, don't give up hope for a boy or a girl who has strayed. Many who have appeared to be completely lost have returned. We must be prayerful and, if possible, let our children know of our love and concern.

Fifth, remember that ours was not the only influence that contributed to the actions of our children, whether those actions were good or bad.

Sixth, know that our Heavenly Father will recognize the love and the sacrifice, the worry and the concern, even though our great effort has been unsuccessful. Parents' hearts are ofttimes broken, yet they must realize that the ultimate responsibility lies with the child after parents have taught correct principles.

Seventh, whatever the sorrow, whatever the concern, whatever the pain and anguish, look for a way to turn it to beneficial use—perhaps in helping others to avoid the same problems, or perhaps by developing a greater insight into the feelings of others who are struggling in a similar way. Surely we will have a deeper understanding of the love of our Heavenly Father when, through prayer, we finally come to know that he understands and wants us to look forward.

The eighth and final point of reminder is that everyone is different. Each of us is unique. Each child is unique. Just as each of us starts at a different point in the race of life, and just as each of us has different strengths and weaknesses and talents, so each child is blessed with his own special set of characteristics. We must not assume that the Lord will judge the success of one in precisely the same way as another. As parents we often assume that, if our child doesn't become an overachiever in every way, we have failed. We should be careful in our judgments. (83–03, pp. 64–65)

Parenthood is of great importance. The responsibilities of parenthood are of the greatest importance. The results of our efforts will have eternal consequences for us and the boys and girls we raise. Anyone who becomes a parent is under strict obligation to protect and love his children and assist them to return to their Heavenly Father. All parents should understand that the Lord will not hold guiltless those who neglect these responsibilities. (83–03, p. 65)

What is a successful parent? There are many in the Church and in the world who are living with feelings of guilt and unworthiness because some of their sons and daughters have wandered or strayed from the fold. . . .

We understand that conscientious parents try their best, yet nearly all have made mistakes. One does not launch into such a project as parenthood without soon realizing that there will be many errors along the way. Surely our Heavenly Father knows, when he entrusts his spirit children into the care of young and inexperienced parents, that there will be mistakes and errors in judgment. . . .

A successful parent is one who has loved, one who has sacrificed, and one who has cared for, taught, and ministered to the needs of a child. If you have done all of these and your child is still wayward or troublesome or worldly, it could well be that you are, nevertheless, a successful parent. Perhaps there are children who have come into the world that would challenge any set of parents under any set of circumstances. Likewise, perhaps there are others who would bless the lives of, and be a joy to, almost any father or mother.

My concern today is that there are parents who may be pronouncing harsh judgments upon themselves and may be allowing these feelings to destroy their lives, when in fact they have done their best and should continue in faith. (83–03, pp. 63, 65)

Children have a responsibility to their parents. "Honour thy father and thy mother: that thy days may be long upon the land which the Lord thy God giveth thee" (Exodus 20:12). Children are admonished to respect and render obedience to their parents, and are expected to provide for them when disabilities arise as their parents did for them as little children. (65–02, p. 511)

Motherhood and Womanhood

Housewives deserve great credit for the load they carry. Our wives deserve great credit for the heavy workload they carry day in and day out within our homes. No one expends more energy than a devoted mother and wife. In the usual arrangement of things, however, it is the man to whom the Lord has assigned the breadwinner's role. (75–02, p. 124)

Women should have educational and vocational training. There are impelling reasons for our sisters to plan toward employment also. We want them to obtain all the education and vocational training possible before marriage. If they become widowed or divorced and need to work, we want them to have dignified and rewarding employment. If a sister does not marry, she has every right to engage in a profession that allows her to magnify her talents and gifts. (75–02, p. 124)

In the Lord's plan women are supremely important. One of the things of interest to women is their place in the social scheme of things. When I read the lessons of the New Testament, it seems to me that women are placed on a very high pedestal. I am somewhat disturbed that there are some who want to bring women down to equality with men. Why would they want to be on a level with men? It is such a simple plan that the Lord has given—women don't walk ahead nor do they walk behind; they walk by the side. Isn't that the way it should be? (79–09)

Sisters deserve credit for spirituality in our families. We depend on you sisters so much and look to you for encouragement. You have great spirituality and testimony and faith. If we of the priesthood were honest in our praise, we would give credit where credit is due for the spirituality in our families that comes from you lovely sisters who encourage us to do the right thing and to fulfill our responsibilities in the priesthood. (79–11)

We must be careful to not confuse the roles of women and men. It seems strange that women want to enter into professions and into work and into places in society on an equality with men, wanting to dress like men and carry on men's work. I don't deny the fact that women are capable of doing so, but as I read the scriptures, I find it hard to reconcile this with what the Lord has said about women—what he has said about the family, what he has said about children. It seems to me that in regard to men and women, even though they might be equal in many things, there is a differentiation between them that we fully understand. I hope the time never comes when women will be brought down to the level with men, although they seem to be making these demands in meetings held . . . all over the world. (79–11)

The Church needs the women and the men to stand together against evil. As our Lord and Savior needed the women of his time for a comforting hand, a listening ear, a believing heart, a kind look, an encouraging word, loyalty—even in his hour of humiliation, agony, and death—so we, his servants all across the Church need you, the women of the Church, to stand with us and for us in stemming the tide of evil that threatens to engulf us. Together we must stand faithful and firm in the faith against superior numbers of other-minded people. It seems to me that there is a great need to rally the women of the Church to stand with and for the Brethren in stemming the tide of evil that surrounds us and in moving forward the work of our Savior. Nephi said, "Ye must press forward with a steadfastness in Christ, having a perfect brightness of hope, and a love of God and of all men, [women, and children]" (2 Nephi 31:20). Obedient to him, we are a majority. But only together can we accomplish the work he has given us to do and be prepared for the day when we shall see him. (92–04, p. 96)

Sisters, visibility does not equate to value. Sisters, continue to seek opportunities for service. Don't be overly concerned with status. Do you recall the counsel of the Savior regarding those who seek the "chief seats" or the "uppermost rooms"? "He that is greatest among you shall be your servant" (Matthew 23:6, 11). It is important to be appreciated. But our focus should be on righteousness, not recognition; on service, not status. The faithful visiting teacher, who quietly goes about her work month after month, is just as important to the work of the Lord as those who occupy what some see as more prominent positions in the Church. Visibility does not equate to value. (92–04, p. 96)

Women have a divine birthright. You are chosen to be faithful women of God in our day, to stand above pettiness, gossip, selfishness, lewdness, and all other forms of ungodliness.

Recognize your divine birthright as daughters of our Heavenly Father. Be one who heals with your words as well as your hands. Seek to know the will of the Lord in your life, and then say, as did that wonderful exemplar Mary, the mother of Jesus, "Behold the handmaid of the Lord; be it unto me according to thy word" (Luke 1:38).

My beloved sisters . . . I testify of the truthfulness and eternal nature of your honored place as women. (94–12, p. 97)

Fatherhood

There must be dedicated leadership in the home. For a family to be successful in the way acceptable to the Lord, there must be dedicated leadership in the home and strong family organization. The Lord has prescribed a patriarchal order for the kingdom, and the family, being the basic unit of the kingdom, must, therefore, be patriarchal in its organization. Under this order the father becomes the head of the family, acting in the spirit of the priesthood, and the mother has the obligation to support, sustain, and be in harmony with that righteous leadership. (74–04, p. 51)

Fathers should have a reverence for motherhood. A man who holds the priesthood has reverence for motherhood. Mothers are given a sacred privilege to "bear the souls of men; for herein is the work of [the] Father continued, that he may be glorified" (D&C 132:63).

The First Presidency has said: "Motherhood is near to divinity. It is the highest, holiest service to be assumed by mankind." (In James R. Clark, comp., *Messages of the First Presidency*, 6 vols. [Salt Lake City: Bookcraft, 1965–75], 6:178.) The priesthood cannot work out its destiny, nor can God's purposes be fulfilled, without our helpmates. Mothers perform a labor the priesthood cannot do. For this gift of life, the priesthood should have love unbounded for the mothers of their children. (94–15, p. 50)

Fathers should help teach and discipline their children. Honor your wife's unique and divinely appointed role as a mother in Israel and her special capacity to bear and nurture children. We are under divine commandment to multiply and replenish the earth and to bring up our children and grandchildren in light and truth (see Moses 2:28; D&C 93:40). You share, as a loving partner, the care of the children. Help her to manage and keep up your home. Help teach, train, and discipline your children. (94–15, p. 50)

Fathers, express your love for your wife and children. You should express regularly to your wife and children your reverence and respect for her. Indeed, one of the greatest things a father can do for his children is to love their mother. (94–15, p. 50)

The father presides in the home with his wife as an equal partner. Effective family leadership, brethren, requires both quantity and quality time. The teaching and governance of the family must not be left to your wife alone, to society, to school, or even to the Church.

A man who holds the priesthood accepts his wife as a partner in the leadership of the home and family with full knowledge of and full participation in all decisions relating thereto. Of necessity there must be in the Church and in the home a presiding officer (see D&C 107:21). By divine appointment, the responsibility to preside in the home rests upon the priesthood holder (see Moses 4:22). The Lord intended that the wife be a helpmeet for man (*meet* means equal)—that is, a companion equal and necessary in full partnership. Presiding in righteousness necessitates a shared responsibility between husband and wife; together you act with knowledge and participation in all family matters. For a man to operate independent of or without regard to the feelings and counsel of his wife in governing the family is to exercise unrighteous dominion. (94–15, pp. 50–51)

No father should ever abuse his wife or children. You who hold the priesthood must not be abusive in your relationship with children. Seek always to employ the principles of priesthood government set forth in the revelations (see D&C 93:40; 121:34–36, 41–45).

President George Albert Smith wisely counseled: "We should not lose our tempers and abuse one another. . . . Nobody ever abused anybody else when he had the spirit of the Lord. It is always when we have some other spirit." (In Conference Report, October 1950, p. 8.)

No man who has been ordained to the priesthood of God can with impunity abuse his wife or child. Sexual abuse of children has long been a cause for excommunication from the Church. (94–15, p. 51)

Fathers should provide for their families. You who hold the priesthood have the responsibility, unless disabled, to provide temporal support for your wife and children. No man can shift the burden of responsibility to another, not even to his wife. The Lord has commanded that women and children have claim on their husbands and fathers for their maintenance (see D&C 83; 1 Timothy 5:8). President Ezra Taft Benson has stated that when a husband encourages or insists that his wife work out of the home for their convenience, "not only will the family suffer in such instances, . . . but [his] own spiritual growth and progression will be hampered" (*Ensign*, November 1987, p. 49).

We urge you to do all in your power to allow your wife to remain in the home, caring for the children while you provide for the family the best you can. (94–15, p. 51)

A father's responsibility is to teach the gospel in the home. Take seriously your responsibility to teach the gospel to your family through regular family home evening, family prayer, devotional and scripture-reading time, and other teaching moments. Give special emphasis to preparation for missionary service and temple marriage. As patriarch in the home, exercise your priesthood through performing the appropriate ordinances for your family and by giving blessings to your wife and children. Next to your own salvation, brethren, there is nothing so important to you as the salvation of your wife and children. (94–15, p. 51)

A husband with his wife determines the spiritual climate for their home. A man who holds the priesthood leads his family in Church participation so they will know the gospel and be under the protection of the covenants and ordinances. If you are to enjoy the blessings of the Lord, you must set your own homes in order. Together with your wife, you determine the spiritual climate of your home. Your first obligation is to get your own spiritual life in order through regular scriptural study and daily prayer. Secure and honor your priesthood and temple covenants; encourage your family to do the same. (94–15, p. 51)

A father's leadership in the home is his most important responsibility. A man who holds the priesthood regards the family as ordained of God. Your leadership of the family is your most important and sacred responsibility. (94–15, p. 50)

Righteous fathers protect and love their children. We encourage you, brethren, to remember that priesthood is a righteous authority only. Earn the respect and confidence of your children through your loving relationship with them. A righteous father protects his children with his time and presence in their social, educational, and spiritual activities and responsibilities. Tender expressions of love and affection toward children are as much the responsibility of the father as the mother. Tell your children you love them. (94–15, p. 51)

Men who abandon their family stand in jeopardy. We further emphasize that men who abandon their family and fail to meet their responsibility to care for those they have fathered may find their eligibility for a temple recommend and their standing in the Church in jeopardy. In cases of divorce or separation, men must demonstrate that they are meeting family support payments mandated by law and obligated by the principles of the Church in order to qualify for the blessings of the Lord. (94–15, p. 51)

Home and Family

Our homes should be holy places in which we can stand against the world. Without doubt there are significant challenges facing the Latter-day Saints, both here and elsewhere in the world. We hope that you will not be overcome with discouragement in your attempts to raise your families in righteousness. Remember that the Lord has commanded this: "But my disciples shall stand in holy places, and shall not be moved" (D&C 45:32).

While some interpret this to mean the temple, which surely it does, it also represents the homes in which we live. If you will diligently work to lead your families in righteousness, encouraging and participating in daily family prayer, scripture reading, family home evening, and love and support for each other in living the teachings of the gospel, you will receive the promised blessings of the Lord in raising a righteous posterity.

In an increasingly wicked world, how essential it is that each of us "stand in holy places" and commit to be true and faithful to the teachings of the gospel of Jesus Christ. (94–17)

If we are to survive as a nation we must have love and strong values in our homes. If we are to survive as a nation, as a people, or even as a fully successful church, we simply must have love and integrity and strong principles in our homes. We must have an abiding commitment to marriage and children and morality. We must succeed where success counts most for the next generation.

Surely that home is strongest and most beautiful in which we find each person sensitive to the feelings of others, striving to serve others, striving to live at home the principles we demonstrate in more public settings. We need to try harder to live the gospel in our family circles. Our homes deserve our most faithful commitments. A child has the right to feel that in his home he is safe, that there he has a place of protection from the dangers and evils of the outside world. Family unity and integrity are necessary to supply this need. A child needs parents who are happy in their relationship to each other, who are working happily toward the fulfillment of ideal family living, who love their children with a sincere and unselfish love, and who are committed to the family's success. (90–03, pp. 61–62)

The family is the most serious business in mortality. [Quotes Genesis 1:27–28.] Thus God placed his own race upon the earth and instituted marriage, not only to multiply, as was commanded of the other animal world, but for the more noble and lofty purposes by which man can obtain eternal life. Marriage, as so instituted by God, is the commencement of the family, the most serious business of lifetime. . . .

To reach success in the family, parents must have love and respect for each other. Husbands, the bearers of the priesthood, should hold their wives in the highest esteem before their children, and wives should love and support their husbands. In return, the children will have love for their parents and for each other. The home will then become a hallowed place where the principles of the gospel can be best lived and where the Spirit of the Lord can dwell. To be a successful father or a successful mother is far greater than to rise to leadership or high places in business, government, or worldly affairs. Home may seem commonplace at times with its routine duties, yet its success should be the greatest of all our pursuits in life. (74–04, p. 51)

The family is the most important unit in time and in eternity. The family is the most important unit in time and in eternity and, as such, transcends every other interest in life. (94–15, p. 50)

Our homes should be a refuge. Our homes should be a refuge from the cares of the world, where there is peace and harmony, where we study the scriptures, where we enjoy love and companionship as husband and wife, where children are taught the values of life by the example of parents. Nothing can separate a man and a woman who are willing to serve the Lord and keep his commandments. Unhappiness or unharmonious relations will not exist if we are willing to follow the example of the Master who gave his life that we might have life everlasting. (58–01)

12

ECONOMICS AND WELFARE PRINCIPLES

The welfare program came by inspiration. There is nothing old or old-fashioned about the welfare program. The principles are old, but the challenges are new. . . .

I am grateful for the inspired leadership which has formulated the course of action that teaches us to help those among us who need assistance. This is religion in action. This is the course ordained of God from the very beginning. I am grateful for the devoted sisters who stand with the Priesthood and, in their compassionate services and assistance, strengthen the great cause in lifting our brothers and sisters by temporal means to spiritual heights.

May we have the vision to clearly see the road ahead. God lives and this is his work. I bear witness that the welfare program comes to us by inspiration and revelation. It is part of living the gospel. (61–06, pp. 236, 239)

Welfare Principles

The Church avoids debt. We don't rely on taxation to take care of our people. We believe that we should take care of our own and not rely upon the help of others. These newspaper reporters were interested in how we build without having any debt. We have built thousands of buildings in the world, and every one is paid for in full. We have no indebtedness. The Church has always taught us that we should live within our income and be free from debt, and it practices what it preaches. (67–04)

The Church is interested in the welfare of its members. There are some who ask why the Church is concerned with temporal affairs. The Church is interested in the welfare of each of its members. This interest therefore cannot be limited to man's spiritual needs alone but extends to every phase of his life. Social and economic needs are important to everyone. Man also has need for physical, mental, and moral guidance. Our lives cannot be one-sided, nor can we separate the spiritual from the temporal. (61–07, p. 962)

Our Heavenly Father has commanded us to work. It is interesting that the first recorded instruction given to Adam after the Fall dealt with the eternal principle of work. The Lord said: "In the sweat of thy face shalt thou eat bread" (Genesis 3:19). Our Heavenly Father loves us so completely that he has given us a commandment to work. This is one of the keys to eternal life. He knows that we will learn more, grow more, achieve more, serve more, and benefit more from a life of industry than from a life of ease. (75–02, p. 122)

There are three major reasons why we must work. There are several principles which undergird the significance of work in the Lord's plan. First, as the covenant people we must be as self-sufficient as possible. We are to be free from dependence upon a dole or any program that might endanger our free agency. Second, we must work to support the families with which the Lord has blessed us. Every true son of God wants to care for his own, and many a noble mother, from whom a husband has been taken, struggles to support her children, both as a breadwinner and a single parent. Finally, we work so we may have the necessities of life, conserving time and energy left over for service in the Lord's work. Sometimes it seems that the men who work the hardest at their occupations are the men most willing to devote time to church service. (75–02, p. 122)

The Church Welfare Program aims to help people help themselves. The Church has established a great welfare program, a system under which the curse of idleness can be done away with, the evil of a dole abolished, and independence, industry, thrift, and self-respect established among the people. The aim of this welfare program is to help the people to help themselves, and work has been enthroned as the ruling principle. (56–01)

Latter-day Saints should avoid indebtedness. Latter-day Saints have always been known as a frugal people; it is part of our history. We have been conservative in our actions and we have lived within our means, but what goes on about us often encourages us to live beyond our means and incur debt. We are proud to be free from bondage in this country and to have many freedoms not enjoyed in other countries. One of the greatest burdens we have had placed upon us and the thing that has taken more of our freedom than any other, perhaps, is indebtedness. Many of us become slaves to debt because we have failed to follow the recommendations of the authorities of the Church. (57–01)

Welfare and work are closely associated with each other. We often refer to the Welfare work of the Church. The word *work* creeps in with the word *Welfare*, and the two seem to be associated together. We know we must work for the things that are worthwhile in life, and if the Welfare Program is to be worthwhile and succeed, we must couple work with high ideals. Faith without works is dead. In the same sense, our success in our Welfare endeavors can only be accomplished by work. (61–06, p. 237)

Both the Welfare Program and work bring pleasure and joy. Is there greater pleasure and joy in the Welfare Program than there is work? It is true our work benefits others, and the Lord has said: "It is more blessed to give than to receive." The great joys in life come from giving, and the greatest gift is the giving of ourselves, our time and energy and efforts. Isn't it a good feeling to know that our efforts have resulted in doing good for someone else? . . .

I have never been on a gloomy welfare project. I have climbed trees and picked lemons, peeled fruit, tended a boiler, carried boxes, unloaded trucks, cleaned the cannery, and a thousand and one other things, but the things I remember most are the laughing and the singing and the good fellowship of people engaged in the service of the Lord. (61–06, p. 238)

A summary of welfare principles. Some of the most important [welfare principles] might be summarized as follows:

1. Righteous living. If we keep the commandments of God, he will bless us with spiritual prosperity.

2. Every person self-sustaining. Church members should sustain themselves to the extent of their ability by their own labors. The Lord has said we shall not be idle.

3. Avoid public relief. We subscribe to the principle that we are our brother's keeper. We should be self-sustaining if possible. Children should be taught their responsibility, where parents are unable to provide for themselves.

4. Avoid debt. President Clark has said: "Let us avoid debt as we would avoid a plague. Where we are now in debt let us get out of debt" (in Conference Report, April 1937, p. 26).

5. Have enough food, clothing, and necessities on hand to take care of any emergency.

6. Live within our income. Families should budget their income so that desires are kept within the ability to pay.

7. Help provide employment where necessary. The Church has always counseled and recommended that mothers be in their home with their children and not seek employment outside of the home. Women should not be unnecessarily employed.

8. Save. Regardless of the size of our income, we should budget our affairs that we might set aside some portion. This becomes our security and independence.

9. Strive to own our own home. Stability comes to the family which owns its own home. We should strive to free our home from mortgage and debt.

10. Gladly accept welfare assignments. Working together in the program brings the strength we need to produce for those who may be less fortunate.

11. Keep the law of the fast. We will be benefited spiritually, and sufficient means will be in the hands of the bishops to take care of all the poor.

12. Be a living testimony. We should so live the principles of the Welfare Program that our example will inspire others. (61–06, p. 239)

Honorable employment involves more than providing an adequate income. The employment we choose should be honorable and challenging. Ideally, we need to seek that work to which we are suited by interest, by aptitude, and by training. A man's work should do more than provide an adequate income; it should provide him with a sense of self-worth and be a pleasure—something he looks forward to each day.

May I suggest a definition of "honorable employment." Honorable employment is honest employment. Fair value is given and there is no defrauding, cheating, or deceit. Its product or service is of high quality, and the employer, customer, client, or patient receives more than he or she expected. Honorable employment is moral. It involves nothing that would undermine public good or morality. For example, it does not involve traffic in liquor, illicit narcotics, or gambling. Honorable employment is useful. It provides goods or services which make the world a better place in which to live. Honorable employment is also remunerative. It provides enough income so that we may be self-sufficient and able to support our families, while leaving us enough time free to be good fathers and church workers. (75–02, pp. 122–23)

Care for the Needy

The Church is unable to support every worthy cause. We find the Church has had to carefully chart its course because it is rapidly expanding throughout the world and has adequate but limited resources. We have had to make choices. The Church cannot undertake to support every worthy cause that is offered, or for which help is requested. The Brethren have had to choose to select those things most consistent with the teaching of the gospel and helping others acquire testimonies of its truth. (90–09)

In giving to the poor we give to the Lord. When we minister to our brethren, we minister to the Lord. In scripture we find this statement: "And inasmuch as ye impart of your substance unto the poor, ye will do it unto me" (D&C 42:31). The principle of giving to the poor is literally giving to the Lord. (58–02)

Wealth and Materialism

True wealth is having something we can share. Are we not wealthy if the Lord has blessed us with something we can share with others? (85–03, p. 74)

The path to Christ leads through poverty or prosperity. You will find, as you follow Christ, that the path to him often leads through poverty. And if you are not struggling financially, your trial may be the greatest of all—prosperity. Whatever your financial circumstances may be, there are some principles that apply to you.

Pay a full tithe and be generous in your other offerings.

Acknowledge that whatever wealth you have, great or small, monetary or otherwise, belongs to the Lord and is to be used as he directs.

Do not covet what you have or what you do *not* have. Brigham Young once said, "I am more afraid of covetousness in our Elders [and sisters] than I am of the hordes of hell" (*Discourses of Brigham Young*, p. 306). Things eventually work out financially; hang on and have faith. (89–03, p. 114)

In a materialistic world we must not aspire to income that leads away from the gospel. It is necessary to say a word about what is "enough income." This is a materialistic world, and Latter-day Saints must be careful not to confuse luxuries with necessities. An adequate income allows us to provide for the basic requirements of life. There are some who unwisely aspire to self-indulgent luxuries that often lead them away from complete commitment to the gospel of our Savior. (75–02, p. 123)

13

GOVERNMENT, LAWS, AND PEACE

Sustaining the Laws of the Land

As Latter-day Saints we must sustain the laws of the land. I suppose just about everyone here drives a car if you are of legal age. We are a nation on wheels. We have just about forgotten how to walk. We ride to church, we ride to school, we ride to town, we even ride around the golf course when we are supposed to be out for our health. I suppose there never was a people who rode so much.

But since we do ride as much as we do, we should not only learn how to operate the cars, but we should be willing to obey the traffic rules and never use a car for any evil purpose.

As Latter-day Saints we are supposed to honor, uphold, and sustain the law. That is one of our Articles of Faith. We can hardly say that we will be Latter-day Saints when we are out of a car and forget the rule of our religion when we are in a car.

If we are Latter-day Saints, we should be Latter-day Saints all the time, whether in a car, or on the football field, on the basketball floor, in the classroom, or in our own homes. Our religion is for all the time. (62–04)

We are duty bound to keep the law. It is a part of our religion to be good drivers, to obey the traffic laws, to support and assist the policeman, not dodge him nor dog him.

Officers are public servants. We would have chaos without them.

As people who honor the law, who believe in being honest,

who believe in doing to others as we would have others do to us, we are duty bound to keep the law. (62–04)

Our Christianity should affect the way we drive. We can't drive a car lawlessly and be a good Christian at the same time. We cannot break the law and be an upholder of the law at the same time.

The Sermon on the Mount is really a sermon on public relations, on how to get along with people. It teaches that we should not be angry with others, nor condemn them, nor call them fools. It teaches honesty, and tells us that if we wrong other people we must become reconciled with them before we can truly come to God in the proper spirit.

All of this fits into the traffic situation, doesn't it?

We can drive cars righteously or unrighteously.

We can drive in a way to make other people angry or pleased with us.

We can build up either good or bad public relations by the way we drive.

Courtesy, kindness, and law obedience make for good feelings.

Anger, rudeness, and disregard for the law make bad feelings.

After teaching his high principles, the Lord said in his sermon: "All things whatsoever ye would that men should do to you, do ye even so to them: for this is the law and the prophets" (Matthew 7:12).

That means that if we are going to be sincere in our religion, we will not serve mammon, as He put it, at any time. We will not be lawbreakers in any degree. (62–04)

We are charged to uphold the laws of the land. We are charged with the duty of sustaining and upholding the laws of the land. It is dishonest to intentionally violate the law. It doesn't make any difference how one may feel personally about the fairness or justness of the rules which have been established by society, one's duty is to respect and sustain the law. The commission of major crimes is condemned by nearly all persons, yet some will intentionally violate lesser laws, such as traffic ordinances, without any sense of guilt.

Is it because of fear of the penalties of law that men observe statutes and ordinances? Is it only because of the great commandments "Thou shalt not!" that he keeps the moral codes? I am of the opinion that there are higher motives—that most persons have a real sense of moral responsibility and duty. . . .

It is not fear of the law, it is not what others may think, but rather the sense of responsibility which causes man to live the higher moral law. He has his free agency, and most men know the difference between right and wrong and are willing to follow what is right. (63–04, p. 17)

In a republic, the government has the sovereign right as well as the duty to protect the rights of the individual and to settle civil disputes or disorders by peaceful means. Citizens do not have the right to take the law into their own hands or exercise physical force. The sovereign laws of the state must be sustained, and persons living under those laws must obey them for the good of the whole. In this regard The Church of Jesus Christ of Latter-day Saints takes a strong position. One of the fundamental tenets of its faith is clearly stated in these words: "We believe in being subject to kings, presidents, rulers, and magistrates, in obeying, honoring, and sustaining the law" (The Articles of Faith 12). (68–03, p. 79)

We owe allegiance to the United States. In the present day . . . , the question might appropriately be asked, what do we owe . . . to the country in which we live? We owe allegiance, respect, and honor. Laws enacted to promote the welfare of the whole and suppress evildoing are to be strictly obeyed. We must pay tribute to sustain the government in the necessary expense incurred in the protection of life, liberty, and property, and in promoting the welfare of all. (68–03, p. 80)

We have a solemn obligation to God and our country. [Quotes D&C 134:1–5.] These words point up the solemn obligation of government and the solemn obligation of those who owe allegiance. This is a day when civil disobedience seems to be prevalent and even advocated from some pulpits, but the position of this Church and its teachings is clear.

I know that God lives, that he is the supreme power of heaven and earth. I bear witness of the divinity of Jesus Christ, the Savior of all mankind. My knowledge of these truths moves me to allegiance to divine sovereignty, also to sustain the law of the land.

There is no conflict between that which is owed to Caesar and the obligation to God. May the God of heaven give inspiration and guidance to those leaders in the world who formulate the policies of earthly sovereignty, and also to those of us who are governed by those powers. May righteousness be placed in proper perspective for the good of every man. (68–03, p. 81)

Moral Decay

That nation is greatest which develops most carefully its people. Given the conditions in the world today, if we want to conserve our nation, its economic security, and everything near and dear to us, we must focus an increased amount of time and interest on strengthening our human values. A nation is not made great by its fruitful acres, its great forests, its rich mineral deposits, but by the men and women who develop those resources, who cultivate the farms, fell the trees, and operate the mines. That nation is greatest which develops most carefully its people, by instilling within their hearts a dedication to the loftiest ideals of the human race. (92–03)

It is important to resist pornography. Pornography is a growing evil in our society. It frequently accompanies immorality and the weakening of the moral fabric of individuals and families. The challenge to oppose this evil is one from which members of the Church, as citizens, cannot shrink. . . .

We encourage members, with other citizens of goodwill, to be aware of the dangers posed by obscene and pornographic materials and to join in thoughtful, appropriate opposition to their production, dissemination, and use. Our voices must be heard in defense of those virtues that, when practiced in the past, made men and nations strong and, when neglected, brought them to decay. (88–07)

When morality is lost, only disaster can result. In spite of the greatness of man and his accomplishments in the modern world, we observe the lack of faith in God and the absence of repentance. . . .

Morality appears to have been lost in the maze of human

philosophies. We see it in the lives of individuals, people in high places in government, and even leaders of industry and labor. Many churches in the world are announcing compromises of their tenets so as not to offend the modern thinking of their membership. The cry has gone up from some pulpits that God is dead. When God ceases to live in the minds and hearts of men and women, moral concepts collapse and only disaster can result. (66–03, p. 516)

Working for Good Government

Government dependency is dangerous. From my own experience in business and as a lawyer and church worker, and from my firsthand observations in this country and other countries of the world, there appears to me to be a trend to shift responsibility for life and its processes from the individual to the state. In this shift there is a basic violation of the law of the harvest, or the law of justice. The attitude of "something for nothing" is encouraged. The government is often looked to as the source of wealth. There is the feeling that the government should step in and take care of one's needs, one's emergencies, and one's future. Just as my friend actually became a slave to his own ignorance and bad habits by refusing to accept the responsibility for his own education and moral growth, so, also, can an entire people be imperceptibly transferred from individuals, families, and communities to the federal government. (66–01, pp. 7–8)

We have a responsibility to sustain our government. We teach our people all over the world, regardless of the countries in which they live, to sustain the policies of their governments. Under the English common law system, we have three branches of government, the executive, the legislative, and the judicial. As citizens we should learn the principle of sustaining these branches of government.

If executive officials have been elected by the vote of the people, after that vote is complete and the majority has spoken, we have the obligation to support and sustain those who have been elected by the majority, and not bring about disharmony. It tears down government when opposition is raised. In the legislative branches of our government, there may be laws enacted that we find difficult to sustain as individuals, yet while they remain law, we have the obligation to abide by and support those laws. It may be that we think the law should be different, but while the statutes stand and until revoked by the people or by legislative or judicial action, we should sustain those laws.

The same is true of judicial bodies. Courts often make decisions we challenge in our own minds, but when we have legislation by judicial edict, as it were, we must follow those decrees of the court until they are reversed by subsequent decisions or set aside by legislative action.

I would hope that as members of the Church we can stand fast on these principles by supporting and sustaining our governments wherever we may live and by sustaining the officers of those governments with our prayers as well. (79–12)

A great nation is one that focuses on strengthening human values. Now is the time for America to decree that no longer shall this terrible waste of our inner strength be allowed to blight our greatness as a nation. We should silently, powerfully, and purposefully determine that no silent hammers of decay shall beat our civilization into dust. We should, with promptness and firmness, decide that the termites of juvenile delinquency and crime shall not eat into the material and spiritual foundations of our country. To continue to permit forces of disintegration to sap our material and spiritual culture of its strength is to stand idly by and watch our civilization become one with Nineveh and Tyre.

To save even our material prosperity, we must show more interest in moral and spiritual values. When civilizations have a decline in moral and spiritual values, material greatness begins to disintegrate.

If we want to conserve our economic security, we must focus an increased amount of time and interest on strengthening our human values. A nation is not made great by its fruitful acres, its great forests, and its rich mineral deposits, but by the men who cultivate the farms, fell the trees, and operate the mines. That nation is greatest which produces the largest number of men dedicated to the loftiest ideals of the human race. (85–02)

We need people to live for democracy. We have often referred to our willingness to die for democracy. The time has come when we ought to be willing to live for democracy. Have we the courage to do it, by directing our lives according to the ideal set forth in the Sermon on the Mount? Can we lend a supporting hand toward reassuring people to follow the high road of life? Others are doing it and have done it throughout our history. (85–02)

Freedom is never free. Someone has said, "To be born free is a privilege. To die free is an awesome responsibility." Freedom is never free. It is always purchased at a great cost. (91–03)

Personal unrighteousness can lead toward a welfare state. What is the real cause of this trend toward the welfare state, toward more socialism? In the last analysis, in my judgment, it is personal unrighteousness. When people do not use their freedoms responsibly and righteously, they will gradually lose these freedoms. . . .

If man will not recognize the inequalities around him and voluntarily, through the gospel plan, come to the aid of his brother, he will find that through "a democratic process" he will be forced to come to the aid of his brother. The government will take from the "haves" and give to the "have nots." Both have lost their freedom. Those who "have," lost their freedom to give voluntarily of their own free will and in the way they desire. Those who "have not," lost their freedom because they did not earn what they received. They got "something for nothing," and they will neither appreciate the gift nor the giver of the gift.

Under this climate, people gradually become blind to what has happened and to the vital freedoms which they have lost. (66–01, p. 9)

Freedom comes through personal righteousness. A thief takes something and gives nothing. He thinks he is free, but sooner or later his freedom vanishes into walls and bars. Likewise, a person becomes a thief of his own soul by deceiving himself that he can live unrighteously, immorally, that he can cheat, lie, and take advantage of his neighbor; but all the while he is imprisoning himself behind bars and walls of his own making. "Be not deceived; God is not mocked" (Galatians 6:7). . . .

The only way we can keep our freedom is through our personal righteousness—by handling that freedom responsibly. We are our brother's keeper. We must be concerned for the social problems of today. We must take that responsibility upon ourselves according to the gospel plan but not according to the socialistic plan. (66–01, p. 10)

We must uphold the principles of freedom. To those who sacrificed for our freedom, the end was worth the painful means. Where would we, who are citizens of the United States of America, be today if there had not been those who counted the cost of freedom and willingly paid for it? Where will we be tomorrow if men and women of integrity do not come forward today and pay the price to uphold those principles of freedom? (91–03)

Our forefathers declared their independence while declaring dependence upon God. We often forget that in declaring dependence from an earthly power, our forefathers made a forthright declaration of dependence upon Almighty God. The words of this document solemnly declare:

"With a firm reliance on the protection of Divine Providence, we mutually pledge to each other our lives, our fortunes, and our sacred honor."

The 56 courageous men who signed that document understood that this was not just high-sounding rhetoric. They knew that if they succeeded, the best they could expect would be years of hardship for a struggling new nation. If they lost, they would face a hangman's noose as traitors. (91–03)

Peace

True peace comes from living the principles of the gospel. A life filled with unselfish service will also be filled with peace that surpasses understanding. The Savior said: "Peace I leave with you, my peace I give unto you; not as the world giveth, give I unto you. Let not your heart be troubled: neither let it be afraid." (John 14:27.) . . .

This peace can come only through living the principles of the gospel. These principles constitute the program of the Prince of Peace, who is also the prince of glory and the prince of eternal progress. May we be ever faithful in observance of our Savior's teachings. (94–20)

Perfect peace is more than the absence of strife. The word *peace* appears frequently in scripture and has many meanings. In classical Greek the word refers to cessation, discontinuance, or absence of hostilities between rival forces. This definition is the antithesis of war and strife. The New Testament, however, has given a far wider range of meaning. This is partly due to the influence of the Hebrew word for peace, which is far more comprehensive of meaning. It was commonly used as a form of greeting when persons met or parted: "May peace be with you" (see Mark 5:34 and John 20:19–21). . . .

The word has also been used in the New Testament in reference to "domestic peace" between husband and wife (1 Corinthians 7:15), to harmonious relationships within the whole family (Matthew 10:34), and in many instances to happy, personal relationships with others. It has also been used to mean "peace of mind" or serenity, and the right relationships between God and man.

Because of the difference in definitions, those who seek peace may be searching for unrelated conditions. The peace for which the world longs is a time of suspended hostilities; but men do not realize that peace is a state of existence that comes to man only upon the terms and conditions set by God, and in no other way.

In a psalm in the book of Isaiah are these words: "Thou wilt keep him in perfect peace, whose mind is stayed on thee: because he trusteth in thee" (Isaiah 26:3). This perfect peace mentioned by Isaiah comes to one only through a belief in God. This is not understood by an unbelieving world. (66–04, pp. 1104–5)

No peace comes to those who reject God. There is no promise of peace to those who reject God, to those who will not keep his commandments, or to those who violate his laws. The Prophet Isaiah spoke of the decadence and corruption of leaders, and then continued in his admonitions by saying: "But the wicked are like the troubled sea, when it cannot rest, whose waters cast up mire and dirt.

"There is no peace, saith my God, to the wicked." (Isaiah 57:20–21.)

The unrighteous and wicked have no peace, and their actions take away the peace of others. Turmoil in the world has usually been caused by a few individuals or a minority, causing millions of innocent persons to suffer. Today, as in eras gone by, those who are the innocent victims of oppressors hopefully look for peace. This cannot come by riots or placards or even the cessation of hostilities. It can come only in the way the Lord gave his peace to the Twelve, "not as the world giveth" (John 14:27).

One of the great writers has penned: "Peace does not dwell in outward things, but within the soul; we may preserve it in the midst of the bitterest pain, if our will remains firm and submissive. Peace in this life springs from acquiescence, not in an exemption from suffering." (Fénelon.) (66–04, p. 1105)

Peace comes by an unconditional surrender. Indifference to the Savior or failure to keep the commandments of God brings about insecurity, inner turmoil, and contention. These are the opposite of peace. Peace can come to an individual only by an unconditional surrender—surrender to him who is the Prince of Peace, who has the power to confer peace. One may live in beautiful and peaceful surroundings but, because of inner dissension and discord, be in a state of constant turmoil. On the other hand, one may be in the midst of utter destruction and the bloodshed of war and yet have the serenity of unspeakable peace. If we look to man and the ways of the world, we will find turmoil and confusion. If we will but turn to God, we will find peace for the restless soul. This was made clear by the words of the Savior: . . .

"Come unto me, all ye that labour and are heavy laden, and I will give you rest.

"Take my yoke upon you, and learn of me; for I am meek and lowly in heart: and ye shall find rest unto your souls." (Matthew 11:28–29.)

This peace shelters us from the worldly turmoil. The knowledge that God lives, that we are his children, and that he loves us soothes the troubled heart. The answer to the quest lies in faith in God and in his Son, Jesus Christ. This will bring peace to us now and in the eternity to follow. (66–04, p. 1105)

Fundamental truths will bring peace. It seems that two eternal truths must be accepted by all if we are to find peace in this world and eternal life in the world to come. (1) That Jesus is the Christ, the very eternal son of our Heavenly Father, who came to earth for the express purpose of redeeming mankind from sin and the grave, and that he lives to bring us back to the presence of the Father. (2) That Joseph Smith was his prophet, raised up in this latter-day to restore the truth which had been lost to mankind because of transgression. If all men would accept and live these two fundamental truths, peace would be brought to the world. (70–04)

The gospel of Jesus Christ provides the only way the world will ever know peace. The world in which we live, whether close to home or far away, needs the gospel of Jesus Christ. It provides the only way the world will ever know peace. We need to be kinder with one another, more gentle and forgiving. We need to be slower to anger and more prompt to help. We need to extend the hand of friendship and resist the hand of retribution. In short, we need to love one another with the pure love of Christ, with genuine charity and compassion and, if necessary, shared suffering, for that is the way God loves us. (92–02, p. 61)

14

LEARNING

Knowledge and Wisdom

How we use knowledge is the most important thing. The knowledge explosion of which the world is so proud is not of man's creation. It is his discovery of portions of the unlimited knowledge and information which is part of God's knowledge. How we use it is determined by whether we are of the eternal kingdom of God or a part of the temporary understanding of the world. The question is simply this: Are we seeking to find our place in the world in the realm of worldly thought, or are we seeking to find our place in the unchanging kingdom of God? (73–06, p. 55)

Wisdom, not knowledge, is the greatest need today. The world needs more knowledge, and we're sweeping rapidly forward in this achievement. But increase in knowledge is not the greatest need of mankind today. Man's greatest need is the ability to properly use or put to use the knowledge which he has already acquired. To the knowledge you have learned must be added wisdom. Knowledge without wisdom may be the pathway to that which is evil unless one is willing to apply the principles of right-doing and follow the commandments of God. This is wisdom. (73–05)

Moral qualities must be added to knowledge to attain our highest potential. Wisdom is the quality of being wise, of discerning in judging soundly with respect to what is true and false, the ability to deal sagaciously with facts as they relate to life and conduct. Sometimes intelligence is used synonymously with wisdom.

If we were speaking mathematically, we would say that knowledge plus the proper use of knowledge equals wisdom. Knowledge, then, becomes one of the steps by which wisdom is attained. Intelligence and wisdom quicken knowledge.

There's still one thing lacking which is essential for the highest pursuits. Moral qualities must be added to knowledge. I refer now to the principles of right and wrong in a man's behavior, just common everyday honesty. A man must be honest with himself and with every person with whom he comes in contact. What a great change would come over the world if we could all rely upon others as far as honesty is concerned. (73–05)

Knowledge is not man's greatest need. Intelligence is the power of understanding, comprehending, reasoning, and judging. It is the power or ability to meet any situation by a proper adjustment. . . .

There has been no other time in the history of the world when knowledge has increased at a more rapid rate than it has in your generation. Today is the sum total of all the knowledge of yesterdays, and the acceleration of learning in the sciences and other fields is staggering to us. We realize that our breakthrough in scientific achievement is the result of discovery, through research, of laws which have always been in existence, but hidden from man until this enlightened day.

The world needs more knowledge and we are sweeping rapidly forward in this achievement, but increase of knowledge is not the greatest need of mankind today. Man's greatest need is the ability to put to use the knowledge which he has already acquired. The welfare of the people of the world is not dependent upon expanding knowledge alone, but upon the just and proper use of what man had learned to the present day.

History is replete with the examples of men and women who have become learned in education and have risen to high places in industry, finance, government, education, science, and other pursuits, yet, because they have wandered into forbidden paths, have fallen to the depths and are held in contempt by those who have a sense of right-doing. The convictions in our criminal courts are not limited to the illiterate. Behind prison walls are many who have reached high educational levels, but their acts and conduct with respect to society have been the very antithesis of their knowledge.

We ask the question: How can men with such learning and knowledge be blinded or misled, and fall from the pinnacles they have reached? The answer is simple. Knowledge alone is not sufficient; to knowledge must be added wisdom. Knowledge without wisdom may be the pathway to that which is evil unless one is willing to apply the principles of right-doing and follow the commandments of God. This is wisdom. (63–04, p. 17)

What is the meaning of the word "intelligence"? Found in the Doctrine and Covenants are these profound words: "The glory of God is intelligence" (D&C 93:36). I've often pondered these words. I've repeated them over and over in my mind. "The glory of God is intelligence." Intelligence is the power of understanding, comprehending, reasoning, and judging. It is the power and ability to meet any situation by a proper adjustment. (73–05)

Intellectual capacity alone is not sufficient. We may admire a man who has knowledge and ability and stands out as an intellectual genius, but our admiration declines if he lacks earnestness in purpose, industry, or persistence. Intellectual capacity alone produces very little of that which is worthwhile unless coupled with work, effort, industry, and perseverance. The combination of these results in achievement if cultivated and put to use. (63–04, p. 17)

One of the chief purposes of education is to develop character. The question is being asked: Is education failing to form desirable traits of character? If it is failing, it is failing in what is one of its chief purposes. (92–03)

The true purpose of education involves far more than acquiring facts. If we examine the reasons why students enter universities and seek higher education, we will probably come to the conclusion that the primary one is for social and economic reasons. We are compelled to admit that there is substantial economic gain resulting from education, but this is not its highest purpose. One of our great leaders has said: "True education does not consist merely in the acquiring of a few facts of science, history, literature, or art, but in the development of character. True education awakens a desire to conserve health by keeping the body clean and undefiled. True education trains in self-denial and self-mastery. True education regulates the temper, subdues passion, and makes obedience to social laws and moral order a guiding principle in life. It develops reason and inculcates faith in the living God as the eternal, loving father of all." (David O. McKay, in Conference Report, April 1928, p. 102.)

At the end of your lives you will not be judged by academic successes, the degrees or diplomas earned, the positions held, the material wealth acquired, or power and prestige, but rather on the basis of what you have become as persons and what you are in conduct and character. Yours is the power individually to transform yourselves into the persons you want to be. (79–03)

We should continue to seek knowledge even after college. Leave school with your books and your minds still open, and make your lives a quest for knowledge. Plato thought knowledge the highest human good, and Matthew Arnold thought the primary purpose of education was to help students to see things as they really are, to see the world about them as it really is. Only as we see the world as it really is can we hope to solve its problems. Only by knowledge can we banish ignorance, superstition, prejudice, fear, and hatred, the evils from which spring most of our world's problems. Therefore it is imperative that you continue to seek knowledge. (79–03)

We need people who know how to apply knowledge in their lives. Men may be turned out of colleges as walking encyclopedias of facts, but if they cannot control their emotions, desires, and way of thinking, they are ships without a rudder, being blown about by the winds until they may be dashed to pieces. The world needs men and women of knowledge, but it has far greater need for men and women who can thoughtfully make application of that knowledge for a better and happier life. (83–02)

Books are among life's prized possessions. Books are among life's most precious possessions. They are among the most remarkable creation of man. Out of the books we get the great literature, the great biography, the great religion. . . . The most powerful ideas, the finest logic, the best good judgment are made immediately available to us. We can learn how to think, how to plan, how to organize, how to worship, and how to work. We have the holy books of scripture through which we may learn about God himself and become familiar with his great doctrines, his standards of value, and his will concerning us. (88–05)

Secular Versus Religious Learning

The greatest quest is a search for God. With the advance of knowledge has come a reliance upon scientific principles of proof, and as a consequence, there are some who do not believe in God because his existence cannot be substantiated by such proof. In reality, scientific research is an endeavor to ascertain truth, and the same principles which are applied to that pursuit are used in the quest to establish the truth of religion as well. . . .

As important as scientific research may be, the greatest quest is a search for God—to determine his reality, his personal attributes, and to secure a knowledge of the gospel of his Son Jesus Christ. It is not easy to find a perfect understanding of God. The search requires persistent effort, and there are some who never move themselves to pursue this knowledge. In place of making the struggle and effort to understand, they follow the opposite course, which requires no effort, and deny his existence. (74–05, p. 96)

The knowledge of God is important. It is a thousand times more important to have a knowledge of God and his laws, than it is to have all the worldly knowledge that can be obtained. (74–02)

The truths of the gospel are eternal and unchanging. Where . . . is hope in this world of frustration and moral decay? It lies in the knowledge and understanding of the truths taught by the Master, which must be taught by the Church of Christ without deviation and believed in and lived by its membership. These are eternal truths and will be so in perpetuity regardless of changing circumstances in society, development of new scientific achievements, or increase of man's knowledge.

I believe we can be modern and enjoy the fruits of a modern world and its high standard of living, and I believe we can have the benefits of modern scholarship and scientific advances without turning to the theories of the modernist. I believe the principles of the gospel announced by the Savior in his personal ministry were true when they were given and are true today. Truth is eternal and never changing, and the gospel of Jesus Christ is ever contemporary in a changing world. (73–06, p. 55)

The tenets of modernism have caused many to abandon true doctrine. Modernism has become the order of the day in some religious thought. Modernists advocate a restatement of traditional doctrine on the grounds that today's modern scholastic and scientific advances require a new critical interpretation of the Bible and the history of dogma. The term "modernism" is often used interchangeably with "liberalism." Its advocates claim that religious truths are subject to constant reinterpretation in the light of modern knowledge; therefore, new and more advanced concepts are required to express modern thought and progress.

The Bible has been the subject of attack by modernists. It is said by some that science refuses to support the authenticity of such Biblical accounts as the creation of the world, placing life upon the earth, Adam and Eve and the Garden of Eden, the flood, and many other happenings in the Old and New Testaments. What is claimed to be superior knowledge in this day of enlightenment causes some men to look upon these accounts as fables. Because of this, can believers in Christ repudiate them? In an attempt to regain the confidence of communicants who have ceased to believe, many liberal churches have abandoned one doctrine after another, even to the extent of failing to stand by the doctrine of the existence of a personal God. They no longer uphold as a reality the resurrection of the crucified Savior, and the doctrine of the atoning sacrifice has lost its credibility. Under such circumstances, how can organized religion maintain its place as a stabilizing influence in society?

In this day of increased knowledge, higher thought, and a modernization of the old, the simple has been overlooked and the profound sought after. The basic, simple, fundamental truths of the gospel are being ignored. (73–06, p. 54)

We should resist the teachings of the modernists. We are entering into, or going through, a period of history in which so-called modern thought is taking precedence in the minds of many persons who classify themselves as advocates of a modern generation. The more extreme of these lean toward free thinking and free action without assuming the responsibility men owe to fellowmen.

Where will we be led if we follow those who advocate freedom of use of drugs and freedom of morality? What will be the result of universal free love, abortions at will, homosexuality, or legalized pornography?

What of spiritual values and the religious ideals of past generations, which have been the great stabilizing influence on society? Modern thinkers claim these have been the great deterrents to man in the freedoms he now seeks. There is a great effort on the part of so-called modernists to change religious beliefs and teachings of the past to conform to modern thought and critical research. They de-emphasize the teachings of the Bible by modern critical methods and deny that scripture is inspired. The modernist teaches that Christ is not the Son of God. He denies the doctrine of the atoning sacrifice by which all men may be saved. He denies the fact of the resurrection of the Savior of the world and relegates him to the status of a teacher of ethics. Where, then, is hope? What has become of faith? . . .

The Church stands firmly against relaxation or change in moral issues and opposes the so-called new morality. Spiritual values cannot be set aside, notwithstanding modernists who would tear them down. We can be modern without giving way to the influence of the modernist. If it is old-fashioned to believe in the Bible, we should thank God for the privilege of being old-fashioned. (70–02, pp. 115, 117)

All types of knowledge are not of equal worth. There is a tendency, as we pursue formal education in institutions of higher learning, to lose ourselves in our quest for knowledge and overlook some of the important things which would bring happiness to us in this life and throughout eternity.

Never before in the history of the world has man possessed as much knowledge as in the present day. Modern achievements in the field of science far exceed the accomplishments of all the preceding centuries.

All types of knowledge, however, are not of equal worth. Education in many fields gives the student nothing to help him in his pursuit for exaltation in the life hereafter. Secular education is an important step in our pursuit for knowledge, but it will never take the place of a knowledge of the Kingdom of God.

William Athern, Dean Emeritus of Boston University, wrote

upon this subject in his book *An Adventure in Religious Education* in these words: "Unless society can build an effective system of religious education to match its system of secular schools, our nation will crumble just as certainly as did Greece and Rome, and for the same reasons. The American people are becoming aroused; wise and far-seeing leaders in all religious bodies are calling the people to a great crusade in the interests of moral and religious education." (54–01)

Secular education must be coupled with religious education. When the Prophet said, "A man is saved no faster than he gets knowledge," he had reference not to the temporal knowledge flowing from research, but to the eternal knowledge coming by revelation. "Hence it needs revelation to assist us," he continued, "and gives us knowledge of the things of God." (*Teachings of the Prophet Joseph Smith,* p. 217.) When he said, "It is impossible for a man to be saved in ignorance" (D&C 131:6), he meant there could be no salvation in ignorance of Jesus Christ and the saving principles of the gospel.

The kingdom of God and the truths that lead the way to eternal life are far more important than all the learning, the training, and the education that can be received in the great universities. As we grow in intelligence, we learn that secular education must be coupled with religious education if we are to become partakers of life eternal. (54–01)

The fulness of truth is not available outside the kingdom of God. No man, no matter how great his education, no matter how much he studies of the things of the world, and no matter what he does in this life, will ever find truth or the fulness of light and understanding outside of the kingdom of God. Fortunate is the student who gains this testimony.

"Ask, and it shall be given you; seek, and ye shall find; knock, and it shall be opened unto you:

"For every one that asketh receiveth; and he that seeketh findeth; and to him that knocketh it shall be opened" (Matthew 7:7–8). (54–01)

We need not be ashamed of spiritual truths. Because of the temptation to intellectual pride, always remember that the sun rises and shines on gentle and simple alike, so the light of truth beams as directly upon the simplest and humblest of God's children as upon you. Do not, therefore, be ashamed of spiritual truths. Do not reject them or think you must amend them because they are common to you and to those who have not had the advantage of higher education. Be not ashamed of Jesus Christ because the poor believe in him and some of the mighty of the world do not. Do not let your scientific intellect discard truths merely because they are not subject to demonstrable proof. Open your hearts and souls so that you may have understanding of spiritual truth. (60–07, pp. 7–8)

We need to return to the simple teachings of Christ. In this world of confusion and rushing, temporal progress, we need to return to the simplicity of Christ. We need to love, honor, and worship him. To acquire spirituality and have its influence in our lives, we cannot become confused and misdirected by the twisted teachings of the modernist. We need to study the simple fundamentals of the truths taught by the Master and eliminate the controversial. Our faith in God needs to be real and not speculative. The restored gospel of Jesus Christ can be a dynamic, moving influence, and true acceptance gives us a meaningful, religious experience. One of the great strengths of the Mormon religion is this translation of belief into daily thinking and conduct. This replaces turmoil and confusion with peace and tranquility. (70–02, p. 117)

Truth is never conflicting. Truth never conflicts with itself. When we understand and work from true principles, we can expect order and agreement. True principles are part of one great whole, as the Savior explained to Joseph Smith:

"The Spirit of truth is of God. I am the Spirit of truth, and John bore record of me, saying: He received a fullness of truth, yea, even of all truth;

"And no man receiveth a fullness unless he keepeth his commandments.

"He that keepeth his commandments receiveth truth and light, until he is glorified in truth and knoweth all things." (D&C 93:26–28.)

When we encounter apparent conflict in our studies and scholarly work, it is because we see only a part of this great whole. Our understanding of the truth we seek may be partial or limited. We may hold an opinion or an idea about the world or human nature that is not entirely true. When we encounter situations of seeming conflict, we should not feel angry or discouraged, but rather we should confront the matter with great optimism and hope. For we know that this apparent conflict is only a prelude to a new understanding and a closer approximation of the ultimate principles we seek, and that this conflict will yield, in God's own time, to those who seek wisdom by study and by faith.

It is inappropriate, especially at this university, to divide learning into secular education and religious education. Truth is, or ought to be, the object of our endeavors throughout the university, and truth is not two things; it is one. Our concern is with true science *and* true religion. Certainly the laws that govern the behavior of both molecules and men are part of the laws known and used by our Heavenly Father. God is the perfect scientist. We must not forget that our knowledge is not yet perfect. Everyone in this life must often look at matters through a glass, darkly.

Nevertheless, all our discoveries in the physical sciences, in the social sciences, even in the workings of human nature testify that there is a set of eternal laws that govern in this universe. We come to realize that God, in his infinite wisdom and power, uses these laws in accomplishing his work. As we come to this awareness we can sense the beauty and majesty and harmony of the gospel. These truths are learned not just by study *or* prayer, but by study *and* prayer. (84–04)

Religious Education

Following Christ is the way to true happiness. You may be successful in the fields for which you have planned your education, but to find true happiness in your endeavors and real success in life, you need to add to your education the elements of spirituality . . . by following in the footsteps of the Master. This will produce the well-balanced individual you hope to become. His invitation to each of you is the same as to the rich young man—"Come, follow me." (85–02)

Teachers at Church schools should couple the academic educa-tion with the spiritual. I know that in your classroom you can spiritually discern the youth with the greatest potential. While ful-filling the needs of all, you can encourage them especially. Teach them to have confidence in themselves. Please couple their formal academic education with an awareness that they are children of a Divine Father. Help them to learn to use their agency wisely. They must learn to avoid temptation. They must learn to be in control of their own lives.

You are the keepers of the gate. You have the vision. You know what it is to be touched with the Spirit. You are in a partnership with the Lord and his church to ignite a flame of faith and to build a foundation of obedience that will lead, guide, motivate, and ma-ture each child.

You can teach them how to memorize, how to respond me-chanically, how to act like everyone else, or you can teach them how to think, how to pray, how to recognize inspiration. You can't do that in a class where you demand them to respond by rote. . . . You must create an atmosphere of freedom, of love, of control, of understanding and willing obedience to the commandments of the Lord so that they can soar, so that they can experiment with the capacity and stirrings that are within them. They can learn to be-lieve in themselves—to live and rise to greater heights and beyond. (90–09)

Teachers should be cautious to avoid counterfeits of the Spirit. Let me offer a word of caution on this subject. I think if we are not careful as professional teachers working in the classroom every day, we may begin to try to counterfeit the true influence of the Spirit of the Lord by unworthy and manipulative means. I get concerned when it appears that strong emotion or free-flowing tears are equated with the presence of the Spirit. Certainly the Spirit of the Lord can bring strong emotional feelings, including tears, but that outward manifestation ought not to be confused with the presence of the Spirit itself.

I have watched a great many of my brethren over the years, and we have shared some rare and unspeakable spiritual experi-ences together. Those experiences have all been different, each special in its own way, and such sacred moments may or may not be accompanied by tears. Very often they are, but sometimes they are accompanied by total silence. Other times they are accompanied by joy. Always they are accompanied by a great manifestation of the truth, of revelation to the heart.

Give your students gospel truth powerfully taught; that is the way to give them a spiritual experience. Let it come naturally and as it will, perhaps with the shedding of tears, but perhaps not. If what you say is the truth, and you say it purely and with honest conviction, those students will feel the spirit of the truth being taught them and will recognize that inspiration and revelation has come into their hearts. That is how we build faith. That is how we strengthen testimonies—with the power of the word of God taught in purity and with conviction.

Listen for the truth, hearken to the doctrine, and let the manifestation of the Spirit come as it may in all of its many and varied forms. Stay with solid principles; teach from a pure heart. Then the Spirit will penetrate your mind and heart, and every mind and heart of your students. (89–01)

Live so you have the Spirit in your teaching. May I also encourage you to prepare and live in such a way that you have the Spirit of the Lord in your teaching. There is so much in our world that destroys the feeling of the Spirit and so much that would keep us from having the Spirit with us. We need to do all we can for these young people who are assaulted and barraged by worldliness all around them. We need to do everything possible to let them feel the sweet, reassuring presence of the Spirit of the Lord. Your classrooms are weekday sanctuaries where they should be able to find that. (89–01)

Religious educators assist directly in the salvation of men. You [seminary and institute teachers] are important agents in this great work. You labor every day in reaching out to our young people, and you do have a profound influence on them. I am sure you have already discovered the truthfulness of President Grant's words—that no financial or worldly dividend of any kind can compare with the satisfaction you feel in shaping these young lives for good. You are making a great investment in these students and a great investment in the future strength of the Church. You will one day enjoy a great personal return on that investment—the knowledge that you assisted directly in the eternal salvation of men and women and in the establishment of the kingdom of God on earth. (89–01)

It is a privilege to be a religious educator. I have often thought how privileged you are, how fortunate you must feel, to be in a profession that not only *allows* you but quite literally *compels* you to be immersed in the holy scriptures every day. There are so many members of the Church who envy you that rare privilege, and on some days my brethren and I envy you as well. We spend a good deal of time in the scriptures ourselves, but we do not have the hour-by-hour privilege you have to study the scriptures in your class preparation and with your students in the classroom. My, what a privilege! What an influence—to feel the word of God rising up from all the dispensations, coming to your eyes and your mind, and lodging permanently in your heart.

Think of the instruction you have received at the feet of the ancients. Think of the company you are able to keep in your daily work—not only the company of wonderful young people and worthy professional colleagues, but the company of Moses and Mosiah and Moroni, Peter and Paul, and Abraham and Isaiah. You may walk and talk with the Lord Jesus Christ, taking counsel from him regarding the gospel plan and empathizing with him over the trials and challenges of his people. And you get to do it all day after day! (89–01)

Those who teach should teach confidence in the scriptures. I strongly encourage you to use the scriptures in your teaching and to do all within your power to help the students use them and become comfortable with them. I would like our young people to have confidence in the scriptures, and I would like you to interpret that phrase two ways.

First, we want the students to have confidence in the strength and truths of the scriptures, confidence that their Heavenly Father is really speaking to them through the scriptures, and confidence that they can turn to the scriptures and find answers to their problems and their prayers. That is one kind of confidence I would hope you give your students, and you can give it to them if you show them daily, hourly, that you trust in the scriptures just that way. Show them that you yourself are confident that the scriptures hold the answers to many—indeed most—of life's problems. So when you teach, teach from the scriptures.

Obviously another meaning implied in the phrase "confidence in the scriptures" is to teach students the standard works so thoroughly that they can move through them with confidence, learning the essential scriptures and sermons and texts contained in them. We would hope none of your students would leave your classroom fearful or embarrassed or ashamed that they cannot find the help they need because they do not know the scriptures well enough to locate the proper passages. Give these young people sufficient experience in the Bible, the Book of Mormon, the Doctrine and Covenants, and the Pearl of Great Price that they have both of the kinds of confidence I have just mentioned. (89–01)

Teachers should turn students to Christ, not to themselves. Let me give a word of caution to you. I am sure you recognize the potential danger of being so influential and so persuasive that your students build an allegiance to you rather than to the gospel. Now that is a wonderful problem to have to wrestle with, and we would only hope that all of you are such charismatic teachers. But there is a genuine danger here. That is why you have to invite your students into the scriptures themselves, not just give them your interpretation and presentation of them. That is why you must invite your students to feel the Spirit of the Lord, not just give them your personal reflection of that. That is why, ultimately, you must invite your students directly to Christ, not just to one who teaches his doctrines, however ably. You will not always be available to these students. You cannot hold their hands after they have left high school or college. And you do not need personal disciples.

Our great task is to ground these students in what can go with them through life, to point them toward him who loves them and can guide them where none of us will go. Please make sure the loyalty of these students is to the scriptures and the Lord and the doctrines of the restored Church. Point them toward God the Father and his Only Begotten Son, Jesus Christ, and toward the leadership of the true Church. Make certain that when the glamour and charisma of your personality and lectures and classroom environment are gone that they are not left empty-handed to face the world. Give them the gifts that will carry them through when they have to stand alone. When you do this, the entire Church is blessed for generations to come. (89–01)

Brigham Young University is unique. The Lord stands at the head of his kingdom on the earth. As an institution of the Church there is no separation of this university [BYU] from the Church itself in government, teaching, or principle. As chairman of the Board of Trustees of this institution stands a prophet of the Lord. We follow this leadership, for from this source comes truth, and the path is pointed out to us. Our course is clear. There can be no deviation from those things which have been revealed. In this we are unified, and this unity distinguishes us from every other religious institution in the world. (68–04)

Teachers should teach for eternity as well as for time. Every teacher must have a personal testimony that God lives, of the divine mission of Jesus Christ, and that the appearance to Joseph Smith of the Father and the Son was a reality. Not only must he have that knowledge and testimony, but he should be anxious to express his belief without equivocation to those who come to learn. There is no need to vacillate from theory to theory, or to rationalize, because truth will always reconcile and come into perfect harmony.

Every person who instructs students in this institution [BYU—Hawaii] should be outstanding in the field of spirituality and teach not only for the limits of time, but that which will give guidance to the student for eternity. (72–01)

15

CHURCH HISTORY AND DESTINY

Joseph Smith

We must accept the revelations that came through Joseph Smith. Time vindicates the words and acts of a prophet. The passing of time has turned faith into knowledge, for these things which Joseph Smith prophesied have largely come to pass. . . . One who accepts the doctrine commonly known or referred to as Mormonism must accept word for word and syllable by syllable, wholly and completely, those writings which have been left to us by the Prophet Joseph Smith—a prophet, seer, and revelator.

This is the time of the year when we are reminded of his birth. I am grateful for his teachings, for his revelations, for the heritage he has left us. Through him the gospel was restored to the earth. There is no story in all of history more beautiful than the simple, sweet story of the lad who went into the woods near his home, kneeled in prayer, and received heavenly visitors. . . .

As time went by, this young man, without scholarly achievements and formal education, was educated by the Lord for the things to come. . . .

I am grateful for my membership in the Church. My testimony of its divinity hinges upon the simple story of the lad under the trees kneeling and receiving heavenly visitors. If it is not true, Mormonism falls. If it is true—and I bear witness that it is—it is one of the greatest events in all history. (60–11)

We praise the man who endured, and endured well. When we sing of Joseph Smith, "Praise to the Man" (*Hymns*, 1985, no. 27), we remember so many praiseworthy things about him.

We praise him for his capacity to commune not only with Jehovah but also with other personages of heaven. So many visited, gave keys, and tutored that "choice seer" raised up in the latter days (see 2 Nephi 3:6–7). When Father Smith blessed young Joseph in 1834, he declared that ancient Joseph in Egypt saw this latter-day seer. Ancient Joseph wept when he realized how the work of the Prophet Joseph would bless the earlier Joseph's numerous posterity.

We praise Joseph Smith, too, for his diligence and capacity to translate and to receive hundreds of pages of revealed scripture. He was the revealing conduit. Through him, it has been estimated, more marvelous pages of scripture passed than through any other human in history.

We praise Joseph not only for his capacity to endure but to "endure it well" (D&C 121:8). . . .

We praise Joseph for enduring bitter and repeated betrayals and disappointments. Thus, he went to Carthage "like a lamb to the slaughter," "calm as a summer's morning," and "void of offense towards . . . all men" (D&C 135:4). He did not go to Carthage bitterly. He did not go to Carthage complainingly. What a marvelous capacity to endure well!

Joseph knew which way he faced. It was toward the Savior Jesus Christ to whom he listened ever since our Heavenly Father first instructed young Joseph, saying, "This is My Beloved Son. Hear Him!" (JS—H 1:17). . . .

I bear solemn testimony of the Prophet Joseph Smith as the Lord's anointed servant in these the latter days. (94–05, pp. 63, 64)

Joseph Smith fearlessly pursued his divine mission. As we sang "We Thank Thee, O God, for a Prophet" (*Hymns*, 1985, no. 19), I thought of the Prophet Joseph Smith. How grateful we are for his life and his mission. Joseph Smith was a man committed to his Heavenly Father's work. He loved his fellowmen, and he spent his life in serving them. Joseph Smith was the instrument through which the Lord restored the fullness of the everlasting gospel. He was the Prophet of the Restoration.

Joseph Smith's greatness consists in one thing—the truthfulness of his declaration that he saw the Father and the Son and that he responded to the reality of that divine revelation. He was directed to reestablish the true and living Church, restored in these modern times as it existed in the day of the Savior's own mortal ministry. The Prophet Joseph Smith was fearless in pursuing this divine mission. (94–06, p. 72)

The Apostasy and the Restoration

There was an apostasy and a restoration. The Gospel was taken from the earth soon after the close of the ministry of Jesus because of the dwindling in belief and the corruption of the ordinances, and for many years the earth was in darkness. It is now our witness that the gospel of Jesus Christ has been restored through the instrumentality of the Prophet Joseph Smith, from the God of Heaven. (56–01)

Christ's church has been restored. This is the witness of the missionaries to the world: that Christ's church has been established in these latter days with the same ordinances, the same officers, and all the other tenets of the Church as were given by Christ. This distinguishes us from other religions in the world. (67–05)

The organization of the Church ranks as one of the most important events since the death of Jesus. On the sixth of April, 1830, 161 years ago yesterday, a group of men and women, acting in obedience to a commandment of God, assembled in the house of Mr. Peter Whitmer to organize The Church of Jesus Christ of Latter-day Saints. . . .

Six men comprised the total membership of the Church that day. . . .

Most of life's momentous hours are recorded, but what these men did on that humble occasion would not have given the world much reason to take note. What they did, however, ranks among the most important events ever to have transpired since the death of Jesus and his Apostles in the meridian of time. (91–02, p. 63)

The Modern Church and Unity

Every program in the Church is in reality an aid to the Church member in helping him attain celestial life. (69–03)

The Church provides us the opportunity to do the work of the Lord. The objectives of the Church are to teach the laws of the Lord and the principles of the gospel, to assist individuals in religious education, to implant the firm testimony that God lives and that Jesus is the Christ and Savior of the world, and to help and encourage each member along the path to celestial and eternal exaltation through the opportunity of "doing." There is a real reason why Christ established his Church during his personal ministry on earth. We need only to listen to his words and the teachings of those he sent into the world in order to understand.

"Not every one that saith unto me, Lord, Lord, shall enter into the kingdom of heaven; but he that doeth the will of my Father which is in heaven" (Matthew 7:21); "And all saints who remember to keep and do these sayings" (D&C 89:18); "But the doers of the law shall be justified" (Romans 2:13); "Whosoever cometh to me, and heareth my sayings, and doeth them" (Luke 6:47)—these are the admonitions.

We must assume from the fact that the Church was established by Christ during his ministry that it is essential for man and not an elective. His life and ministry were to set the pattern and create the model. The things established by him were given with the admonition that we follow them.

I submit that the Church of Jesus Christ is as necessary in the lives of men and women today as it was when established by him, not by passive interest or a profession of faith, but by an assumption of active responsibility. In this way the Church brings us out of the darkness of an isolated life into the light of the gospel, where belief is turned into doing according to the admonitions of scripture. (67–07, pp. 46–47)

We are following a carefully charted course. The course we have charted over the past few years has been prayerfully and carefully conceived. . . . We have sought to measure everything we do on the basis of whether or not it was vital to our mission of assisting our Father in Heaven and his Son Jesus Christ in bringing to pass the immortality and eternal life of mankind (see Moses 1:39).

We have a singular mission with three dimensions: proclaiming the gospel; perfecting the Saints, which includes seeking after their temporal and spiritual welfare; and redeeming the dead. To this end we have sought to focus our efforts on making the saving covenants and ordinances of the gospel available to all mankind: to the nonmember through our fellowshipping and missionary work; to the less-active through activation efforts and to all members through participation and service in the Church; to those who have passed beyond the veil through the work of redemption for the dead. . . .

The whole purpose of the Church operating smoothly at the local level is to qualify individuals to return to the presence of God. That can only be done by their accepting the covenants, receiving the ordinances, and then living in accordance with all they have covenanted to do in the temples of our Lord. (91–01)

The Church must be united to continue to grow. As we think of the great growth of the Church and the monumental tasks that yet lie before us, we wonder if there is any more important objective before us than to so live that we may enjoy the unifying Spirit of the Lord. As Jesus prayed, we must be united if the world is ever to be convinced that he was sent by God his Father to redeem us from our sins. It is unity and oneness that has thus far enabled us to bear our testimonies around the globe. . . .

. . . I know of no stronger weapons in the hands of the adversary against any group of men or women in this Church than the weapons of divisiveness, faultfinding, and antagonism. The key to a unified Church is a unified soul—one that is at peace with itself and not given to inner conflicts and tensions. (94–22)

The Church is a worldwide church. The Church of Jesus Christ of Latter-day Saints, is now a world religion, not simply because its members are now found throughout the world, but chiefly because it has a comprehensive and inclusive message based upon the acceptance of all truth, restored to meet the needs of all mankind. (94–06, p. 73)

The need for unity in the Church is great. However great the need may be for unity within nations, there is even greater need for harmony and interdependence within the worldwide Church of Jesus Christ of Latter-day Saints. . . .

Within this Church there is a constant need for unity, for if we are not one, we are not his (see D&C 38:27). We are truly dependent on each other, "and the eye cannot say unto the hand, I have no need of thee: nor again the head to the feet, I have no need of you" (1 Corinthians 12:21). Nor can the North Americans say to the Asians, nor the Europeans to the islanders of the sea, "I have no need of thee." No, in this Church we have need of every member. . . .

As we think of the great growth of the Church, the diversities of tongues and cultures, and the monumental tasks that yet lie before us, we wonder if there is any more important objective before us than to so live that we may enjoy the unifying Spirit of the Lord. As Jesus prayed, we *must* be united if the world is ever to be convinced that he was sent by God his Father to redeem us from our sins. (76–01, pp. 105–6)

The great purposes of the Church could not be accomplished without unity. It is unity and oneness that has thus far enabled us to bear our testimony around the globe, bringing forward tens of thousands of missionaries to do their part. More must be done. It is unity that has thus far enabled the Church, its wards and stakes, branches and districts, and members, to construct temples and chapels, undertake welfare projects, seek after the dead, watch over the Church, and build faith. More must be done. These great purposes of the Lord could not have been achieved with dissension or jealousy or selfishness. Our ideas may not always be quite like those who preside in authority over us, but this is the Lord's church and he will bless each of us as we cast off pride, pray for strength, and contribute to the good of the whole. (76–01, p. 106)

The key to a unified Church is a unified soul. The key to a unified church is a unified soul—one that is at peace with itself and not given to inner conflicts and tensions. So much in our world is calculated to destroy that personal peace through sins and temptations of a thousand kinds. We pray that the lives of the Saints will be lived in harmony with the ideal set before us by Jesus of Nazareth.

We pray that Satan's efforts will be thwarted, that personal lives can be peaceful and calm, that families can be close and concerned with every member, that wards and stakes, branches and districts can form the great body of Christ, meeting every need, soothing every hurt, healing every wound until the whole world, as Nephi pleaded, will "press forward with a steadfastness in Christ, having a perfect brightness of hope, and a love of God and of all men. . . .

"My beloved brethren," continued Nephi, "this is the way; and there is none other way." (2 Nephi 31:20–21.)

For the entire worldwide Church, for the great body of Saints to the east and to the west, to the north and to the south, we pray that we may be one. (76–01, p. 106)

Unity makes the Church strong. One of the things that has made the Church strong is the great principle of unity. We support and sustain each other. When I hear the counselors to President David O. McKay express their great love and appreciation for him with the statement that they sustain him with all their strength, I gain respect for the leadership of the Church. This same principle is demonstrated by the Council of the Twelve where there is absolute unity within the Council and the First Presidency. The ward is strong because the members sustain and support the bishop. Stakes are strong because the stake president is supported by the bishops of the wards and the membership of the wards. The Church becomes strong because the general authorities are supported by the presidents of stakes, the bishops of wards, and the membership of the Church. This same principle carries into all of the organizations of the Church. (61–05)

Unity is the spirit of the gospel. We live in a world of controversy and contention. Seldom do we read of things which are good, virtuous, and praiseworthy. It seems as though what is placed before us, both to view and to read, contains the controversy of our modern day. It is good to have the feeling of sustaining and supporting rather than raising our voices or hearing other voices raised in opposition.

Unity is the spirit of the gospel—the spirit of the kingdom. (79–10)

The Church and Continuing Revelation

Revelation to the Church has continued from Joseph Smith to the present. From the early nineteenth century through our day, the Lord has revealed his mind and will to his anointed prophets. There is an unending stream of revelation flowing constantly from the headwaters of heaven to God's anointed servants on earth. Since the death of the Prophet Joseph Smith, the voice of the Lord to his prophets has continued as before. (88–08)

The Church has always been led by continuous revelation. A study of the revelations of the Lord in holy writ confirms the fact that it is continuous revelation that guides prophets and the Church in any age. Were it not for continuous revelation, Noah would not have been prepared for the deluge that encompassed the earth. Abraham would not have been guided from Haran to Hebron, the land of promise. Continuous revelation led the children of Israel from bondage back to their promised land. Revelation through prophets guided missionary efforts, directed the rebuilding of Solomon's temple, and denounced the infiltration of pagan practices among the Israelites. (81–01, p. 65)

Christ's Church is founded on the rock of revelation. Some writers, seeking a doctrinal beginning rather than a specific event for the commencement of the Church of Christ, give great weight to the reply of the Lord when Peter bore his testimony that Jesus was the Christ. It was on the occasion when they were near Caesarea Philippi that Jesus asked his disciples, "Whom do men say that I the Son of man am?" (Matthew 16:13). It doesn't seem reasonable to suppose that he didn't know what people thought and were saying about him. He was giving his disciples the opportunity to express their faith and to be strengthened. "And they said, Some say that thou art John the Baptist: some, Elias; and others, Jeremias, or one of the prophets" (Matthew 16:14).

"He saith unto them, But whom say ye that I am?" (Matthew 16:15). The Master may have been prompted to ask this question because of their surroundings. Caesarea Philippi is near the grotto and the temples of the Greek god Pan, a center of pagan worship, and he may have wanted his disciples to think about the contrast between pagan gods and the true God. "And Simon Peter an-

swered and said, Thou art the Christ, the Son of the living God"
(Matthew 16:16). In answer to this positive testimony of Peter,
"Jesus answered and said unto him, Blessed art thou, Simon Bar-
jona: for flesh and blood hath not revealed it unto thee, but my
Father which is in heaven.

"And I say also unto thee, That thou art Peter, and upon this
rock I will build my church; and the gates of hell shall not prevail
against it" (Matthew 16:17–18).

This is a very significant statement. The Lord in effect said to
Peter that this knowledge that Jesus was the Christ did not come
to him from mortal men or from the reasoning or learning of men,
but by revelation from on high, that is, direct, divine revelation of
the divinity of the Master. In answer to the statement "Thou art
the Christ," Jesus replied, "Thou art Peter" in friendly acknowl-
edgment of his disciple. The Lord then added, "And upon this
rock I will build my church." Upon what rock? Peter? Upon a
man? No, not upon a man, upon the rock of revelation, the thing
which they were talking about. He had just said, "Flesh and blood
hath not revealed it unto thee, but my Father which is in heaven."
This revelation that Jesus is the Christ is the foundation upon
which he would build his Church. (65–03, p. 1145)

The Lord reigns in our midst through revelation. In a revelation to a modern oracle, Joseph Smith, the Lord said: . . .

"And also the Lord shall have power over his saints, and shall
reign in their midst" (D&C 1:36).

The Savior is reigning in the midst of the Saints today through
continuous revelation. I testify that he is with his servants in this
day and will be until the end of the earth. (81–01, p. 65)

The rise and progress of the Church is due to revelation. Some
have attempted to explain the origin and operation of The Church
of Jesus Christ of Latter-day Saints without acknowledging the
principle of revelation. That is like trying to explain the operation
of a vehicle without mentioning the fact that the vehicle has an en-
gine. To attempt to account for the rise and progress of this
Church on any basis other than revelation will prove to be naïve.
Anyone . . . who attempts to tell our history and omits the detail
of revelation in the narration will not be giving a truthful nor accurate account. The Spirit will not ratify such a history. (83–06)

Revelation is the distinguishing characteristic of the Church of Jesus Christ. A distinguishing characteristic of the Church of Jesus Christ in any age is revelation to prophets and the operation of the gifts of the Spirit among the Saints. It has been the design of the Almighty from the very beginning to regulate the affairs of his kingdom on earth according to heavenly patterns. Thus Adam, Noah, Enoch, Melchizedek, Abraham, Moses, Elijah, Lehi, Nephi, Mormon, and others received wisdom and instruction from the God of heaven to guide the affairs of mankind.

The guiding principle of Church government is revelation. The Church of Jesus Christ operates under the premise that man, unaided by revelation, cannot discover God's mind and will. The most important function, therefore, of a Church administrator is to find out the will of God and then do it. (83–06)

16

PREPARING IN THE LAST DAYS

As Latter-day Saints we have no excuse for despair. I am here tonight to tell you that despair, doom, and discouragement are not an acceptable view of life for a Latter-day Saint. However high on the charts they are on the hit parade of contemporary news, we must not walk on our lower lip every time a few difficult moments happen to confront us.

I am just a couple of years older than most of you [university students], and in those few extra months I have seen a bit more of life than you have. I want you to know that there have always been some difficulties in mortal life and there always will be. But knowing what we know, and living as we are supposed to live, there really is no place, no excuse, for pessimism and despair. (93–01, p. 68)

Life's difficulties are designed to make us better people. Here are some actual comments that have been made and passed on to me in recent months. This comes from a fine returned missionary:

Why should I date and get serious with a girl? I am not sure I even want to marry and bring a family into this kind of a world. I am not very sure about my own future. How can I take the responsibility for the future of others whom I would love and care about and want to be happy?

Here's another from a high school student:

I hope I die before all these terrible things happen that people are talking about. I don't want to be on the earth when there is so much trouble.

And this from a recent college graduate:

I am doing the best I can, but I wonder if there is much reason to even plan for the future, let alone retirement. The world probably won't last that long anyway.

Well, isn't that a fine view of things. Sounds like we all ought to go and eat a big plate of worms.

I want to say to all within the sound of my voice tonight that you have every reason in this world to be happy and to be optimistic and to be confident. Every generation since time began has had some things to overcome and some problems to work out. Furthermore, every individual person has a particular set of challenges that sometimes seems to be earmarked for us individually. We understood that in our premortal existence.

Prophets and apostles of the Church have faced some of those personal difficulties. I acknowledge that I have faced a few, and you will undoubtedly face some of your own now and later in your life. When these experiences humble us and refine us and teach us and bless us, they can be powerful instruments in the hands of God to make us better people, to make us more considerate of other people in their own times of difficulty. (93–01, pp. 68–69)

Even in these latter days faithful members need not fear. The scriptures also indicate that there will be seasons of time when the whole world will have some difficulty. We know that in our dispensation unrighteousness will, unfortunately, be quite evident, and it will bring its inevitable difficulties and pain and punishment. God will cut short that unrighteousness in his own due time, but our task is to live fully and faithfully and not worry ourselves sick about the woes of the world or when it will end. Our task is to have the gospel in our lives and to be a bright light, a city set upon a hill that reflects the beauty of the gospel of Jesus Christ and the joy and happiness that will always come to every people in every age who keep the commandments.

In this last dispensation there will be great tribulation (Matthew 24:21). We know that from the scriptures. We know there will be wars and rumors of wars and that the whole earth will be in commotion (D&C 45:26). All dispensations have had their perilous times, but our day will include genuine peril (2 Timothy 3:1). Evil men will flourish (2 Timothy 3:13), but then evil men have very often flourished. Calamities will come and iniquity will abound (D&C 45:27).

Inevitably, the natural result of some of these kinds of prophecies is fear, and that is not fear limited to a younger generation. It is fear shared by those of any age who don't understand what we understand.

But I want to stress that these feelings are not necessary for faithful Latter-day Saints, and they do not come from God. (93–01, p. 69)

The Lord has power over his Saints and thus we should have hope. I promise you tonight in the name of the Lord whose servant I am that God will always protect and care for his people. We will have our difficulties the way every generation and people have had difficulties. Your life as a young college student or working person in the 1990s is no different than any young person's life has been in any age of time. But with the gospel of Jesus Christ you have every hope and promise and reassurance. The Lord has power over his Saints and will always prepare places of peace, defense, and safety for his people. When we have faith in God we can hope for a better world—for us personally and for all mankind. The prophet Ether taught anciently (and he knew something about troubles):

"Wherefore, whoso believeth in God might with surety hope for a better world, yea, even a place at the right hand of God, which hope cometh of faith, maketh an anchor to the souls of men, which would make them sure and steadfast, always abounding in good works, being led to glorify God" (Ether 12:4).

Disciples of Christ in every generation are invited, indeed commanded, to be filled with a perfect brightness of hope (2 Nephi 31:20). (93–01, p. 71)

Preparation for the Second Coming does not require a preoccupation with the future. Jesus taught his disciples to watch and pray; however, he taught them that prayerful watching does not require sleepless anxiety and preoccupation with the future, but rather the quiet, steady attention to present duties. (74–01, p. 18)

All of the ancient prophets have looked forward to our day with delight. Let me close tonight with one of the greatest statements I have ever read from the Prophet Joseph Smith, who faced such immense difficulties in his life and who of course paid the ultimate price for his victory. But he *was* victorious, and he was a happy, robust, optimistic man. Those who knew him felt his strength and courage, even in the darkest of times. He did not sag in spirits or long remain in any despondency.

He said about our time—yours and mine—that ours is the moment "upon which prophets, priests and kings [in ages past] have dwelt with peculiar delight; [all these ancient witnesses for God] have looked forward with joyful anticipation to the day in which we live; and fired with heavenly and joyful anticipations they have sung and written and prophesied of this our day; . . . we are the favored people that God has [chosen] to bring about the Latter-day glory. [HC 4:609–10.]

That is a thrilling statement to me: that the ancients whom we love and read and quote so much—Adam and Abraham, Joshua and Joseph, Isaiah and Ezekiel and Ezra, Nephi and Alma, and Mormon and Moroni—all of these ancient prophets, priests, and kings focused their prophetic vision "with peculiar delight" on our day, on our time. It is this hour to which they have looked forward "with joyful anticipation," and "fired with heavenly and joyful anticipation they have sung and written and prophesied of this our day." They saw us as "the favored people" upon whom God would shower his full and complete latter-day glory, and I testify that is our destiny. What a privilege! What an honor! What a responsibility! And what joy! We have every reason in time and eternity to rejoice and give thanks for the quality of our lives and the promises we have been given. (93–01, pp. 72–73)

Things will always get better if we live and love the gospel. In my lifetime I have seen two world wars plus Korea plus Vietnam and all that you are currently witnessing. I have worked my way through the depression and managed to go to law school while starting a young family at the same time. I have seen stock markets and world economies go crazy and have seen a few despots and tyrants go crazy, all of which causes quite a bit of trouble around the world in the process.

So I am frank to say tonight that I hope you won't believe all the world's difficulties have been wedged into your decade or that things have never been worse than they are for you personally, or that they will never get better. I reassure you that things have been worse and they *will* always get better. They always do—especially when we live and love the gospel of Jesus Christ and give it a chance in our lives. (93–01, p. 68)

17

TEACHING IN
THE CHURCH

The Sunday School has the greatest product in the world. The Sunday School has the greatest product in all the world to sell—a product needed by every living person: the Gospel of Jesus Christ.

The Sunday School is big business. It spreads throughout the whole world. The results are not measured in dollars nor in dividends to stockholders; the results are measured in joy and happiness to the givers of those things which the Sunday School has to give. And this joy and happiness is known only to those who devote themselves, their time, and their lives to the service of others. The benefits to the receiver are well known to us, because we have been the beneficiaries of others who have so devoted themselves for our benefit. . . . What a great privilege is ours to teach the principles of the Gospel and to help others find the path of eternal exaltation. We stand in this modern day as representatives of the organization with the world's most precious product. (60–05, p. 289)

Teachers can perform miracles. When a teacher performs as the Lord intended, a miracle takes place. The miracle of the Church today is not the healings which are so profuse, not that the lame shall walk, the blind see, the deaf hear, or the sick be raised up. The great healing of the Church and kingdom of God in our day and in our time is the transformation of the human soul. As we journey throughout the stakes and missions of the Church, this is what we see, the transformation of the human soul because someone has taught the principles of truth. (65–01)

The purpose of teaching is to change hearts. "Have ye spiritually been born of God? Have ye received his image in your countenances? Have ye experienced this mighty change in your hearts?" (Alma 5:14.)

This is the purpose of teaching. This is the reason we labor so hard, seek the Spirit, and prepare our minds with good things as the Lord has commanded, that we might be an instrument in the hands of the Lord in changing the heart of an individual. Our aim is to plant in the hearts of the children the desire to be good, the desire to be righteous, the desire to keep the commandments of the Lord, the desire to walk in humility before him. If we can be an instrument in the hands of the Lord in bringing to pass this mighty change in the hearts of the youth of Zion, then we have accomplished the great miracle of a teacher. And truly it is a miracle. We do not understand how the Lord changes the hearts of men, but he does. Through a teacher, he can change the hearts of children almost overnight. (65–01)

It is a privilege to teach children. President Brigham Young, on one occasion, said: "Some of the brightest spirits who dwell in the bosom of the Father are making their appearance among this people of whom the Lord will make a royal priesthood, a peculiar nation that he can own and bless, talk with, and associate with" (*Discourses of Brigham Young*, p. 130). Some of these children whom we teach in our Primaries, whom we lead, are these very bright spirits whom President Brigham Young said were being sent to the earth in our time and in our day. . . .

What a great privilege we who are associated with the Church and kingdom of God have in teaching the principles of truth, the light of heaven, to the hearts and minds of children. (65–01)

Teaching Youth

We must teach youth the joy of worthy accomplishment. If you want to make it hard for the youth later, make it easy for them now. Instead, teach them the joy that results from worthy accomplishment. (90–09)

We must teach by example. Let me take just a moment to men-tion a little incident that made an impression upon me when I was a boy. This came to my mind when it was mentioned that there are with us this afternoon a large group of dedicated people who teach our youth.

It was on a summer day early in the morning. I was standing near the window. The curtains obstructed me from two little creatures out on the lawn. One was a large bird and the other a little bird, obviously just out of the nest. I saw the larger bird hop out on the lawn, then thump his feet and cock his head. He drew a big fat worm out of the lawn and came hopping back. The little bird opened its bill wide, but the big bird swallowed the worm.

Then I saw the big bird fly up into a tree. He pecked at the bark for a little while and came back with a big bug in his mouth. The little bird opened his beak wide, but the big bird swallowed the bug. There was squawking in protest.

The big bird flew away, and I didn't see it again, but I watched the little bird. After a while, the little bird hopped out on the lawn, thumped its feet, cocked its head, and pulled a big worm out of the lawn.

God bless the good people who teach our children and our youth. (72–02, p. 85)

We serve youth best when we help them live better lives. We serve youth best when we help them to live the better and more abundant life—when we help them to know God. Young people like to have fun, to dance and play, and the MIA program is built around the things they like to do. The great genius of the program is to couple those things with spirituality. . . .

As leaders we hold in trust the treasures of the gospel of Jesus Christ for the young men and young women of the Church. These beneficiaries will receive in direct proportion to our devotion and faithfulness to this great charge. (60–08)

A Primary teacher needs the inspiration that comes from prayer. The sacredness of the call to be a Primary worker becomes awesome when one comes to the realization of the great responsibility of playing a part in the spiritual development of God's children. If we are sincere, we cannot take any other course than that which we know the Lord would have us take. We need inspiration. Inspiration and prayer go hand in hand. If we can grow close to the Lord in prayer, we can be assured of the inspiration to accomplish our task. (67–01)

Boys need models to follow. A boy has a greater need for a model than he has for a critic. Someone has said, "Boys will be boys," but he forgot to add, "Boys will also be men." (67–01)

Primary teachers are keepers of the jewels. What a glorious thing it is to have received the call to serve in the Primary. The Lord showed his love for the little children and he blessed them. Surely he loves those who teach them of his commandments and of his kingdom—those who bring them out of darkness into the light of the gospel. What a joy it is to share with our co-workers and those we teach, the testimony that God lives; that Jesus is the Christ, the Savior of all mankind; that there is a prophet of the Lord on the earth in our day. This knowledge brings to us peace in a troubled world. Troubles vanish and are replaced by joy in the hearts of those who work with little people so fresh from the presence of God and still untouched by the corruptions of the world. You are the keepers of the jewels—the preservers of our wealth. (67–01)

Our challenge is to treat youth as responsible adults. We would be naive to believe that our young people could grow up in the world without coming in contact with or even being tempted by drugs, liquor, the sophisticated cigarette, immorality, youthful crime, and a thousand other things that destroy and tear down moral stability. Our place is to show them and teach them the way which is best. I have confidence in their decisions when we treat them as responsible adults and not refute, deride, and denounce them because the acts of their minority have been given such prominence. (67–03)

There is something special about Primary. As I travel about in the stakes and the missions and review their reports and the statistics, I am always pleased to note that the percentage of attendance at Primary is higher than any of the other organizations in the Church. Children love Primary. Teachers love to teach children. This is a choice organization, and our calls to serve are great blessings to us. Of course, we would be glad to serve wherever we might be called, but Primary is something special because it pertains to God's little children—these little wide-eyed, questioning, eager boys and girls who are facing life. . . . There is something special about the little ones, and I have the feeling that there is something special about those who give of themselves to help them—especially in teaching them to find God and to talk with him in prayer. (69–02)

The potential influence of Primary is far-reaching in effect. There are thousands who are the beneficiaries of Primary, and as they grow and take their places in the world, there will come millions of beneficiaries from the seeds you sow. . . .

What a glorious thing it is to take part in a movement in the world for good, in molding character in little people, in teaching them the principles of righteous living, and in finding the real happiness in life. People who understand children know how important it is to inculcate into their young lives a feeling of affection for the Church. No moral influence in the lives of young men and young women is more beautiful than the sentiment they possess for the Church. As they go away from home to school or to work, or take their place in marriage with a new family, the lessons they learned and the affection for the Church learned in childhood lead them to look for that sacred association. Your efforts create the desire for young men to hold the priesthood and to accept the call to go on missions. Your willingness to help them turns the hearts of boys and girls towards the temples of God when they reach those important years. (69–02)

We must not fail to strengthen the youth of the Church. In preparing our members to receive the ordinances and covenants of the temple, we must not neglect our youth. We cannot afford to wait until youth are mature in years before teaching them eternal truths and values in preparation for their making sacred covenants in holy places. Our youth face great challenges in this respect. These are difficult and trying times, especially for those who are young.

Youth must be taught to live high moral standards and to love those holy beings who have established these standards, even our Father in Heaven and his Son, our Savior Jesus Christ. Parents are the first line of defense in arming our youth against the evils of the world. Priesthood and auxiliary leaders stand ready to assist. . . .

As our youth live clean lives, we will have more who will serve missions and more who will be worthy to have their marriages sealed in the house of the Lord. In turn, we will have more fathers and mothers who will honor their sacred vows of fidelity one to another, and who will raise righteous children of their own. (91–01)

Responsibilities of Teachers

The best teaching is often done individually. I have always been impressed that the Lord deals with us personally, individually. We do many things in groups in the Church, and we need organizations of some size to allow us to administer the Church well, but so many of the important things—the *most* important things—are done individually. We bless babies one at a time, even if they are twins or triplets. We baptize and confirm children one at a time. We take the sacrament, are ordained to the priesthood, or move through the ordinances of the temple as individuals—as one person developing a relationship with our Father in Heaven. There may be others nearby us in these experiences, just as there are others in your classroom, but heaven's emphasis is on each individual, on every single person.

When Christ appeared to the Nephites, he said:

"Arise and come forth unto me, that ye may thrust your hands into my side, and also that ye may feel the prints of the nails in my hands and in my feet. . . .

"And it came to pass that the multitude went forth, and thrust their hands into his side, and did feel the imprints of the nails in his hands and in his feet; and this they did do, *going forth one by one* until they had all gone forth, *and did see with their eyes and did feel with their hands*, and did know of a surety and did bear record" (3 Nephi 11:14–15; emphasis added).

That experience took time, but it was important that each individual have the experience, that each set of eyes and each pair of hands have that reaffirming, *personal* witness. Later Christ treated the Nephite children exactly the same way. "He took their little children, *one by one*, and blessed them, and prayed unto the Father for them" (3 Nephi 17:21; emphasis added).

It will be hard for you to give all of the personal attention some of your students both want and need, but try the best you can to think of them individually, to let them feel something personal and special in the concern of you, their teacher. Pray to know which student needs what kind of help, and remain sensitive to those promptings when they then come. . . .

Remember that the very best teaching is one on one and often takes place out of the classroom. (89–01)

Those who are struggling need special attention. In your search for individually teaching each student, you will most certainly discover that some are not doing as well as others and that some are not making it to class at all. Take personal interest in such students; give extra-mile effort to invite and help the lost sheep back into the fold. "Remember the worth of souls is great in the sight of God" (D&C 18:10). An incalculable price has been paid by our Savior for *every* one of us, and it is incumbent on us to do all we can to assist him in his work. It is incumbent on us to make sure that the gift of the Atonement is extended to *every* young man or woman we have responsibility for. In your situation, that means keeping them in full activity in your classes.

Give special attention to those who may be struggling, and go out as necessary to find the lost sheep. A written postcard, a telephone call, or, if possible, a personal visit to a home in many cases will have a wonderful result. Personal attention to a young person just beginning to stray may save hours and hours—indeed, years and years—of effort later in our attempt to reclaim that person to activity. Do all you can to fortify the strong ones and reanchor the wayward ones at this age. It will be infinitely more difficult to successfully reach them later. (89–01)

We cannot teach without the Spirit. In one of the most basic revelations of this dispensation, the Lord said, "And the Spirit shall be given unto you by the prayer of faith; and if ye receive not the Spirit ye shall not teach" (D&C 42:14).

I take this verse to mean not only that we *should not* teach without the Spirit, but also that we really *cannot* teach without it. Learning of spiritual things simply cannot take place without the instructional and confirming presence of the Spirit of the Lord. Joseph Smith would seem to agree: "All are to preach the Gospel, by the power and influence of the Holy Ghost; and no man can preach the Gospel without the Holy Ghost" (Joseph Smith, *Teachings of the Prophet Joseph Smith*, sel. Joseph Fielding Smith [Salt Lake City: Deseret Book Co., 1976], p. 112). (89–01)

There is a thrill that comes from helping others know the Savior. Some of us have wished that we could have been on the bank of the Jordan that day when Jesus came to John to be baptized of him. . . .

We also think of those occasions when he sat in a small boat on the Sea of Galilee a short distance from the shore and taught the multitudes which came to him. . . .

We would have been thrilled, of course, if we could have been present; but these things occurred in a day which has long passed.

Think of the thrill, however, that we can bring to others in this day by teaching them to know the Savior and to know the things which he taught. This is the spirit of the Sunday School. (60–05, pp. 288–89)

Teachers have a sacred responsibility. Before me now I see some of the choice spirits of the earth—faithful Sunday School workers. Your very presence here indicates this truth. I see you, after this conference, scattered over wide fields of labor. I try to visualize each one of you at work in your own specific assignment. I wonder what kind of fruit your labor will bring forth. Will some of that fruit be blighted because you have failed to till or cultivate the soil entrusted to your care; or will all the soil be cultivated so it will yield a maximum of good fruit?

Out in your respective wards and stakes, to which you will shortly return, reside many of our Father's children. Like you, they are choice in his sight; but, unlike you, many are inexperienced and many are new in the Gospel. Your responsibility toward them is great indeed. Their lives are pliable, easily bent, easily molded, easily led, if you can gain their confidence and win their hearts. You are their "shepherd." You must guide them to "green pastures." . . .

What a challenge, what a joyous task, what a sacred responsibility is yours now as you return to your fields of labor! How thoughtful, how considerate, how kind, how tender, how pure in heart, how possessed of that unselfish love as our Lord possessed, how humble, how prayerful you must be as you assume anew your work to feed the lambs as the Lord is telling you to do! (63–03, pp. 240–41)

A great teacher walks in holiness before God. The formula for a great teacher is not only to live the commandments of the Lord, and to advocate the commandments of the Lord, but to obtain the spirit of teaching by prayer. When we obtain that spirit and observe the commandments of the Lord, walking in holiness before him, then the lives of those whom we touch will be changed and they will be motivated to live lives of righteousness. (65–01)

Teachers should be examples. It is so needful for us [teachers] to set the proper example, to be diligent and vigilant in our own lives, to keep the Sabbath Day holy, to honor the leadership of the ward, the stake, and the Church. Nothing unseemly should come from our lips that would give any child the right or the privilege to do wrong. Surely if we say or do something wrong, they have all the license in the world to follow.

Example carries with it an influence much more forceful than precept. He who would persuade others to do right should do right himself. It is true that he who practices good precepts because they are good, and does not suffer himself to be influenced by the unrighteous conduct of others, will be more abundantly rewarded than one who says and does not. (65–01)

As teachers, priesthood bearers have significant responsibilities. From the scriptures I have just read [D&C 42:12–13, D&C 88:118–19] and the many others that might be cited, several things are made abundantly clear:

1. Every bearer of the priesthood within his sphere of influence and responsibility is to teach the gospel through precept and example. That is, he should be teaching by the example of living the gospel; also through words, learning experiences, and instructional materials.

2. Every bearer of the priesthood is to prepare himself to be an effective teacher by study, prayer, and faith.

3. Every bearer of the priesthood should seek the direction of the Spirit to guide him in his own life and to inspire him in his teaching efforts.

4. Every bearer of the priesthood has a sacred stewardship in the kingdom of God. Our time, our talents, our property, our priesthood callings are part of this stewardship.

Thus, in our teaching responsibilities we are blessed with the opportunity to respond by participating in the divine plan of saving men's souls. (71–03, p. 51)

General Conference

Listen to and ponder the messages of conference. We would say to the world: "Listen to and weigh the words of this conference; consider the direction and counsel that come from those who speak. Then, after prayerful pondering, that sweet warm conviction that comes from the Holy Spirit will testify to you of its truthfulness." (81–03, p. 13)

The Lord speaks to us through chosen servants. Much inspired counsel by prophets, seers, revelators, and other General Authorities of the Church is given during general conference. Our modern-day prophets have encouraged us to make the reading of the conference editions of our Church magazines an important and regular part of our personal study. Thus, general conference becomes, in a sense, a supplement to or an extension of the Doctrine and Covenants. In addition to the conference issues of the Church magazines, the First Presidency writes monthly articles that contain inspired counsel for our welfare.

We would do well to recognize that the Lord speaks to us through his chosen servants. He has reminded us that "whether by mine own voice or by the voice of my servants, it is the same" (D&C 1:38). (88–08)

General conference is a time for spiritual renewal. Conference time is a season of spiritual revival when knowledge and testimony are increased and solidified that God lives and blesses those who are faithful. It is a time when an understanding that Jesus is the Christ, the Son of the living God, is burned into the hearts of those who have the determination to serve him and keep his commandments. Conference is the time when our leaders give us inspired direction in the conduct of our lives—a time when souls are stirred and resolutions are made to be better husbands and wives, fathers and mothers, more obedient sons and daughters, better friends and neighbors. (81–03, p. 12)

The Lord reveals his will at conference time. As I have pondered the messages of the conference, I have asked myself this question: How can I help others partake of the goodness and blessings of our Heavenly Father? The answer lies in following the direction received from those we sustain as prophets, seers, and revelators, and others of the General Authorities. Let us study their words, spoken under the spirit of inspiration, and refer to them often. The Lord has revealed his will to the Saints in this conference. (94–16, p. 87)

18

PRIESTHOOD AND MEMBER ACTIVATION

Priesthood in the Church

What does it mean to hold the priesthood? I have reflected upon the expression we often use of "holding the priesthood." What do we mean by "holding the priesthood"? I suppose we could say that we hold the priesthood in our hands and in our heads and in our hearts.

First, our hands. Will we always use them for good . . . will we use them to do his work? We magnify the priesthood as we lay our hands on other's heads in ordination. We anoint, we bless, and through our hands his power is passed on to others. We should hold out our hands in fellowship. . . .

We also hold the priesthood in our heads. We must seek knowledge. No one is saved in ignorance. We must know his word. Besides knowing his word, we must understand his will and put his counsel into action. Brothers in the priesthood, we must constantly study—our knowledge then will become wisdom, and to utilize wisdom properly is priesthood in action. This wisdom will guide our actions. This wisdom will help our brethren accomplish that which the Lord has placed them upon the earth to do.

Brethren, we hold the priesthood in our hearts. It is through love that we actuate this great power. Not only must we love one another, but it is our responsibility to teach each other how to love one another. Each day our love can be shown by understanding another's problems or needs. One man is bound to another by his heart strings. This bond is made strong by serving those who are weak.

We must love kindly, we must love totally. We must love the brethren in our quorums as our Heavenly Father loves us. Our brothers in the Priesthood quorums of the Church must be concerned with one another. A priesthood quorum must have strong bonds of friendship, like bridges built from one brother to another in the greatest common bond of all—the power of God that we hold. (69–01)

The priesthood is a guide. The priesthood is a guide to a young man as he grows to maturity and he is strengthened throughout these years by the priesthood quorums. As he realizes that he holds the priesthood and that he is here on earth to do God's will, his actions are tempered. His priesthood will serve as an insurance to him, and he will find a happy life. He will act in accordance with our Heavenly Father's wishes. He will seek out his talents and develop them. (69–01)

Love of the Lord and our fellowmen is the key to priesthood power. To love the Lord and our fellowmen is the key by which we unlock the power of the priesthood so that it may become active in our lives. (71–06, p. 98)

The Lord gives revelation to those he calls. The Lord never calls a man to any office in his Church but what he will by revelation help that man to magnify his calling, for "the Lord giveth no commandments unto the children of men, save he shall prepare a way for them that they may accomplish the thing which he commandeth them" (1 Nephi 3:7). (83–06)

All who serve should strive to be governed by revelation. All priesthood officers should strive to be governed by the spirit of revelation, which is the manifestation of the Holy Ghost to their minds and hearts (see D&C 8:2–3). This will require fasting, prayer, meditation, personal effort to magnify one's calling, obedience, and experience. "By learning the Spirit of God and understanding it, [they] may grow into the principle of revelation, until [they] become perfect in Christ Jesus" (*Teachings of the Prophet Joseph Smith*, p. 151). (83–06)

Aaronic and Melchizedek Priesthoods

Preparing young men to receive and advance in the priest-hood is a sacred trust. We trust that young men are being properly tutored before receiving the Aaronic Priesthood at the age of twelve and that their parents and advisors are preparing them to advance within the priesthood at the appropriate age and then be ordained to the Melchizedek Priesthood at the proper time. (94–11)

The Lord shares the priesthood with men. The Lord has faith in young people. He shares with young men one of their most prized possessions—his priesthood, the power to act in the name of and by the authority of God. This trust has been imposed in young men throughout history. Noah was ordained when only ten years of age. Samuel must have been ordained at an early age. Joseph was only seventeen when he was sold into Egypt, and it is evident that he received the priesthood prior to that time. The record tells us that Nephi was visited by the Lord when he was "exceeding young." He must have held the priesthood in his youth. God the Father and the Son appeared to a boy in this dispensation of time. (67–03)

We must give greater emphasis to the callings of Melchizedek Priesthood leaders. As we have pondered the important responsibility placed upon our Melchizedek Priesthood quorum leaders, we have felt the need to give greater emphasis to the calling and installing of these great brethren as well as to their ongoing training.

We believe that the work will prosper if Melchizedek Priesthood leaders are given more visibility and recognition in their respective assignments. Members of the ward need to know who they are. We feel it would add dignity to the office of an elders quorum president or a high priests group leader if they were given greater visibility and recognition. (89–04)

Home Teaching

Home teaching is a way to show our faithfulness. What greater opportunity comes to us to show our priesthood faithfulness than to participate in home teaching? In so doing we truly demonstrate our love for our fellowmen by bringing to their homes spiritual and material help. (71–06, p. 99)

Member Activation

Members as well as leaders are responsible for the forward movement of the Church. As leaders we must help the members of our group realize that it is just as much the task of a member, to help the group reach its goals, as it is the task of the formal leader. (66–02)

The saving of souls is serious business. Remember that statistics represent people—individuals endowed with the blessing of agency. We urge you to respect that gift of agency. The work of the priesthood is to be done "only by persuasion, by long-suffering, by gentleness and meekness, and by love unfeigned" (D&C 121:41).

Please do not look upon the work of the mission of the Church as a regimented program. Seeking after the lost, the wayward, and the straying is the Lord's business. (90–02)

We have a priesthood responsibility to go after those who are lost. The Prophet Joseph Smith significantly altered one verse in the Joseph Smith Translation [of Luke 15:4–7]. It reads: "What man of you, having an hundred sheep, if he lose one of them, doth not leave the ninety and nine, *and go into the wilderness after that which is lost*, until he find it?" (JST, Luke 15:4; emphasis added.)

That translation suggests that the shepherd leave his secure flock and go out into the wilderness—that is, go out into the world after him who is lost. Lost from what? Lost from the flock where there is protection and security. I hope the message of that parable will be impressed on each of us who has priesthood responsibility. (86–01, p. 8)

We should help those who have lost their way. What should we do to help those who have lost their way in the wilderness?

Because of what the Master has said about leaving the ninety-nine and going into the wilderness to seek the one that is lost, and because of the invitation of the First Presidency to those who have ceased activity or have been critical to "come back," we invite you to become involved in saving souls. Reach out to the less active and realize the joy that will come to you and those you help if you and they will take part in extending invitations to come back and feast at the table of the Lord.

The Lord, our Good Shepherd, expects us to be his under-shepherds and recover those who are struggling or are lost. We can't tell you how to do it, but as you become involved and seek inspiration, success will result from efforts in your areas, stakes, and wards. (86–01, p. 9)

The whole purpose of the Church is to qualify individuals to return to the presence of God. The whole purpose of the Church operating smoothly at the local level is to qualify individuals to return to the presence of God. That can only be done by their receiving the ordinances and making covenants in the temple. (87–02)

The ordinances and covenants are to help us come unto Christ. We hope you can see that by emphasizing the mission of the Church in a three-fold manner, we are leading toward one objective for each individual member of the Church. That is for all to receive the ordinances of the gospel and make covenants with our Heavenly Father so they may return to his presence. That is our grand objective. The ordinances and covenants are the means to achieving that divine nature that will return us into his presence again. . . .

Keep in mind the purpose: to invite all to come unto Christ. . . .

I testify, my brethren and sisters, to his divinity and power to save those who will come to him with broken hearts and contrite spirits. Through the ordinances and his Holy Spirit, each individual may become clean. (87–02)

The purpose of activation is to restore people to their covenants to the Savior. We must ever remember to what end and purpose we labor in these efforts to activate a person to the gospel. It is to restore them again to their covenants with our Lord and Savior Jesus Christ. (88–02)

Christmas 2002

Dear Associate:

We are pleased to present to you this book of teachings of President Howard W. Hunter. As you read and study his teachings, we hope that you will be inspired to accept his invitation to "live with ever-more attention to the life and example of the Lord Jesus Christ, especially the love and hope and compassion he displayed" (*The Teachings of Howard W. Hunter,* 44).

We also affirm the reality of the Redeemer's mission and matchless sacrifice and testify that He is "the way, the truth, and the life" (John 14:6).

We extend our sincere gratitude for all that you do to assist in this great work. May the Savior's love and peace be with you at this special season and throughout the coming new year.

Sincerely,

The First Presidency

We have a responsibility to invite those who have strayed to come back. We now ask you as priesthood leaders and undershepherds of the Lord's flock to join us in inviting those who have transgressed or been offended to come back. To those who are hurt and struggling and afraid, we say let us stand by you and dry your tears. To those who are confused and assailed by error on every side, we say come to the God of all truth and the Church of continuing revelation. Come back. Feast at the table laid before you in The Church of Jesus Christ of Latter-day Saints and strive to follow the Good Shepherd who has provided it. (94–10)

Our efforts in activation are to save souls. Over the years the Church has made some monumental efforts to recover those who are less active because of their preoccupation with the world, neglect by Church leaders, and willful rebellion. And all to what end? It is to save the souls of our brothers and sisters and see that they have the ordinances of exaltation. (94–10)

19

LEADERSHIP AND FOLLOWING THE BRETHREN

Effective Leadership

A leader's resolution should be to do his very best. When we are called to service, there should also be an unqualified resolution to do our very best. Three things should be included in this resolution.

1. The determination to give the time, energy, and talents as may be required to produce the expected results. If we are not willing to give of ourselves fully, the program is bound to suffer. . . .

2. The determination to seek for greater excellence. It is not sufficient to perform only the task which is assigned to us, but to constantly seek ways and means to do it better and more effectively. We should always remember that our assignment is to result in increasing spirituality. . . .

3. The determination to serve others without thought of praise. Every parent knows that seldom are efforts rewarded by praise from children, and this is true of leaders. . . . Every leader must understand the principle that "it is more blessed to give than receive," and know that joy in leadership comes from service to others and by tasks well done. (63–01)

There are two kinds of leadership in the world. We have two kinds of leadership—one we see demonstrated in the world today, leadership from an unrighteous plan for unrighteous purposes. In contrast to this, there is a good leadership, a leadership for good in the world of which you are a part. We must be more than leaders. We must be leaders with direction and purpose that we might give others vision and determination to do right and to do good; otherwise we will be overwhelmed by an unrighteous leadership which has been demonstrated even before the foundations of this world. . . . Our leadership must be directed in the lines of righteousness that we might bring to the world our influence for good. (61–05)

Leaders need the spirit of their calling. The prime question we may ask ourselves as we work at being leaders is this: "Will what I am about to do help the group in moving toward its goals or purposes?" . . .

We may study and work hard, yet there will be a deficiency unless we have the spirit of our calling. You may possess a wealth of ideas and information—you may know the program perfectly—you may have the ability to teach and direct and to show others how, but the great attribute which will make you successful as a leader is to have the spirit of your calling. (66–02)

Leaders of youth inspire gratitude. I have a feeling of gratitude for the leaders of youth who follow the example of the Lord, having a faith and trust in young people, and who envision in them the spark of goodness and greatness and are willing to help them find the way. (67–03)

A good leader must first be a good follower. We can never be a leader in life until we first learn to be a good follower and follow rules. (62–00)

Following Church Leaders

The Latter-day Saints can avoid spiritual famine. Most important is the fact that down through its history, including this very day, the Church has had a prophet, seer, and revelator. At the head of the Church is Jesus Christ, who directs his prophet. . . . His counselors and the members of the Council of the Twelve . . . are also prophets, seers, and revelators. The . . . members of the Church do not have to listen to an uncertain trumpet. They can believe the voice of their leaders, knowing they are guided by the Lord. . . .

Hundreds are going daily from the darkness and uncertainty of unbelief and disbelief into the eternal life of the gospel by having faith, complying with the law of repentance, and accepting of baptism. Their lives are made bright and luminous by the gift of the Holy Ghost, and their souls are lifted up by their service to God and man.

There is hope—God does live—and there is a believable voice to those who have faith and the will to believe. Certainly we live in a day of famine, as described by Amos, when "they shall run to and fro to seek the word of the Lord, and shall not find it" (Amos 8:12). Nevertheless, in what appears to be a spiritual famine, there are many who have found a spiritual abundance. (72–03, p. 65)

We need loyalty if we are to have the spirit of unity. I have always been grateful I had the privilege of attending the Solemn Assembly in the Tabernacle when David O. McKay was sustained as President of the Church. Prior to that time, President J. Reuben Clark had served as first counselor to President Grant and to President Smith, and David O. McKay had served as second counselor. On that occasion, when the names of the General Authorities were presented to us, the name of David O. McKay was presented as President of the Church, then followed Stephen L Richards as first counselor and J. Reuben Clark as second counselor. Many people present had questions in their minds regarding the order in which the counselors were named. It might have appeared to some that this was a demotion for President Clark.

President McKay explained his reasons for calling President Richards as first counselor, and when President J. Reuben Clark was called upon to address the conference, he made a significant statement. I would like to read it to you because it is impressive and teaches us a great lesson: "In the service of the Lord, it is not where you serve, but how. In The Church of Jesus Christ of Latter-day Saints, one takes the place to which one is duly called, which place one neither seeks nor declines. I pledge to President McKay and to President Richards the full, loyal, devoted service to the tasks that may come to me, to the full measure of my strength and abilities, and so far as they will enable me to perform them, however inadequate I may be." (In Conference Report, April 1951, p. 154.)

Those are the words of a great man. Those are the words that exemplify a great principle in Church government. . . . There is a unity when we are loyal to one another. Unless we are loyal, the principles of the priesthood cannot be served. There is nothing we cannot do or accomplish if we have the spirit of loyalty and unity— unity of purpose, loyalty to those who preside over us, loyalty to the cause we represent. (54–03)

If we follow the counsel of Church leaders we will not be led astray. If we follow the advice, counsel, and teachings of the leaders of the Church in their instruction to us, we will not go amiss in that which is important for our own personal salvation and exaltation. (59–02)

The principle of sustaining is important. Anyone who has come close enough to the Church to be able to observe finds that one of the distinguishing features is that we support and sustain those who have been called to preside and those who are in authority. . . .

When the bishop of the ward or the president of the branch is presented to us for our sustaining vote, we raise our hands in a body. He might not have been our choice personally, but because he was called under the influence of prayer and through the direction of revelation, we feel that we must support and sustain so there might be unity and harmony. We raise our hands to sustain and then in our prayers, we ask the Lord to bless and sustain him. I am sure the revelation, given to the Prophet in the early days of the Church, that we sustain is a true principle of the kingdom.

The principle doesn't apply in the Church only; it is a principle by which we conduct the affairs of our own families. A wife must support her husband by her sustaining attitude in his responsibilities, in his business affairs, in his conduct of the family, and in those offices in which he serves in the Church. A man cannot serve adequately unless he has that sustaining influence of the one who is his wife. He sustains her also in those responsibilities which are hers in the affairs of the household and of the children.

Children must sustain their parents as parents sustain the children. When we have this kind of unity in the family, we prosper and grow strong and there is love and affection; then we commence to understand the admonition of the Lord that we love one another—that we sustain one another. When we can do this in our families, petty contentions seem to disappear, love prospers, and we have a sweet association. (79–06)

The unity of the Brethren should increase your testimony. I only wish that you could have the same privilege that I have each week of meeting with the Twelve and the First Presidency in the upper room of the temple. I think if you could catch the vision of the great harmony there is at the top of the Church by men who love each other and would give their lives if called upon for the thing which they so firmly believe, that it would increase your testimony. (62–00)

The Role of the Prophet and General Authorities

What is the definition of a prophet, seer, and revelator? The terms *prophet* and *seer* and *revelator* are often used interchangeably and are thought by many to be one and the same thing. They are not the same, however. These three terms have separate and distinct meanings.

Dr. John A. Widtsoe defines a prophet as a teacher—one who expounds truth. "He teaches . . . [truth . . . as] revealed by the Lord to man; and under inspiration explains it to the understanding of the people" (John A. Widtsoe, *Evidences and Reconciliations* [Salt Lake City: Bookcraft, 1960], p. 257). The word *prophet* is often used to designate one who receives revelation and direction from the Lord. Many have thought that a prophet is essentially a fore-teller of future events and happenings, but this is only one of the many functions of a prophet. He is a spokesman for the Lord.

A seer is one who sees. This does not mean that he sees through his natural eyes but rather through spiritual eyes. The seeric gift is a supernatural endowment. Joseph was like unto Moses, the ancient seer, who saw God face to face, but he explains how he saw him in these words: "But now mine own eyes have beheld God; but not my natural, but my spiritual eyes, for my natural eyes could not have beheld; for I should have withered and died in his presence; but his glory was upon me; and I beheld his face, for I was transfigured before him" (Moses 1:11).

We should not suppose that to see spiritually is not to see literally. Such vision is not fancy or imagination. The object is actually beheld, but not with the natural eyes. . . .

By the power of the Holy Ghost, certain persons, sent to the earth for that purpose, are able to see and behold the things which pertain to God. "A seer can know of things which are past, and also of things which are to come, and by them shall all things be revealed" (Mosiah 8:17). In short, he is one who sees, who walks in the light of the Lord with spiritual eyes opened and quickened by the power of the Holy Ghost. Moses, Samuel, Isaiah, Ezekiel, and many others were seers, because they were privileged to have a nearer view of the divine glory and power than other mortals have.

A revelator makes known something presently unknown or which has been known previously by man and taken from his memory. Always the revelation deals with truth, and always it comes with the divine stamp of approval. Revelation is received in various ways, but it always presupposes that the revelator has so lived and conducted himself as to be in tune or harmony with the divine spirit of revelation, the spirit of truth, and therefore capable of receiving divine messages. (60–11)

Only the President of the Church receives revelation for the entire Church. Only the President of the Church has the right to receive revelations for the entire Church or to give official interpretations of the scriptures or the doctrines of the Church:

"No one shall be appointed to receive commandments and revelations in this church excepting [the President of the Church], for he receiveth them even as Moses" (D&C 28:2). (83–06)

The responsibility of a prophet is to lead God's children. A prophet is one who has been called and raised up by the Lord to further God's purposes among his children. He is one who has received the priesthood and speaks with authority. Prophets are teachers and defenders of the gospel. They bear witness of the divinity of the Lord Jesus Christ. Prophets have foretold future happenings, but this is not the most important of their responsibilities, although it may be some evidence of prophetic power.

Righteous leadership has been needed in each dispensation of time, and God chose prophets for this purpose long before they came to this mortal existence (see Abraham 3:23, Jeremiah 1:5). (63–06, p. 1098)

For spiritual safety we must heed the prophet's warnings. As the prophets from the beginning to the present day pass in review before our memory, we become aware of the great blessing which comes to us from the influence of a living prophet. History should teach us that unless we are willing to heed the warnings and follow the teachings of a prophet of the Lord, we will be subject to the judgments of God. (63–06, pp. 1099–1100)

The organization of the First Quorum of the Seventy was important. [Previously quotes D&C 107:33–34, 38.] With the rapid growth of the Church and the heavy demands on the Twelve to provide leadership and administration and teach all nations, it becomes clear why the Lord has directed the building up of the First Quorum of the Seventy. The recent decision [1978] to do so by the First Presidency and the Quorum of the Twelve reminds us of an interesting historical parallel of an episode recorded by Luke in the Acts of the Apostles. The foreign or Hellenistic Jews in Jerusalem were complaining that their widows were being neglected and not taken care of like the widows of the native Jews. When the apostles heard of this murmuring, a significant thing happened:

"Then the twelve called the multitude of the disciples unto them, and said, It is not reason that we should leave the word of God, and serve tables.

"Wherefore, brethren, look ye out among you seven men of honest report, full of the Holy Ghost and wisdom, whom we may appoint over this business.

"But we will give ourselves continually to prayer, and to the ministry of the word." (Acts 6:2–4.)

In other words, the Twelve told the meeting that it was not reasonable for them to leave their important office of teaching the gospel to provide for the daily welfare of the widows and serve their tables. There were other good men who could look after these duties so the Twelve could continue to devote themselves to the charge of teaching the gospel to all persons. The result of the decision to call others to assist with the details was this: "And the word of God increased; and the number of the disciples multiplied in Jerusalem greatly; and a great company of the priests were obedient to the faith" (Acts 6:7).

In the brief statement of that episode, we learn these facts: First, that the Twelve determined they were not to "serve tables" or, in other words, occupy their time in the details of administration; second, they appointed seven men, "full of the Holy Ghost and wisdom," to look after the day-to-day needs; third, the Twelve then devoted their energies to the "ministry of the word"; fourth, the word of God increased, and the gospel was carried to greater numbers.

In December 1978, the First Presidency and Quorum of the Twelve made a similar determination that it was no longer advisable for the Twelve to occupy their time in the details of administration of the many Church departments. They delegated seven men, designated as the presidents of the First Quorum of the Seventy, to give supervision to these details so that the Twelve could devote their full energies to the overall direction of the work, and, as directed by the Doctrine and Covenants, "To build up the church, and regulate all the affairs of the same in all nations."

I fully believe that in the near future we will see some of the greatest advancements in spreading the gospel to all nations that have ever taken place in this dispensation or any previous dispensation. I am sure that we will be able to look back in retrospect—as a result of the decision recently made—and record as Luke did, "And the word of God increased." (79–01, pp. 34–35)

The prophet is an instrument in the hands of the Lord. Jesus Christ is the head of this Church. He leads it in word and deed. I am honored beyond expression to be called for a season to be an instrument in his hands to preside over his Church. But without the knowledge that Christ is the head of the Church, neither I nor any other man could bear the weight of the calling that has come. (94–14, p. 7)

The Lord has established the divine pattern by which the Church is governed. I am overcome with gratitude for the revelations which have established the marvelous system by which his Church is governed. Each man who is ordained an Apostle and set apart as a member of the Quorum of the Twelve is sustained as a prophet, seer, and revelator. The First Presidency and the Quorum of the Twelve Apostles, called and ordained to hold the keys of the priesthood, have the authority and responsibility to govern the Church, to administer its ordinances, to teach its doctrine, and to establish and maintain its practices.

When a President of the Church is ill or not able to function fully in all of the duties of his office, his two counselors, who, with him, comprise a Quorum of the First Presidency, carry on the work of the Presidency. Any major questions, policies, programs, or doctrines are prayerfully considered in council by the counselors in the First Presidency and the Quorum of the Twelve Apostles. No decision emanates from the First Presidency and the Quorum of the Twelve without total unanimity among all concerned.

Following this inspired pattern, the Church will move forward without interruption. The governance of the Church and the exercise of the prophetic gifts will always be vested in those apostolic authorities who hold and exercise all of the keys of the priesthood. (94–14, p. 7)

Prophets were chosen before they were born. Those who rejected the Savior when he came to earth with the declaration that he was the Son of God said of him: "Is not this the carpenter's son?" (Matthew 13:55.) When Joseph announced that he had seen a vision and had seen the Father and the Son, the query came to the minds and lips of the neighbors, the ministers, and the townspeople: "Is not this the farmer's son?" Christ was persecuted and put to death, but time has been his vindicator. As with the carpenter's son, so it has been with the farmer's son. History does not indicate that prophets have been chosen for their great learning, for their acquisition of worldly culture, or for their social position. They have been called from the more humble stations of life; they were chosen before they were born. (60–11)

An Apostle is a special witness of Christ. In our day the Lord has again called Apostles. These Apostles have been ordained as special witnesses of Christ in all the world. They know of the reality of Christ and his redemption with a certainty born of the Spirit. . . .

As an ordained Apostle and special witness of Christ, I give to you my solemn witness that Jesus Christ is in fact the Son of God. He is the Messiah prophetically anticipated by Old Testament prophets. He is the Hope of Israel, for whose coming the children of Abraham, Isaac, and Jacob had prayed during the long centuries of prescribed worship. . . .

He suffered in the Garden of Gethsemane and died on the cross, giving his sinless life as a ransom for every soul who enters mortality. He did in very fact rise from the dead on the third day, becoming the firstfruits of the resurrection and overcoming death. . . .

It is by the power of the Holy Ghost that I bear my witness. I know of Christ's reality as if I had seen with my eyes and heard with my ears. I know also that the Holy Spirit will confirm the truthfulness of my witness in the hearts of all those who listen with an ear of faith. (83–05, pp. 69, 70)

20

TEMPLE AND FAMILY HISTORY WORK

Temple Ordinances for the Dead

We must do temple work for ourselves and our own kindred dead. The building of temples has deep significance for ourselves and mankind, and our responsibilities become clear. We must accomplish the priesthood temple ordinance work necessary for our own exaltation; then we must do the necessary work for those who did not have the opportunity to accept the gospel in life. Doing work for others is accomplished in two steps: first, by family history research to ascertain our progenitors; and second, by performing the temple ordinances to give them the same opportunities afforded to the living.

Yet there are many members of the Church who have only limited access to the temples. They do the best they can. They pursue family history research and have the temple ordinance work done by others. Conversely, there are some members who engage in temple work but fail to do family history research on their own family lines. Although they perform a divine service in assisting others, they lose a blessing by not seeking their own kindred dead as divinely directed by latter-day prophets. . . .

I have learned that those who engage in family history research and then perform the temple ordinance work for those whose names they have found will know the additional joy of receiving both halves of the blessing.

Furthermore, the dead are anxiously waiting for the Latter-day Saints to search out their names and then go into the temples to officiate in their behalf, that they may be liberated from their prison house in the spirit world. All of us should find joy in this magnificent labor of love. (95–01, pp. 4–5)

We must seek after our dead. If the Jews were to answer for the blood of their progenitors because they neglected the salvation of their dead, then may we not in propriety ask if we will not also have to answer for the blood of our righteous dead if we neglect these ordinances in their behalf? (See *History of the Church* 4:599.)

From Joseph Smith the Prophet to our present-day prophet, seer, revelator, and president . . . we have been admonished to seek after our dead and perform for them those ordinances which are needed for their exaltation in the celestial kingdom of God.

The Prophet Joseph Smith said, "Those Saints who neglect it in behalf of their deceased relatives, do it at the peril of their own salvation" (*History of the Church* 4:426). (67–06)

Work for the dead is a great responsibility. Those engaged in genealogical research and temple work are giving of themselves, their time and their efforts, for the benefit of others. They find the joy and happiness which must have come to the Savior after his resurrection, knowing what he had accomplished for the benefit of his brothers and sisters. . . .

We have a great obligation, a great responsibility. There is no question in my mind but what the Prophet knew exactly what he was talking about when he stated that this is our "greatest responsibility." (*Teachings of the Prophet Joseph Smith*, p. 356.) I presume that no greater blessing comes to us than to become saviors of others. This is our privilege and opportunity if we would accept of it. (62–11)

We are foreordained to be saviors on Mount Zion. We who live in this day are those whom God appointed before birth to be his priesthood representatives on the earth in this dispensation. We are the House of Israel. In our hands lie the sacred powers of bringing to pass the ennobling work of being saviors on Mount Zion in the latter days. (66–05)

Laboring for our dead is the most important work we can do. Let us help all members of the Church qualify for and receive these heavenly blessings [of the temple]. After they have received them, teach them the high and holy opportunities that await them if they will search out their genealogies and minister for their loved ones in the Houses of the Lord. The Lord expects each of us to qualify as a savior on Mount Zion and labor in love for our families who have passed beyond the veil not having had the privilege of accepting the principles of the gospel.

I desire to bear my witness to you that this work is of God and is the most important work that he has revealed for the salvation of mankind as has been so clearly explained by the Prophet Joseph Smith (see *History of the Church* 6:313). (66–05)

We are obligated to do the work for our dead. Through the means of revelation in the beginning of the re-establishment of the Church, there was clarified to all future members what Joseph Smith the Prophet later declared was our most important responsibility while in this world (see Joseph Smith—History 1:36–39). He further emphasized this truth by saying: "It is necessary that those who are going before and those who come after us should have salvation in common with us; and thus hath God made it obligatory upon man" (*History of the Church* 6:313).

Man was not given a choice to do this work when and if he pleased, or when he had time, but the work was given as an obligation to be filled. (67–06)

Temple work breaks down the barriers of the grave. Genealogical research and temple ordinance work are required of every Latter-day Saint. . . .

Our dead are anxiously waiting for this people to search out their names and then go into the temples of God to officiate for them, that they may be liberated from their prison house in the spirit world. The keys of this great power given to the Prophet Joseph Smith are with us today. This power, to officiate for the dead, breaks down the barriers of the grave. All of us should find the joy of this magnificent labor of love. (71–01, p. 5)

Ordinances can be performed vicariously. In centuries past many people have lived and died without knowing of the gospel. How will they be judged in the absence of this knowledge? Peter said that after Christ was crucified, "but quickened by the Spirit

. . . he went and preached unto the spirits in prison" (1 Peter 3:18–19). Then he adds, "For for this cause was the gospel preached also to them that are dead, that they might be judged according to men in the flesh, but live according to God in the spirit" (1 Peter 4:6). Thus, those who die without knowledge of the gospel will have the opportunity to hear and accept it and to accept baptism.

Does it seem reasonable that persons who have lived upon the earth and died without the opportunity of baptism should be deprived throughout eternity? Is there anything unreasonable about the living performing the baptisms for the dead? Perhaps the greatest example of vicarious work for the dead is the Master himself. He gave his life as a vicarious atonement, that all who die shall live again and have life everlasting. He did for us what we could not do for ourselves. In a similar way we can perform ordinances for those who did not have the opportunity to do them in [their] lifetime. (71–08, p. 71)

The great work of this dispensation is to seal family units. Not only may baptisms be performed for the dead, but endowments; also sealings, by which wives become eternal companions to husbands and their children are sealed to them as a family. The sealing of family units can be continued until the family of God is made perfect. This is the great work of the dispensation of the fullness of times, by which the hearts of the fathers are turned to the children and the hearts of the children to the fathers (see D&C 110:13–15). The uniting and redemption of the family of God was the divine plan before the foundations of the earth were laid. (71–08, pp. 71–72)

Temple and family history work must be hastened. We who live in this day are those whom God appointed before birth to be his representatives on earth in this dispensation. We are of the house of Israel. In our hands lie the sacred powers of being saviors on Mount Zion in the latter days.

With regard to temple and family history work, I have one overriding message: This work must hasten. The work waiting to be done is staggering and escapes human comprehension. Last year we performed proxy temple endowments for about five and a half million persons, but during that year about fifty million persons died. This might suggest futility in the work that lies before us, but we cannot think of futility. Surely the Lord will support us if we use our best efforts in carrying out the commandment to do family history research and temple work. (94–18, p. 64)

Temple work must expand. We know that our responsibility is for every son and daughter of God even though they have left mortality. No one really dies. The great work of the temples, and all that supports it, must expand. It is imperative! (77–01)

Why do we perform baptisms for the dead? When . . . people from all over the world . . . come and look at our temples, the question these people most frequently ask is, what are the ordinances that are performed in temples?

In response, we often first explain the ordinance known as baptism for the dead. We note that many Christians believe that at the time of death, our status before the Lord is determined for all eternity, for did not Christ say to Nicodemus, "Verily, verily, I say unto thee, Except a man be born of water and of the Spirit, he cannot enter into the kingdom of God" (John 3:5)? Yet we know that many people have died without the ordinance of baptism, and thus, according to Christ's statement to Nicodemus, they would be eliminated from entering into the kingdom of God. This raises the question, is God just?

The answer is, of course God is just. It is evident that the Savior's statement to Nicodemus presupposes that baptisms may be done for those who have died who have not been baptized. Latter-day prophets have told us that baptism is an earthly ordinance that can be performed only by the living. How then can those who are dead be baptized if only the living can perform the ordinance? That was the theme of the Apostle Paul's writing to the Corinthians when he asked this question:

"Else what shall they do which are baptized for the dead, if the dead rise not at all? why are they then baptized for the dead?" (1 Corinthians 15:29).

In fact, as we study ecclesiastical history, we find that baptism for the dead was practiced by the early Christians. There was vicarious work for the dead at that time, and there is today. Indeed, vicarious work is not something new or strange to us. We remember that the Savior himself in a vicarious manner atoned for the sins of all mankind. Today, baptisms are again performed by the living in behalf of individuals who have died, as is also the laying on of hands for the bestowal of the gift of the Holy Ghost for these same deceased people. These ordinances for the deceased, however, are performed only in the house of the Lord. (95–01, p. 2)

Importance of the Temple and Temple Ordinances

In the ordinances of the temple, the foundations of the eternal family are sealed in place. Our first great purpose in this work is to save ourselves and our own families. The Lord has not given me the responsibility to save your family, but he has given me the responsibility of saving my own family. My own family will be the unit through which I may obtain exaltation and continuation of the seeds. . . .

Joseph Smith the Prophet said: "If you have power to seal on earth and in heaven, then we should be wise. The first thing you do, go and seal on earth your sons and daughters unto yourself, and yourself unto your fathers in eternal glory." (*History of the Church* 6:253.) This is the real work of what we call priesthood genealogy. It is the work of saving and exalting all of Father's children if they will hearken unto his commandments and obey his laws and ordinances.

Our purpose is to see that every man lives worthy of receiving, in the House of the Lord, those great and marvelous blessings which will associate him in an eternal family unit. We long to see the day when every Melchizedek Priesthood bearer will love his wife, and the family which he expects or may now have, enough to stand together in sacred places and be sealed together as an eternal family. When this has been performed in our own behalf, we should then labor unceasingly to provide these same blessings for those who gave us the opportunity to be born into mortality and died without the privilege of hearing these sacred truths. (66–05)

The temple is the gate of heaven. Even the temple where Jesus taught and worshipped in Jerusalem was built in such a way as to establish respect for and devotion to the Father. . . . God must be approached carefully, respectfully, and with great preparation.

Never did Jesus show a greater tempest of emotion than in the cleansing of the temple. . . .

The reason for the tempest [Christ's fury against the money exchangers in the temple] lies in just three words: "My Father's house." It was not an ordinary house; it was the house of God. It was erected for God's worship. It was a home for the reverent heart. It was intended to be a place of solace for men's woes and troubles, the very gate of heaven. (77–04, pp. 52–53)

The temple should be our ultimate earthly goal. Let us truly be a temple-attending and a temple-loving people. We should hasten to the temple as frequently, yet prudently, as our personal circumstances allow. We should go not only for our kindred dead but also for the personal blessing of temple worship, for the sanctity and safety that are within those hallowed and consecrated walls. As we attend the temple, we learn more richly and deeply the purpose of life and the significance of the atoning sacrifice of the Lord Jesus Christ. Let us make the temple, with temple worship and temple covenants and temple marriage, our ultimate earthly goal and the supreme mortal experience. (95–01, p. 5)

The endowment consists of instructions and covenants. The endowment is another ordinance performed in our temples. It consists of two parts: first, a series of instructions, and second, promises or covenants that the person receiving the endowment makes—promises to live righteously and comply with the requirements of the gospel of Jesus Christ. The endowment is an ordinance for the great blessing of the Saints—both living and dead. Thus it is also an ordinance performed by the living in behalf of deceased individuals; it is performed for those for whom baptismal work has already been performed. (95–01, p. 2)

There is no work equal to that done in the temple. The objective of family history work is to make the blessings of the temple available to all people, living and dead. As we attend the temple and perform work for the dead, we acquire a deep sense of alliance with God and a better understanding of his plan for the salvation of the human race. We learn to love our neighbors as ourselves. Truly there is no work equal to that done in the temple. (94–18, p. 65)

The temple helps us to see clearly our priorities in life. In the temple we learn the things of eternity and make sacred covenants which, if fulfilled, will bring us back into the presence of the Lord. The knowledge we gain in this holy house helps us to see clearly our priorities in life and our place among the purposes of God. (94–19)

It is in the temple where things of heaven and earth are joined. Temples are sacred for the closest communion between the Lord and those receiving the highest and most sacred ordinances of the holy priesthood. It is in the temple that things of the earth are joined with the things of heaven. In a letter written by Paul to the Saints at Ephesus, he made a very significant statement about the day in which we live, that there would be a gathering of all things in Christ that are on earth and in heaven:

"Having made known unto us the mystery of his will . . .

"That in the dispensation of the fullness of times he might gather together in one all things in Christ, both which are in heaven, and which are on earth" (Ephesians 1:9–10).

The doctrine that all creation will ultimately be united in Christ is the major theme of Paul's epistle. The things of earth will become one with the things of heaven. The great family of God will be united through the saving ordinances of the gospel. Vicarious work for the dead and ordinances for the living are the purposes of temples. (94–13, p. 2)

Parents must teach their children the importance of the temple. Let us share with our children the spiritual feelings we have in the temple. And let us teach them more earnestly and more comfortably the things we can appropriately say about the purposes of the house of the Lord.

Let us prepare every missionary to go to the temple worthily and to make that experience an even greater highlight than receiving the mission call. Let us plan for and teach and plead with our children to marry in the house of the Lord. Let us reaffirm more vigorously than we ever have in the past that it does matter where you marry and by what authority you are pronounced man and wife. (94–16, p. 88)

The temple is at the center of the mission of the Church. All of our efforts in proclaiming the gospel, perfecting the Saints, and redeeming the dead lead to the holy temple. This is because the temple ordinances are absolutely crucial; we cannot return to God's presence without them. (94–16, p. 88)

The temple should be the great symbol of our membership. We should strive to "be partakers of the divine nature." Only then may we truly hope for "peace in this world, and eternal life in the world to come" (D&C 59:23).

In that spirit I invite the Latter-day Saints to look to the temple of the Lord as the great symbol of your membership. It is the deepest desire of my heart to have every member of the Church worthy to enter the temple. It would please the Lord if every adult member would be worthy of—and carry—a current temple recommend. The things that we must do and not do to be worthy of a temple recommend are the very things that ensure we will be happy as individuals and as families. (94–14, p. 8)

I also invite the members of the Church to establish the temple of the Lord as the great symbol of their membership and the supernal setting for their most sacred covenants. (94–03, p. 14)

Personal blessings come from temple attendance. And we again emphasize the personal blessings of temple worship and the sanctity and safety that are provided within those hallowed walls. It is the house of the Lord, a place of revelation and of peace. As we attend the temple, we learn more richly and deeply the purpose of life and the significance of the atoning sacrifice of the Lord Jesus Christ. Let us make the temple, with temple worship and temple covenants and temple marriage, our ultimate earthly goal and the supreme mortal experience. (94–16, pp. 87–88)

We should be a temple-attending people. Let us be a temple-attending people. Attend the temple as frequently as personal circumstances allow. Keep a picture of a temple in your home that your children may see it. Teach them about the purposes of the house of the Lord. Have them plan from their earliest years to go there and to remain worthy of that blessing.

If proximity to a temple does not allow frequent attendance, gather in the history of your family and prepare the names for the sacred ordinances performed only in the temple. This family research is essential to the work of the temples, and blessings surely will come to those who do that work. (94–14, p. 8)

Every adult member should be temple worthy. The Lord desires that his people be a temple-motivated people. It would be the deepest desire of my heart to have every member of the Church be temple worthy. I would hope that every adult member would be worthy of—and carry—a current temple recommend, even if proximity to a temple does not allow immediate or frequent use of it.

Let us be a temple-attending and a temple-loving people. Let us hasten to the temple as frequently as time and means and personal circumstances allow. Let us go not only for our kindred dead, but let us also go for the personal blessing of temple worship, for the sanctity and safety which is provided within those hallowed and consecrated walls. The temple is a place of beauty, it is a place of revelation, it is a place of peace. It is the house of the Lord. It is holy unto the Lord. It should be holy unto us. (94–13, p. 5)

We can make the temple the symbol of our discipleship. To have the temple indeed be a symbol unto us, we must desire it to be so. We must live worthy to enter the temple. We must keep the commandments of our Lord. If we can pattern our life after the Master, and take his teaching and example as the supreme pattern for our own, we will not find it difficult to be temple worthy, to be consistent and loyal in every walk of life, for we will be committed to a single, sacred standard of conduct and belief. . . .

The ability to stand by one's principles, to live with integrity and faith according to one's belief—that is what matters. That devotion to true principle—in our individual lives, in our homes and families, and in all places that we meet and influence other people—that devotion is what God is ultimately requesting of us. It requires commitment—whole-souled, deeply held, eternally cherished commitment to the principles we know to be true in the commandments God has given. If we will be true and faithful to the Lord's principles, then we will always be temple worthy, and the Lord and his holy temples will be the great symbols of our discipleship with him. (94–13, p. 5)

Temple attendance creates spirituality. Temple attendance creates spirituality. It is one of the finest programs we have in the

Church to develop spirituality. This turns the hearts of the children to their fathers and the hearts of the fathers to their children (Malachi 4:6). This promotes family solidarity and unity. (68–01)

There are many blessings of temple attendance. Several things are accomplished by our attendance at the temple—we comply with the instructions of the Lord to accomplish our own ordinance work, we bless our families by the sealing ordinances, and we share our blessings with others by doing for them what they cannot do for themselves. In addition to these, we lift our own thoughts, grow closer to the Lord, honor our priesthood, and spiritualize our lives.

When I contemplate the temple, I think of this definition:

"The temple is a place of instruction where profound truths pertaining to the Kingdom of God are unfolded. It is a place of peace where minds can be centered upon things of the Spirit and the worries of the world can be laid aside. In the temple we take covenants to obey the laws of God, and promises are made to us, conditioned upon our faithfulness, which extend into eternity." (*The Priesthood and You*, p. 293.) (71–06, p. 100)

Temple worthiness is the key to building the kingdom. Earlier this month I began my ministry by expressing a deep desire to have more and more Church members become temple worthy. As in Joseph [Smith's] day, having worthy and endowed members is the key to building the kingdom in all the world. Temple worthiness ensures that our lives are in harmony with the will of the Lord, and we are attuned to receive his guidance in our lives. (94–05, pp. 62–63)

All are encouraged to hold a current temple recommend. We hope that every adult member of the Church is worthy of and carries a current temple recommend. Even our young people can qualify to receive a temple recommend to do baptisms for the dead. We encourage the adults present, who have received the ordinances of the temple, to live according to the covenants they have made. We should be obedient to the sacred and eternal promises made with the Lord in his holy house.

To those who have not received their temple blessings, or who do not hold a current temple recommend, may I encourage you in humility and love to work towards the day that you can enter into the house of the Lord. He has promised those who are faithful to their covenants, "If my people will hearken unto my voice, and unto the voice of my servants whom I have appointed to lead my people, behold, verily I say unto you, they shall not be moved out of their place" (D&C 124:45). (94–11)

Blessings come from regular temple attendance. May I encourage the adults who have current temple recommends to attend the temple on a regular basis. Make sure in your planning that you include a visit to the temple as often as personal circumstances will allow. I promise you that your personal spirituality, relationship with your husband or wife, and family relationships will be blessed and strengthened as you regularly attend the temple. (94–11)

Increased temple attendance will result in stronger families. Many of our temples are still underused, except on weekends. Much work remains to be done, and we continue to encourage you to attend the temple as often as is feasible. Stronger marriages, more attentive parents, and more faithful children will come as a result of following this counsel. (95–02)

Temples are special places of worship. If we define a temple as a building where God is worshipped, then every cathedral, church, chapel, synagogue, or religious meetinghouse would qualify; but a temple is not just a building in which one worships. Temples have always served a special purpose. As we read history we learn that they were extraordinary places, consecrated to the most solemn rituals of worship, and were never used as ordinary places of worship or for the general assembly. (69–06)

Family History Work

The Lord has had a hand in bringing forth technology to accelerate family history work. In recent years we have begun using information technology to hasten the sacred work of providing

ordinances for the deceased. The role of technology in this work
has been accelerated by the Lord himself, who has had a guiding
hand in its developments and will continue to do so. However, we
stand only on the threshold of what we can do with these tools. I
feel that our most enthusiastic projections can capture only a tiny
glimpse of how these tools can help us and of the eternal consequences of these efforts. (94–18, p. 65)

Our family history records should be accurate. In our [family
history] work, we are establishing records that will be used for
years to come. We believe in the divine purpose of searching our
pedigrees and must be willing to employ every resource in making
our record complete, accurate, and factual for the purpose of accomplishing the responsibility of effective temple work, and to
compile a record upon which others can rely. (73–04)

We have a responsibility to both the living and the deceased.
Although genealogical research is an interesting and fascinating
pastime, requiring specialized knowledge and skills, let us never
forget the ultimate purposes for being engaged in its pursuit. We
have been given a responsibility to the living and the dead. The
Prophet Joseph Smith, in an epistle to the Church dated September 6, 1842, had this to say: "And now, my dearly beloved
brethren and sisters, let me assure you that these are principles in
relation to the dead and the living that cannot be lightly passed
over, as pertaining to our salvation. For their salvation is necessary
and essential to our salvation, as Paul says concerning the fathers—
that they without us cannot be made perfect—neither can we
without our dead be made perfect." (D&C 128:15.)

This seems to say that it is not sufficient for a woman to be
sealed to her husband only, without continuing the sealing chain
to the families that have gone before who had no opportunity to
accomplish these ordinances in their lifetimes. The law has been
clearly given to us. The family is a divine institution, and we are
charged with the responsibility of chaining our ancestral families,
by the sealing power, to the great family of God. Thus our task is
to take the steps necessary to diligently, conscientiously, and accurately identify our ancestors by research, and then to complete the
prescribed ordinances in the House of the Lord so that our obligation is accomplished. (73–04)

The purpose of genealogical research is to increase temple work. The priesthood genealogical program is just simply to get people to the temples and keep them going there.

Brother Widtsoe termed temple service as a labor of love. First, because we love Jesus Christ. It is his house. We want to serve him and keep his commandments. Second, we love our progenitors—those who made it possible for us to come here. We want to make these ties eternal, these ties which will bind us to them and to the family of God. Now this is why we are interested in searching genealogy. (68–01)

The Spirit motivates people to do genealogy. We have talked about genealogy for years. Beyond just talking about it, what do we do about it to motivate people to want to do it? We know that preaching will not accomplish the objective. We must touch their hearts in order to make them want it. This was what Alma was talking about. . . .

"And now behold, I ask of you, my brethren of the church, have ye spiritually been born of God? Have ye received his image in your countenances? Have ye experienced this mighty change in your hearts?" (Alma 5:14.)

Now this is the thing we are talking about, changing people, changing attitudes, changing hearts. (68–01)

One purpose of family history records is to bring us to a knowledge of our ancestors. One reason for our attempt to preserve the vital records of mankind is because we believe that we should learn of "things both in heaven and in the earth, and under the earth; things which have been, things which are, things which must shortly come to pass; things which are at home, things which are abroad; the wars and perplexities of the nations, and the judgments which are on the land; and a knowledge also of countries and of kingdoms" (D&C 88:79). It would appear that the reason for constant mistrust and misunderstanding among nations is that the boundary lines of countries have blinded us to the extent that we have forgotten that each person who lives upon the earth has something in common with another. The Genealogical Society has always fostered the idea that wars would become unheard of, men would beat their swords into plowshares, and the earth could easily become a delightful garden for all men if we could only learn enough about each other and something about our origin to understand and appreciate one another.

Another prominent reason for the Genealogical Society to devote its efforts toward the gathering and preserving of mankind's records is the literal belief that men were created by a beneficent Father whose purpose was to create man that he might have joy (see 2 Nephi 2:25). The joy we speak of is the joy of family association. With this in mind we seek out our family lines so we may know who our ancestors and family members are. Thus the work goes on until we have identified all our people as far back as records are available. (69–07)

More spiritual growth occurs when we do temple work for our own ancestors. Our Saints will get more spiritual growth from the temple if they submit names for temple ordinance work, then go to the temple and do that work for their kindred dead themselves. (69–04)

No priesthood bearer is exempt from family history research and temple work. [Family history] research and temple work go hand in hand because genealogical data is necessary for the ordinances to be performed in the house of the Lord. This sacred work has not been entrusted to any other people in the world, and no priesthood bearer is exempt from its obligation. (71–06, p. 99)

Temple and family history work must hasten. With regard to temple work and genealogy I have one overriding message: *This work must hasten.* All that I say today will revolve around that message. President Kimball has told us that it is on his mind constantly, and it should be so with the rest of us as well. The pressing urgency of this work needs to get into the minds of the leaders and members out in the stakes and missions and the wards and branches.

I have a fear that the urgency will not be felt until the Saints really sense that it is *their* responsibility to make the work go forward. Many of our people feel that genealogy and temple work depends upon Church headquarters for its success. It is easy to understand this attitude because in many ways the Genealogical Department has acted as if *it* were responsible for the work. This was necessary for a time, but we have come to a point where there should be a change. (77–01)

21

SPREADING
THE GOSPEL

Our responsibility is to teach the gospel to all nations. The Church, being the kingdom of God on earth, has a mission to all nations.

"Go ye therefore, and teach all nations, baptizing them in the name of the Father, and of the Son, and of the Holy Ghost:

"Teaching them to observe all things whatsoever I have commanded you" (Matthew 28:19–20).

These words from the lips of the Master know no national boundaries; they are not limited to any race or culture. One nation is not favored above another. The admonition is clear—"teach all nations." (79–01, p. 33)

Member Responsibilities

Member involvement in missionary work is more important than the number of full-time missionaries. Generally, the number of converts in a geographical area is more related to the number of Church members than to the number of full-time missionaries. Of all the things we can do to lift dramatically the number of convert baptisms, more effective involvement of Church members in missionary work tops the list. (*Ensign*, May 1979, p. 104)

We should focus on making the saving ordinances available to all mankind. Our efforts focus on making the saving covenants and ordinances of the gospel available to all mankind: to the nonmember through our missionary work; to the less-active through fellowshipping and activation efforts; to active members through participation and service in the Church, and to those who have passed beyond the veil through the work of redemption for the dead. (90–02)

We must not hide behind self-made walls to avoid missionary work. As we try to understand the spirit of reconciliation sweeping the globe and to give it meaning within the gospel context, we have to ask ourselves: Could this not be the hand of the Lord removing political barriers and opening breaches in heretofore unassailable walls for the teaching of the gospel, all in accord with a divine plan and a divine timetable? Surely taking the gospel to every kindred, tongue, and people is the single greatest responsibility we have in mortality. In 1974, President Spencer W. Kimball, speaking on this theme, said: "I can see no good reason why the Lord would open doors that we are not prepared to enter." He concluded by saying that the doors to nations would open "when we are ready for them." *(Ensign,* October 1974, p. 7.)

As the walls in Eastern Europe, the Soviet Union, Africa, China, India, South America, and many other parts of the world come tumbling down, the corresponding need for more missionaries to fulfill the divine commission to take the gospel to all the earth will certainly go up! Are we ready to meet that contingency?

To satisfy the new demands being made upon us in this great missionary work of the last days, perhaps some of us (particularly the older generation whose families are raised) need to take stock to determine whether "walls" that we have built in our own minds need to come down.

For example, how about the "comfort wall" that seems to prevent many couples and singles from going on a mission? How about the "financial wall" of debt that interferes with some members' ability to go, or the "grandchildren wall," or the "health wall," or the "lack of self-confidence wall," or the "self-satisfied wall," or the "transgression wall," or the walls of fear, doubt, or complacency? Does anyone really doubt for a minute that with the help of the Lord he or she could bring those walls crashing down?

We have been privileged to be born in these last days, as opposed to some earlier dispensation, to help take the gospel to all the earth. There is no greater calling in this life. If we are content to hide behind self-made walls, we willingly forgo the blessings that are otherwise ours. The Lord in modern-day revelation explains the great need:

"For behold the field is white already to harvest; and lo, he that thrusteth in his sickle with his might, the same layeth up in store that he perisheth not, but bringeth salvation to his soul" (D&C 4:4).

An all-wise Heavenly Father goes on to explain in that same revelation the qualifications that we need to be good missionaries. Knowing full well of our weaknesses and of our reservations as we stand before the huge gate of our self-made wall, he reassures us that divine help to overcome all obstacles will be forthcoming if we will only do our part, with the simple promise:

"Ask, and ye shall receive; knock, and it shall be opened unto you" (D&C 4:7).

May the Lord bless us that the walls of our minds may not obstruct us from the blessings that can be ours. (90–05, pp. 8–11)

We should be grateful for the opportunity to teach the gospel. There has never been a period in the history of the Church when missionaries were not called and set apart to fulfill missions somewhere in the world. Each one of us who is here today has been introduced to the Church directly or indirectly through the efforts of some humble missionary. We should be grateful for this—for the part our forefathers played in it and for the opportunity we have today in teaching the gospel to others. . . .

A great opportunity is ours to pass on to others the message of the gospel which has come into our lives. The Lord has said, "It is more blessed to give than to receive" (Acts 20:35). We feel real joy and pleasure when we have the privilege of giving to someone else. This principle is exemplified when we go to the baptismal service on the Saturday preceding Fast Sunday and see converts to the Church, who have been taught by stake missionaries or others, go into the waters of baptism. Great is the joy and satisfaction of the person who first gave them an understanding of the gospel. Many opportunities are ours, each day we live, to spread the Gospel of Jesus Christ. (54–02)

The greatest missionaries are those who live their religion. Some of the greatest missionaries the Church has are those who live their religion and teach it to others by their actions. (55–01)

We should all be missionaries. What a wonderful thing it will be when the work is carried throughout the world, and the message of the gospel of Jesus Christ taken to all people. We should devote ourselves to missionary effort and not be content to let the missionaries carry the banner alone. As members of the Church, it is incumbent upon each one of us to teach the message of the restoration of the gospel of Jesus Christ to everyone with whom we associate, by example and by righteous living. . . . Shouldn't we be willing to devote ourselves, our time, and our energy in the Lord's work? (58–03)

Our responsibility is to share the gospel. The program of the Church is a vital, vibrant force in the lives of its members. We hold the conviction that this is the Church of Christ, which imposes upon us the responsibility of sharing that witness with others. (71–02, p. 1)

We must love all people and teach them the gospel. To our brothers and sisters of all nationalities: We bear solemn witness and testify that God has spoken in our day and time, that heavenly messengers have been sent, that God has revealed his mind and will to a prophet, Joseph Smith. And, as Andrew beckoned his brother, Simon Peter, to come and hear the Messiah, we say to one and all: "Come and see" (see John 1:35–42).

As our Father loves all his children, we must love all people— of every race, culture, and nationality—and teach them the principles of the gospel that they might embrace it and come to a knowledge of the divinity of the Savior. Only they are favored who keep his commandments. (79–01, p. 36)

How does the Atonement relate to missionary work? What does the Atonement have to do with missionary work? Any time we experience the blessings of the Atonement in our lives, we cannot help but have a concern for the welfare of our brethren.

Examples abound in the Book of Mormon that illustrate this principle. When Lehi partook of the fruit of the tree, symbolic of partaking of the Atonement, he said, "I began to be desirous that my family should partake" (1 Nephi 8:12). When Enos experienced his conversion and received a forgiveness of his sins, because of his faith in Jesus Christ he said, "I began to feel a desire for the welfare of my brethren, the Nephites" (Enos 1:9). Then he prayed for the Lamanites, the implacable enemies to the Nephites. Then there is the example of the four sons of Mosiah—Ammon, Aaron, Omner, and Himni—who received a forgiveness of sins through the Atonement and then labored for years among the Lamanites to bring them to Christ. The record states that they could not bear the thought that any soul should perish (see Mosiah 28:3).

This supernal example of the covenanted one desiring to share the gospel with others is best illustrated by the example of Alma the Younger [quotes Alma 36:12–24]. . . .

A great indicator of one's personal conversion is the desire to share the gospel with others. For this reason the Lord gave an obligation to every member of the Church to be missionaries. (88–04)

Missionary work is one way to take upon us the Savior's name. We are to stand as witnesses of God at all times in all places, even until death [see Mosiah 18:8–9]. We renew that covenant during the sacrament when we covenant to take the name of Christ upon us.

Missionary service is one important way we take upon ourselves his name. The Savior has said if we desire to take upon us his name, with full purpose of heart, we are called to go into all the world and preach his gospel to every creature (see D&C 18:28). . . .

Those of us who have partaken of the Atonement are under obligation to bear faithful testimony of our Lord and Savior. For he hath said, "I will forgive you of your sins with this commandment—that you remain steadfast in your minds in the solemnity and the spirit of prayer, in bearing testimony to all the world of those things which are communicated unto you" (D&C 84:61). (88–04)

Qualified members should serve missions. We are thrilled with the continuing expansion of the Church worldwide. Our membership now exceeds nine million people who live in 156 countries and territories. Our missionary force [1995] is 47,300 strong in 303 missions, and more missionaries are needed. We call upon every able, worthy young man of eligible age to respond to a call from the Lord to serve as a full-time missionary. Many more mature couples are needed to assist as full-time ambassadors of the

Lord. While full-time missionary work is primarily a priesthood calling, young women who reach the age of twenty-one and have no immediate plans for marriage are also welcome to serve as full-time missionaries. (95–02)

Preparation for Missions

More missionaries are needed. Earlier prophets have taught that every able, worthy young man should serve a full-time mission. I emphasize this need today. We also have great need for our able, mature couples to serve in the mission field. Jesus told his disciples, "The harvest truly is great, but the labourers are few: pray ye therefore the Lord of the harvest, that he would send forth labourers into his harvest" (Luke 10:2). (94–16, p. 88)

Our challenge is to teach the need of faith. We don't go into the mission field with tangible, concrete evidence that Joseph Smith was instructed by heavenly visitors. If everything could be proven by positive evidence there would be no need for faith. If the element of faith is taken out of the gospel, the plan is destroyed. Faith becomes the bridge by which the unbeliever can cross over and become a believer. Your challenge is to teach faith. There will be times in your teaching when your eyes will meet the eyes of your investigator. In this moment of interest you will say to him, "I know this is the truth." Your testimony will pierce him like an arrow, just as your hearts have been pierced, not by tangible evidence, but bridged by faith. (73–02)

Missionary success depends on your level of spirituality. Our assignment as missionaries is to plant faith and testimony in the hearts of other people. Some of you will be greatly successful and I will tell you why. You have been set apart as a personal representative of the Lord to teach his children in the mission field. I don't know of a higher calling that could come to any person. You are set apart from all worldly things, worldly influences and thoughts, to a higher plateau—a spiritual plateau where you can live, think, act, and portray the gospel to others. When you can do this and leave all worldly influences behind and live on the new higher plateau, you will be successful. (73–02)

Young men—plan for a mission. Boys—plan for a mission. The Lord expects you to fill an honorable mission for the Church. President [David O.] McKay has said that filling a mission is an obligation which every one of us owes to the Lord. We should plan for it. (62–06)

Missionary Work

Dress and grooming standards are important before and after missions. I compliment you on the dress and grooming standards which you uphold as ambassadors of the Lord. I hope that you recognize the importance of this matter, not only while you are serving as missionaries, but throughout your lives. Too often we see returned missionaries who forget the standard of excellence they once had in this regard. As General Authorities, we are striving to set a standard that the members of the Church can follow in this matter. (94–09)

A mission is a great learning experience. What a magnificent opportunity is yours to serve as full-time missionaries of the Lord Jesus Christ. I feel a missionary who has taken leave from educational or employment pursuits to serve in the mission field will have no regret for such a decision. If you take advantage of the lessons there are to learn, there is no university anywhere in the world that will teach you the lessons you will learn in the mission field.

Employers are constantly looking for men and women who are above average, who are a head higher than others. Those who are effective as missionaries and have learned these lessons have less difficulty finding employment and are more likely to be successful in their professions. I think every missionary in the Church ought to be above average. If you take advantage of the lessons you can learn in the mission field, you will be. (94–09)

To be successful, missionaries must avoid worldly things. Remember that you have a relatively short time to serve the Lord full-time, and the rest of your life to think about it.

You can't be a part of worldly things and also carry out your role as a representative of the Lord. The two are not compatible.

Your objective has been clearly defined for you. From the day you were set apart, you were charged to not be of the world, meaning that you were transferred then from worldly things into a spiritual climate for the duration of your mission. If you have found yourself in this new climate, you are on your way. If you haven't, then you've got some work to do. Satan is always present and will do everything he can to hinder and block and defeat. We encourage you as companionships to help each other in this matter. Two persons dedicated, living in faith, and being prayerful can be an awesome force in the work of the Lord. (94–09)

Missionaries must obey mission rules and learn to be good followers. We encourage you to obey the mission rules. Follow them specifically all the way through and you will be successful. You will learn that to be a leader you must first learn to be a good follower. You will never learn the principles of leadership until you learn how to follow them. You may feel that you know a lot more than your senior companion, but he is your senior companion and you should follow him in righteousness. This is one of the greatest lessons in life—to learn how to follow your district leader and zone leader and especially your mission president. (94–09)

Missionaries should do all they can to ensure that converts remain faithful. You may recall that the sons of Mosiah were so effective in their teaching, with "the power of God working miracles in them," that "as many of the Lamanites as believed in their preaching, and were converted unto the Lord, never did fall away" (Alma 23:6). We trust that your efforts will be as fruitful. As you teach potential converts, make sure they have a sufficient foundation of faith, understanding, conviction, and commitment to keep themselves faithful when they become members of the Church. Please be certain there is coordination with the ward mission leader and stake missionaries so that new converts are warmly fellowshipped by ward or branch members. (94–09)

The parable of the sower is really a parable of hearers. In the parable [of the sower, Matthew 13:1–8], the different soils on which the seed fell become the subject—four different kinds of soil describing four classifications of persons.

As the sower cast the seed, some fell along the path by the

wayside and the birds came and devoured it. The seed on the smooth, hard pathway didn't get to the soil where it could grow, and it soon disappeared. When minds are closed and tramped down by other forces, like the path along the wayside, they lose their receptiveness to new truth and new ideas. Thoughts or ideas that could have been useful are snatched away.

Other seed cast by the sower fell on rocky ground where the soil was thin. It immediately sprang up, but because the roots could not go deep, it withered away when the sun came out. Every day we see casualties of those whose roots are in shallow soil and they become withered. People often become rootless when they migrate to what appears to be the greener pastures of large industrial cities. They become cut off from the nourishment of homes and family and the familiar places. New life may spring up quickly with the enthusiasm of a fresh beginning, whether it be a change of business activity or other circumstances, but unless roots can be sent deep for nourishment, the sun of adversity may wither the quick growth.

Some of the seed which was sown fell among the thorns. The roots were deep but there were so many weeds that the growing grain was strangled and yielded no fruit. Many of us become strangled by the extraneous things that overcome us. I heard a story of a boy who read a list of the number of deaths from various diseases and he was surprised to learn of so many under the heading of miscellaneous. He had never heard of such a disease, yet millions have died from it. We become buried under a landslide of miscellaneous things that close in about us until we are strangled. One needs to know where he is going and conscientiously free himself of obstructions and the domination of influences that make him a servant instead of a master.

After telling of the seed that fell along the path and was snatched away by the birds, the seed that lodged in the rocks, and that which fell where there were weeds, the parable tells of seed that found good soil in which to grow. There is a lesson in the proportion—three kinds of bad soil and only one kind of soil that is favorable. Sowing involves the loss of some seed, but the fact that the greater bulk of attention was given to the poor soils should not obscure the emphasis placed on the fact that good soil produces abundant fruit.

This is not really a parable of the sower, but rather a parable of four classes of hearers identified with four different kinds of soil. Its very purpose is to show how various listeners respond. There are as many differences in those who listen as there are differences in the soils in which seed is sown. (73–03)

Fear is a hindrance to missionary work. Why should we fear any person in the world when we have such a great thing to give them? But it has been fear that has prevented missionaries from doing their best in the field, and you felt this when you first went out. . . . Fear is engendered by the adversary, and when we once cast aside fear and find what our potential is, that means there's just no limitation. (62–00)

Missionaries, don't return and settle back into old ways. Now the time's going to come when your missions will be terminated and you will be given an honorable release. As soon as you come out of the mission field, a new life ahead, it's going to be a change. . . . You won't feel at ease at first, coming back into civilian life, because it's going to be different, different than what you had expected. . . . There's going to be a question as to whether you are going to come home and fall in with the rest, or whether you're going to keep the enthusiasm for missionary work that you have today. Oh, I'd be disappointed in any elder here who came home . . . and settled back into old ways. (62–00)

22

THE GOSPEL
IN OUR LIVES

Character

A successful life requires commitment to divine principles. A successful life, the good life, the righteous Christian life requires something more than a contribution, though every contribution is valuable. Ultimately it requires commitment—whole souled, deeply held, eternally cherished commitment to the principles we know to be true in the commandments God has given. (90–03, p. 62)

An understanding heart is a power that could cure the ills of the world. If the Lord was pleased because of that which Solomon had asked of him [an understanding heart; see 1 Kings 3:6–13] surely he would be pleased with each of us if we had the desire to acquire an understanding heart. This must come from conscious effort coupled with faith and firm determination. An understanding heart results from the experiences we have in life if we keep the commandments of God. . . .

The ills of the world would be cured by understanding. Wars would cease and crime disappear. The scientific knowledge now being wasted in the world because of the distrust of men and nations could be diverted to bless mankind. Atomic energy will destroy unless used for peaceful purposes by understanding hearts.

We need more understanding in our relationships with one another, in business and in industry, between management and labor, between government and the governed. We need understanding in that most important of all social units, the family; understanding between children and parents and between husband and wife.

Marriage would bring happiness, and divorce would be unknown if there were understanding hearts. Hatred tears down but understanding builds up.

Our prayer could well be as was Solomon's, "Lord, give me an understanding heart." (62–01, p. 443)

Having a spiritual consciousness is the ultimate enrichment in life. Every human being has the natural instinct to seek and acquire food for himself. But when he comes to the point that he earnestly and sincerely desires that there be food for others, his life has been enriched by what might be termed a moral or a spiritual consciousness. . . . The development of moral or spiritual consciousness or real religion is, of course, the ultimate enrichment in life. It transforms human life from the earth to the skies, from the clod to the cloud, from the beast to the god. (73–05)

Poor is the man who does not have compassion for his fellowman. Poor, indeed, and destitute is the man who disclaims being religious because he does not have sufficient love for his fellowmen to be concerned and have compassion. The Lord will say: "Inasmuch as ye did it not to one of the least of these, ye did it not to me.

"And these shall go away into everlasting punishment: but the righteous into life eternal." (Matthew 25:45–46). (78–04, p. 13)

Ambition must be properly directed if we are to find true success. A man must have the ambition to succeed if he is to keep faith with himself, but ambition must be properly directed, not associated with evil, and the motivation must come from a worthy purpose. Joy and happiness in life are promised to those who have the right kind of success. We know that eternal joy is the purpose of man's creation, for the Lord said: "Men are, that they might have joy" (2 Nephi 2:25).

If we properly approach success, we can obtain the greatest rewards; we can be genuinely concerned for other people; we can carry forward a good cause. (79–04)

Courtesy is the medium of social exchange. Courtesy is not the whimsical invention of a past generation, but a long-standing manner of life. . . .

Courtesy is a habit that is useful toward success in any business or project. It provides the ability to work efficiently and pleasantly with other people. The aggressive, domineering personality, careless of the rights or even the susceptibilities of others, is an extreme to be avoided at all costs. It is worth making an effort to treat everyone you meet with such consideration that his memory of you will be pleasant.

Indifference is the most hurtful affront we can give people. They crave personal recognition. It is ill-mannered to ignore people in the home or office, to pass others without greeting, to look at them with blank eyes, to talk around them as if they were not there. Here is one way everyone can contribute to the pleasantness of life: by recognizing people as fellow human beings with a greeting or a good-bye or a wave of the hand. Courtesy, after all, consists of little things. It is lacking in any masterful quality, but it wins friends in the collisions and minor adjustments of daily life. No one is likely to say "thank you" too often.

We think of money or gold as the medium of economic exchange, but courtesy, defined as gentleness and politeness, is the settled medium of social exchange. (81–02)

Achieving true greatness is a long-term process. The achievement of true greatness is a long-term process; it may involve occasional setbacks. The end result may not always be clearly visible, but it seems that it always requires regular, consistent, small, and sometimes ordinary and mundane steps over a long period of time.

True greatness is never a result of a chance occurrence or a one-time effort or achievement. It requires the development of character. It requires a multitude of correct decisions for the everyday choices between good and evil that Elder Boyd K. Packer spoke about when he said, "Over the years these little choices will be bundled together and show clearly what we value." (*Ensign,* November 1980, p. 21.) Those choices will also show clearly what we are. (82–02, p. 20)

Gospel Living

Let us be Latter-day Saints all the time. It is the only way to lasting happiness. (62–04)

Living one's religion should bring joy. Religion is often regarded as opposed to pleasure, but God's reason for creating man is that he might have joy.

"Adam fell that men might be; and men are, that they might have joy" (2 Nephi 2:25).

There is no reason why joy should be turned out-of-doors before religion can come in. Many people think of a religious person as one with a sad countenance and draped in black, but this is not so. When the angel of the Lord appeared to the shepherds to announce the birth of the Savior, he said:

"Fear not: for, behold, I bring you good tidings of great joy, which shall be to all people" (Luke 2:10).

Christ, himself, said:

"I am come that they might have life, and that they might have it more abundantly" (John 10:10).

Joy existed in the pre-existence before the foundations of the earth were laid: "And all the sons of God shouted for joy" (Job 38:7).

Peter, in his epistle, speaking of the appearance of Jesus Christ, said:

"Though now ye see him not, yet believing, ye rejoice with joy unspeakable and full of glory" (1 Peter 1:8).

There is nothing sad or gloomy about a person who accepts the truths of the gospel and incorporates these principles in his daily living. God wants all of his children to be joyous and glad, and we can have this blessing if we are willing to keep his commandments and live by his word in all that we do. (61–07, p. 962)

The gospel should influence us in business, at home, and at church. There are those who would say don't mix business with religion. Business is as much living our religion as is our home life and our church life. It's part of living. (90–04)

Mormonism is a way of life. Mormonism is not a Sunday religion. It's not a religion confined to a chapel where people sing and pray, and where preaching is done. It is our way of life, for we were placed here as God's children for a specific purpose, and everything we do is in response to carrying out that purpose. (58–02)

The gospel is a call to action. The best goals, the best of friends, and the best of opportunities are all meaningless unless they are translated into reality through our daily actions.

Belief must be realized in personal achievement. Real Christians must understand that the gospel of Jesus Christ is not just a gospel of belief; it is a plan of action. His gospel is a gospel of imperatives, and the very nature of its substance is a call to action. He did not say "observe" my gospel; he said "live" it! He did not say, "Note its beautiful structure and imagery"; he said, "Go, do, see, feel, give, believe!" The gospel of Jesus Christ is full of imperatives, words that call for personal commitment and action—obligatory, binding, compulsory. (67–02, p. 101)

The gospel provides long-range as well as short-term objectives. There must be reasons for action and guides for action in the form of real goals and objectives. That is why we are given a plan of salvation and progression. Because the gospel is a long-range—even an eternal—goal, it must be broken up into short-range, immediate objectives that can be achieved today and tomorrow and the next day. The gospel imperatives constitute an immediate challenge to action in our lives right now, today, as well as a plan for action eternally. (67–02, p. 101)

Success in life comes by setting and working toward definite goals. In order to accomplish the things we desire and for which we have been set apart, we must have positive and definite goals in mind. Success in life, school, marriage, business, or any other pursuit doesn't come by accident, but as the result of a well-defined plan and a concentrated effort to bring about a realization of the plan. (56–02)

It is essential that we put gospel imperatives into action. If the gospel of Jesus Christ is truly to become a part of ourselves, then there are several things we must keep in mind in putting the gospel imperatives into action.

First, it is essential to remember that it is more important to be able to *think* and hence to *act* in terms of gospel principles and teachings than it is to merely memorize gospel facts. Remember the injunction from Proverbs: "Wisdom is the principle thing; therefore get wisdom: and with all thy getting get understanding" (Proverbs 4:7). Solomon's great blessing was "an understanding heart." We should study gospel principles with the purpose of understanding how they apply and may be used in our life today, not just to be able to remember them.

Second, don't be afraid to put them into action. Courage—and this is as true of spiritual courage as it is of physical courage—is not acting in the absence of fear. Courage is acting in spite of fear. If we stood tall in the gospel, we would soon find that it is easier to act than it is to remain idle or to cower in a corner.

Third, remember that our attitudes are most important tools to success. Knowledge is power only when it is used constructively. We should extend a positive belief in the gospel into a positive belief in our own ability to live the gospel as an effective factor in our lives and in the lives of those about us. Businessmen have proven that the difference between the successful and the unsuccessful usually reduces down to a difference in attitudes. This is just as true of gospel living. "As [a man] thinketh in his heart, so is he" (Proverbs 23:7) ought to be a prime tenet in every gospel lesson.

Fourth, be assured that one kind of ability we must have is "stick-ability." No matter how good the beginning, success comes only to those who "endure to the end."

Fifth, whenever we tackle a gospel imperative, immediate goals will help us master it. Our decision to read scripture becomes quite practical when we decide to read a chapter at night before we go to sleep. We should set up long-range and eternal goals, to be sure—they will be the guides and inspiration of a lifetime; but we should not forget the countless little immediate objectives to be won tomorrow and tomorrow and tomorrow. To win and pass these objectives marks our progress toward the greater goals and insures happiness and the feelings of success along the way.

Gospel imperatives are action words challenging every Latter-day Saint to gospel living. They are the active pathway to personal participation in the laws of the gospel, and every one leads to rewards and blessings. (67–02, pp. 102–3)

Ethics alone are not sufficient. There is a great difference between ethics and religion. There is a distinction between one whose life is based on mere ethics and one who lives a truly religious life. We have a need for ethics, but true religion includes the truths of ethics and goes far beyond. True religion has its roots in the belief in a supreme being. Christian religion is based upon a belief in God the Eternal Father and in his Son Jesus Christ and in the word of the Lord as contained in scripture. Religion also goes beyond theology. It is more than just a belief in Deity; it is the practice of the belief. James E. Talmage said, "One may be deeply versed in theological lore, and yet be lacking in religious and even in moral character. If theology be theory then religion is practice; if theology be precept religion is example." (*The Articles of Faith*, p. 5.)

True religion to the Christian is demonstrated by a real belief in God and the realization that we are responsible to him for our acts and conduct. A person who lives such religion is willing to live the principles of the gospel of Christ and walk uprightly before the Lord in all things according to his revealed law. This brings to a man or a woman a sense of peace and freedom from confusion in life and gives an assurance of eternal life hereafter. The Lord said, "Man shall not live by bread alone, but by every word that proceedeth out of the mouth of God" (Matthew 4:4). A code of morals is not wholly sufficient. For the same reason man cannot be saved by bread alone, he cannot be saved by a code of ethics.

In order to be effective in one's life, religion must be a vibrant influence. It must be an influence that becomes a part of one's thinking and conduct. . . .

A true religious faith teaches us that there are certain principles that must be accepted and obeyed. We must have faith in God the Eternal Father and in his Son Jesus Christ and his atoning sacrifice. This must be followed by repentance from all sin, then baptism by immersion after the example of the Savior by one having authority, and the laying on of hands for the gift of the Holy Ghost. Other things are necessary, including a contrite spirit, a humble heart, obedience to the ordinances and principles of the gospel, and faithfulness to the end. This encompasses the choosing of right over wrong, following good, and abstaining from evil.

Ethics alone will not accomplish all these things for us, but an active religion will add to ethics the principles and ordinances of the gospel, which, if obeyed, will open the doors of eternal salvation, provided such religion is ordained of God and not of man's creation. (69–09, pp. 96–97)

Our religion should influence all we do. If religion means anything to us, it should be something that motivates our lives. I don't believe religion can be relegated to a minister's sermon for an hour on Sunday and mean anything in our lives. If it doesn't enter into our individual life—our family life—our business life—and everything that we do, then religion means little to us and it becomes merely an idol to be set in a high place and worshipped only occasionally. (71–05)

We will be held accountable for how we use our talents. The meaning of the parable [of the talents, Matthew 25:26–30] . . . is clear, and we have seen the application of its principles in our own experiences. The special talents with which we have been blessed—our intelligence, physical abilities, time, money, and the many opportunities given to us—have come from the Lord. They have been entrusted to us to be used, not for safekeeping or to be hidden away. These were given to us according to our ability to use—not for our own gain, but for the Lord's purposes here upon earth. We are like tenant farmers, who, given the use of the land, make their own selection as to the crop they will raise, and they work according to their own skill and desire to work. Some have the ability to sow, cultivate, and raise a bounteous crop, but others are less successful. There are some persons who will work hard and produce, while others, lacking initiative and desire, will fail. The day comes, however, when an accounting must be made. (71–07, pp. 170–71)

There are many who are unwilling to work for the Master. Now [in the parable of the talents] we come to the one-talent servant (see Matthew 25:26–30). We are saddened and disappointed in this part of the drama because first there was an excuse, then a display of the fear that caused him to hide the talent. He had been afraid to assume the responsibility. His attitude was one of resentment and faultfinding, saying he found the master to be a hard man, even harvesting where he had not sown. There are many in the world like this servant, idle and unwilling to work for their master—interested only in themselves. There are those who become so involved in the things of the world and their own selfish interests that they will not make the attempt or put forth the effort to magnify one little talent entrusted to them by the Lord. (71–07, p. 171)

There are two major aspects of true religion. James tells us that true religion is a devotion to God, demonstrated by love and compassion for fellowmen, coupled with unworldliness [see James 1:27]. Such a statement seems too simple to be sufficient, but in its simplicity it speaks an important truth. Restated, it may be said that true religion consists not only in refraining from evil (that is, remaining unspotted), but in deliberately and purposefully doing acts of kindness and service to others. (78–04, p. 12)

Enter ye in at the strait gate. The word "strait" being spelled s-t-r-a-i-t, meaning narrow or a restricted passage. Every worthiness has a narrow entrance. To surrender worthiness is easy, but the true way is strait and the Lord admonishes us to avoid the wide gate and enter at the narrow portal. "Enter ye in at the strait gate: for wide is the gate, and broad is the way, that leadeth to destruction, and many there be which go in thereat:

"Because strait is the gate, and narrow is the way, which leadeth unto life, and few there be that find it" (Matthew 7:13–14).

The strait gate and narrow way leadeth unto life, that is, eternal life to dwell in the presence of God. The reason that few will find the narrow way is because it requires stern self-discipline, determination, and self-denial. Not many are willing to pay the price in work and effort. Most are content to drift with the crowd and follow the easy ways of the world.

What then shall be our course? Shall we live after the manner of the world—the way that people of the world generally are in the habit of living? Or shall we overcome the world, rise above its carnal allurements, become Saints in deed, and qualify for spiritual blessings?

Shall we be a truly distinct and heaven-approved people because we have come out of the darkness of worldly living into the illuminating light of Christ? (80–02)

"Am I a true and living member?" is a question of eternal significance. On November 1, 1831, at a conference of the Church in Hiram, Ohio, the Lord revealed in the preface to the Doctrine and Covenants that this is the "only true and living church upon the face of the whole earth." Then he added, "with which I, the Lord, am well pleased, speaking unto the church collectively and not individually" (D&C 1:30). This should raise a question in our minds of eternal significance: We know that this is the true and living church institutionally, but am I a true and living member individually?

This question may appear as a play on the words of the Lord when he said this is the true and living church. When I ask, "Am I a true and living member?" my question is, am I deeply and fully dedicated to keeping the covenants I have made with the Lord? Am I totally committed to live the gospel and be a doer of the word and not a hearer only? Do I live my religion? Will I remain true? Do I stand firm against Satan's temptations? He is seeking to cause us to lose our way in a storm of derision and a tide of sophistry. We can have victory, however, by responding to that inner voice calling "stand firm!"

To answer affirmatively the question, "Am I a living member?" confirms our commitment. It means that we now and always will love God and our neighbors as ourselves. It means our actions will reflect who we are and what we believe. It means that we are every day Christians, walking as Christ would have us walk.

Living members are those who strive to have a total commitment. . . .

Living members give heed to the Spirit, which quickens the inner life. They constantly seek its direction. They pray for strength and overcome difficulties. Their hearts are not set upon the things of this world but upon the infinite. Spiritual renewal is not sacrificed for physical gratification.

Living members put Christ first in their lives, knowing from what source their lives and progress come. (87–03, pp. 16–17)

We should practice Christianity at every opportunity. How are we supposed to act when we are offended, misunderstood, unfairly or unkindly treated, or sinned against? What are we supposed to do if we are hurt by those we love, or passed over for promotion, or are falsely accused, or have our motives unfairly assailed?

Do we fight back? Do we send in an ever-larger battalion? Do we revert to an eye for an eye and a tooth for a tooth, or, as Tevye says in *Fiddler on the Roof,* do we come to the realization that this finally leaves us blind and toothless?

We all have significant opportunity to practice Christianity, and we should try it at every opportunity. (92–05, p. 18)

The gospel will change people's lives. You have seen [the gospel] change the lives of people, you've seen them change their habits and their thinking and their living. You know what it does for families; just think what it would be if all people of the world would have this same understanding, what a great change would come to the human family here upon the earth. We would live in peace and in plenty, and there would be happiness for all people who live. . . . Peace will never come to the world nor will men ever learn to live together in peace and harmony except by the principles of the restored gospel of Jesus Christ. He came into the world with the message of peace, but people have never learned to live the principles. (62–00)

We must be prepared to qualify for revelation. To qualify for revelation, we must learn to recognize the spirit of revelation, prepare our minds for spiritual things, and be virtuous and pure in heart. (83–06)

Example

Great is the man who sets an example worth following. Great is the man who so conducts himself and his affairs that if others would follow his example, the world would live on a higher plane. This today becomes your challenge. (73–05)

No time is quite as dark as when the light of the gospel is extinguished. Christ said, "Let your light so shine before men, that they may see your good works, and glorify your Father which is in heaven" (Matthew 5:16). There is no time so dark as when individuals and nations extinguish the light of the gospel of Jesus Christ. We see examples of this each day as we live and associate with others. (59–04)

We should recognize and develop our own strengths. Each person has different capabilities, and it is important to recognize them and build on them. It seldom works to our benefit when we try to be just exactly like someone else. We need models, and heroes, and ideals, but we must recognize our own strengths and develop them. (69–01)

Humility

Contrition is costly. Contrition is costly—it costs us our pride and our insensitivity, but it especially costs us our sins. (93–02, p. 64)

Meekness is the right way. What of the meek? In a world too preoccupied with winning through intimidation and seeking to be number one, no large crowd of folk is standing in line to buy books that call for mere meekness. But the meek shall inherit the earth, a pretty impressive corporate takeover—and done *without* intimidation! Sooner or later, and we pray sooner *than* later, everyone will acknowledge that Christ's way is not only the *right* way, but ultimately the *only* way to hope and joy. Every knee shall bow and every tongue will confess that gentleness is better than brutality, that kindness is greater than coercion, that the soft voice turneth away wrath. In the end, and sooner than that whenever possible, we must be more like him. (93–02, p. 64)

Pride, conceit, and vanity all contain the seeds of self-destruction. "Learn of me," [the Savior] continued, "for I am meek and lowly in heart" (Matthew 11:29). Surely the lessons of history ought to teach us that pride, haughtiness, self-adulation, conceit, and vanity contain all of the seeds of self-destruction for individuals, cities, or nations. The ashes and rubble of Chorazin, Bethsaida, and Capernaum are the silent witnesses of the Savior's unheeded warnings to that generation. Once majestic and powerful cities, they no longer exist. Would we add our names or the names of our families to such a list? No, of course not; but if we would not, we must be truly meek and lowly. (90–07, p. 18)

Humility is an attribute possessed by true Saints. Humility is an attribute of godliness possessed by true Saints. It is easy to understand why a proud man fails. He is content to rely upon himself only. This is evident in those who seek social position in fields of business, government, education, sports, or other endeavors. Our genuine concern should be for the success of others. The proud man shuts himself off from God, and when he does he no longer lives in the light. The Apostle Peter made this comment:

"Be clothed with humility: for God resisteth the proud, and giveth grace to the humble.

"Humble yourselves therefore under the mighty hand of God, that he may exalt you in due time." (1 Peter 5:5–6.) (84–02, p. 66)

Joy and Happiness

Happiness comes from serving others. He is the most happy and successful in life whose interests are coupled with giving assistance to others and helping them find the way.

The sign at the railroad crossing that warns us to stop, look, and listen could be a guide for us. Stop as we rush through life. Look for all the friendly, thoughtful, courteous things we can do, and all the little human needs we can fill. Listen to others and learn of their hopes and problems so that we will be able to contribute in little ways to their success and happiness. (60–06)

Too many are pursuing the course of temporal pleasures. We live in difficult times, in a permissive age—difficult for parents and extremely difficult for young people. There has never been a time when the evils of Satan have been more prevalent in the world. Parents are confused in trying to stem the tide of corruption. Children are confused when outside influences dictate to them that their parents are old-fashioned and that this is a new day of so-called modern freedom. They are told that in this new day they should not be restrained by a belief in God, the fables of the Bible, or a belief in a hereafter; that today is the day to live without restrictions.

Can there be any answer other than that these are the teachings of Satan? Millions of people today are pursuing the course of temporal pleasures. They seek happiness in desperation, but their broken lives are sacrificed on the rubbish heaps of a modern society. On the other hand, we observe that those willing to keep the commandments of the Lord find the real values, which the Lord promised would bring joy and happiness. (74–04, pp. 50–51)

Joy comes only by obedience. Joy commenced in the pre-existence, for it was there that "all the sons of God shouted for joy" (Job 38:7) as we are told in the book of Job. They shouted for joy because of the prospects of coming to earth and undergoing the probationary period that mortality affords us. Here in mortality men gain joy only by obedience to the gospel law. The gospel itself, as we are told in Luke, is the "good tidings of great joy" (Luke 2:10). Obtaining exaltation consists of gaining a fulness of joy; it is to "enter into the joy of the Lord" (D&C 51:19). A "fulness of joy" is found only among the resurrected, exalted beings (see D&C 93:33). The Prophet on one occasion made this statement: "Happiness is the object and design of our existence; and will be the end thereof, if we pursue the path that leads to it; and this path is virtue, uprightness, faithfulness, holiness, and keeping all the commandments of God" (*Teachings of the Prophet Joseph Smith,* p. 255).

As Latter-day Saints, have we commenced to find the joy that will come to us from day to day and from year to year, by seeking understanding of the principles of the gospel? In addition to acquiring the understanding, are we willing to devote ourselves to the principles of the gospel? Many have understanding but not the motivation to do the things which will bring blessings. There are some who stumble in living the Word of Wisdom and the law of tithing. These simple requirements should give us no problem. If we understood the joy there is ahead for us, these would be quickly complied with, and we would find ourselves contemplating and meditating upon the things which will bring us joy in our eternal lives. (59–01)

Latter-day Saints should be happy and optimistic. Of all people on the face of the earth, Latter-day Saints, with the perspective given them by the gospel, ought to be happy and optimistic. (92–01, p. 39)

Standards of the Gospel Versus the World

The Church is becoming a refuge from the world. As we become more removed from the lifestyle of the world, the Church becomes more the welcome refuge for hundreds of thousands who come each year and say, "Let us go up to the mountain of the Lord, to the house of the God of Jacob; and he will teach us of his ways, and we will walk in his paths: for out of Zion shall go forth the law, and the word of the Lord from Jerusalem" (Isaiah 2:3). (94–14, p. 9)

All around us we can see the tragic effects of modernism. Society has made a great effort to modernize the world in education, communication, travel, health, commerce, housing, and in many other ways, so as to increase the standard of living; but what has this socialization and modernization done to the family—the basic institution of society? Never before has there been greater instability. The divorce rate is higher now than at anytime in history. Modernization has transferred the responsibility of education from the family to public institutions where modern thought has become paramount and moral principles have become abandoned. The crime rate has increased alarmingly. Drug addiction, disobedience to law, increase in venereal disease, and corruption in all forms seem to be accepted. In this day of modernization, freedom of thought and action is sponsored and promoted without consideration of the responsibilities that must accompany such freedoms if society is to be stabilized. Surely we would agree that the family institution has been seriously, if not irreparably, damaged in our society. (73–06, p. 54)

Joining worthy causes alone will not enable people to reach their ultimate potential. We recognize that much good comes from individuals and organizations who reach out to remedy the ills of the world. We encourage you to follow the scriptural admonition to be anxiously engaged or actively involved in good causes in the Church and in your neighborhoods, communities, and even throughout the world (see D&C 58:27). Yet we also maintain that without taking Christ into their lives and accepting his gospel, with its saving ordinances and covenants, people will not reach their true potential in this life or in the hereafter. (92–04, p. 96)

The Real Spirit of Christmas

The real spirit of Christmas is centered in Christ. The real Christmas comes to him who has taken Christ into his life as a moving, dynamic, vitalizing force. The real spirit of Christmas lies in the life and mission of the Master. I continue with what [one] writer defines as the real spirit of Christmas:

"It is a desire to sacrifice for others, to render service and to possess a feeling of universal brotherhood. It consists of a willingness to forget what you have done for others, and to remember what others have done for you; to ignore what the world owes you . . . to close your book of grievances against the universe, and look about you for a place to sow a few seeds of happiness, and go your way unobserved." (Clarence Baird, "The Spirit of Christmas," *Improvement Era*, 23:154 [December 1919].) (72–04, p. 68)

All must mature in their view of Christmas. It has been said that Christmas is for children; but as the years of childhood fancy pass away and an understanding maturity takes their place, the simple teaching of the Savior that "it is more blessed to give than to receive" (Acts 20:35) becomes a reality. The evolution from a pagan holiday transformed into a Christian festival, to the birth of Christ in men's lives, is another form of maturity that comes to one who has been touched by the gospel of Jesus Christ. (72–04, p. 69)

Christmas is a time when we can give the greatest gifts. Christmas is a time for giving. Someone once said he couldn't think of what to give for Christmas. The next day in the mail he received an anonymous list which read:

> Give to your enemy forgiveness,
> To your opponent tolerance,
> To your friend your heart,
> To all men charity, for the hands that help
>   are holier than lips that pray,
> To every child a good example,
>   and to yourself—respect.

All of us need to follow the example of the Savior in giving these kinds of gifts. . . .

This Christmas, "Mend a quarrel. Seek out a forgotten friend. Dismiss suspicion and replace it with trust. Write a letter. Give a soft answer. Encourage youth. Manifest your loyalty in word and deed. Keep a promise. Forgo a grudge. Forgive an enemy. Apologize. Try to understand. Examine your demands on others. Think first of someone else. Be kind. Be gentle. Laugh a little more. Express your gratitude. Welcome a stranger. Gladden the heart of a child. Take pleasure in the beauty and wonder of the earth. Speak your love and then speak it again." (Adapted from an unknown author.) Christmas is a celebration, and there is no celebration that compares with the realization of its true meaning—with the sudden stirring of the heart that has extended itself unselfishly in the things that matter most. (94–20)

You can find the true spirit of Christmas by turning your heart to God. If you desire to find the true spirit of Christmas and partake of the sweetness of it, let me make this suggestion to you. During the hurry of the festive occasion of this Christmas season, find time to turn your heart to God. Perhaps in the quiet hours, and in a quiet place, and on your knees—alone or with loved ones—give thanks for the good things that have come to you, and ask that his Spirit might dwell in you as you earnestly strive to serve him and keep his commandments. He will take you by the hand and his promises will be kept. (72–04, p. 69)

SOURCES

The following is a list of 240 sermons or writings used in selecting the passages included in this book. References in the text are keyed to the four-digit codes that precede each source listing. The first two digits in the code indicate the year, and the last two digits refer to the order within that year. In many cases sermons were published in more than one place, and for the most part these duplications have been listed together under the original delivery or publication date (for example, see 87–04 or 90–06).

A few of the sermons have been published in collections of sermons by General Authorities, *Hope* (Deseret Book Co., 1988) and *Youth of the Noble Birthright* (Deseret Book Co., 1960). One book containing a collection of Howard W. Hunter's addresses has been published, entitled *That We Might Have Joy* (Deseret Book Co., 1994, cited below as MHJ). The book is a collection of 32 complete talks rather than topically arranged excerpts, as in this volume.

Sermons and Articles

41–01 "Keep the Father's Commandment." Pasadena Stake Conference, MIA Session, 23 February 1941.

45–01 "Thoughts at Christmas." Wilshire Ward, Los Angeles Stake, 23 December 1945.

51–01 "Job: A Perfect and Upright Man." Monrovia Ward, Pasadena Stake, 22 January 1951.

52–01 "Train Up a Child." Faith in Action Series, NBC Radio Network, 7 September 1952.

54–01 "The Pursuit of Knowledge." Institute of Religion, University of Southern California, 23 April 1954.

54–02 "Opportunity for Missionary Work." Conference Address, Pasadena Stake, 12 September 1954.

54–03 "There Is Strength in Unity and Loyalty." Conference Address, Pasadena Stake, 12 September 1954.

55–01 "If Ye Have Desires to Serve God." Conference Address, Pasadena Stake, 11 September 1955.

56–01 "The Restoration of the Gospel." Great Churches of Golden West Series, KNX–TX, from Los Angeles Temple and Westwood Ward, 4 March 1956.

56–02 "We Believe in You the Leaders." Southern California MIA Conference, South Gate Ward, South Los Angeles Stake, 30 June 1956.

56–03 "Things for Which We Are Thankful." Conference Address, Pasadena Stake, 25 November 1956.

57–01 "Temple Marriage, Debt, and the Sabbath." Conference Address, Pasadena Stake, 23 February 1957.

57–02 "Our Heritage from Pilgrims and Pioneers." Conference Address, Pasadena Stake, 24 November 1957.

58–01 "Marriage Ordained of God." Conference Address, Pasadena Stake, 1 March 1958.

58–02 "Thou Shalt Love Thy Neighbor." Conference Address, Pasadena Stake, 2 March 1958.

58–03 "Report of Church Activity in the World." Conference Address, Pasadena Stake, 14 September 1958.

58–04 "Faith in Youth." Conference Address, Pasadena Stake, 30 November 1958.

59–01 "Men Are That They Might Have Joy." Conference Address, Pasadena Stake, 1 March 1959.

59–02 "Missionary Work and Faithfulness." Conference Address, Pasadena Stake, 17 May 1959.

59–03 Conference Report, 11 October 1959, pp. 120–21; "What Is in My Heart." *Improvement Era* 62 (December 1959): 962.

59–04 "The Light of the World." Faith in Action Series, NBC Radio Network, 20 December 1959; *Church News* (2 January 1960): 5.

60–01 "Faith as the Foundation of Accomplishment." Institute of Religion, University of California at Berkeley, 20 February 1960; *Instructor* 95 (February 1960): 42–43.

60–02 "Dating—When and Whom." Youth Fireside Series Address, 28 February 1960; *Church News*, 5 March 1960, p. 3; *Youth of the Noble Birthright*, pp. 101–9.

60–03 "A Girl's Responsibility." Youth Fireside Series Address, 6 March

1960; *Church News*, 12 March 1960, pp. 3, 17; *Youth of the Noble Birthright*, pp. 111–19.

60–04 Conference Report, 3 April 1960, pp. 124–26; "As He Thinketh." Church of the Air Address, CBS Radio, 3 April 1960.

60–05 "Dear Are the Sheep of His Fold." General Sunday School Conference Address, 3 April 1960; *Instructor* 95 (September 1960): 288–89.

60–06 "Success Through Service." Sales Congress of Utah Association of Life Underwriters, Hotel Utah, 11 May 1960.

60–07 *Speeches of the Year 1959–1960*, pp. 1–8, "Be Not Disobedient unto the Heavenly Vision." Baccalaureate Address, Brigham Young University, 2 June 1960.

60–08 "Leaders Hold Gospel Treasures in Trust for Youth." General MIA Conference Address, 10 June 1960.

60–09 "Will Few or Many Be Saved?" Church of the Air Address, KNX, 12 June 1960.

60–10 Conference Report, 9 October 1960, pp. 107–9; "Secretly a Disciple?" *Improvement Era* 63 (December 1960): 948–49; *MHJ*, ch. 12, pp. 63–67.

60–11 "Joseph Smith the Seer." Joseph Smith Memorial Service Address, Institute of Religion, Utah State University, 15 December 1960.

61–01 Conference Report, 6 April 1961, pp. 16–18; "Put Your Hand to the Plow." *Improvement Era* 64 (June 1961): 398–99; *MHJ*, ch. 28, pp. 164–68.

61–02 *Speeches of the Year 1960–1961*, pp. 1–6, "Gifts That Money Cannot Buy." Devotional Address, Brigham Young University, 26 April 1961; also given at Rick's College, 1 September 1992.

61–03 "Business Is Dependent upon Confidence." Business Week Address, Brigham Young University, 26 April 1961.

61–04 "Funeral Services for Bessie Gudmundson Hale." Larkin Mortuary, Salt Lake City, Utah, 10 July 1961.

61–05 "Destined for Greatness." Student Leadership Conference, Brigham Young University, 10 September 1961.

61–06 "Welfare and the Relief Society." General Relief Society Conference Address, 28 September 1961; *Relief Society Magazine* 49 (April 1962): 236–39.

61–07 Conference Report, 1 October 1961, pp. 107–9; "An Everyday Religion." *Improvement Era* 64 (December 1961): 962–63.

62–00 Talk given to missionaries of Central British Mission, 19 January 1962, in the Sutton Coldfield Town Hall Building.

62–01   Conference Report, 7 April 1962, pp. 74–76; "An Understanding Heart." *Improvement Era* 65 (June 1962): 442–43; *MHJ*, ch. 32, pp. 186–90.

62–02   "Too Much Too Soon." Youth Fireside Series, 10 April 1962. Talks 62–02 thru 62–09 were produced as part of a series for the youth of the Church. Sound recordings of the talks and slides produced to accompany them were distributed to wards and stakes in November 1962.

62–03   "Mormonism Helps Us to Succeed." Youth Fireside Series, 10 April 1962.

62–04   "Our Automobile Manners." Youth Fireside Series, 10 April 1962.

62–05   "If You Date—Don't Drink." Youth Fireside Series, 10 April 1962.

62–06   "We Are a People of Destiny." Youth Fireside Series, 10 April 1962.

62–07   "Science Supports the Golden Plate Story." Youth Fireside Series, 10 April 1962.

62–08   "Except Ye Be Agreed." Youth Fireside Series, 10 April 1962.

62–09   "We Believe in Being Honest." Youth Fireside Series, 10 April 1962.

62–10   "Feed My Sheep." *Instructor* 97 (September 1962): 294–95.

62–11   "A New Day in Genealogy." Genealogical Conference Address, Salt Lake Tabernacle, 4 October 1962.

62–12   Conference Report, 5 October 1962, pp. 22–24; "To Believe Is to See." *Improvement Era* 65 (December 1962): 914–15.

62–13   *Speeches of the Year 1962–1963*, pp. 1–5, "Basic Concepts of Honesty." Devotional Address, Brigham Young University, 12 December 1962. See also "Basic Concepts of Honesty," *New Era* 8 (February 1978): 4–5.

63–01   "Who Plants the Seeds of Childhood Faith Is Serving Best of All." General Primary Conference Address, 3 April 1963.

63–02   Conference Report, 7 April 1963, pp. 104–6; "Evidences of the Resurrection." *Improvement Era* 66 (June 1963): 512–13.

63–03   "By Their Fruits Ye Shall Know Them." General Sunday School Conference Address, 7 April 1963; *Instructor* 98 (July 1963): 240–41.

63–04   "Intelligence Quickens Knowledge." Baccalaureate Address, University of California, Berkeley, California, 7 June 1963; *Church News*, 22 June 1963, pp. 17–18; also titled "Men's Greatest Need—Ability to Use Knowledge Already Acquired."

63–05   "Remember the Sabbath Day." Church of the Air Address, CBS Radio, 14 July 1963; *Church News*, 20 July 1963, p. 14; also titled

"Admonition to Keep the Sabbath Day Holy Has Never Been Retracted."

63–06   Conference Report, 6 October 1963, pp. 99–101; "Prophets in This Dispensation." *Improvement Era* 66 (December 1963): 1098–1100.

63–07   *Speeches of the Year 1963–1964*, pp. 1–7, "Pray Always." Devotional Address, Brigham Young University, 15 October 1963.

64–01   Conference Report, 4 April 1964, pp. 33–36; "The Law of the Tithe." *Improvement Era* 67 (June 1964): 475–77; also titled "The Windows of Heaven."

64–02   Conference Report, 4 October 1964, pp. 106–10; "The Road to Damascus." *Improvement Era* 67 (December 1964): 1086–88.

64–03   "The Oakland Temple: Culmination of History." Dedication Address, Oakland Temple, 17–19 November 1964; *Improvement Era* 68 (February 1965): 140–42.

65–01   "Formula for a Great Teacher." General Primary Conference Address, 2 April 1965.

65–02   Conference Report, 5 April 1965, pp. 55–58; "And God Spake All These Words." *Improvement Era* 68 (June 1965): 510–12.

65–03   Conference Report, 3 October 1965, pp. 111–15; "Organization of the Church of Christ." *Improvement Era* 68 (December 1965): 1145–47.

66–01   *Speeches of the Year 1965–1966*, pp. 1–11, "The Law of the Harvest." Devotional Address, Brigham Young University, 8 March 1966.

66–02   "To Have the Spirit of One's Calling Makes Dynamic Leaders." General Primary Conference Address, 5 April 1966.

66–03   Conference Report, 6 April 1966, pp. 46–49; "Motivations for Good: Fear, Duty, Love." *Improvement Era* 69 (June 1966): 515–17.

66–04   Conference Report, 30 September 1966, pp. 14–17; "Where Is Peace?" *Improvement Era* 69 (December 1966): 1104–5; *MHJ*, ch. 6, pp. 27–31.

66–05   "An Appeal to Do Genealogical Research." General Priesthood Genealogy Conference Address, 30 September 1966.

67–01   "Sacredness of the Call to Primary Leadership." General Primary Conference Address, 5 April 1967.

67–02   Conference Report, 9 April 1967, pp. 115–18; "Gospel Imperatives." *Improvement Era* 70 (June 1967): 101–3; *MHJ*, ch. 22, pp. 131–37.

67–03 "Faith in Youth." General MIA Conference Address, 25 June 1967.

67–04 Dedication Address, Goteborg Chapel, Goteborg, Sweden, 10 September 1967.

67–05 Dedication Address, Malmo Chapel, Malmo, Sweden, 11 September 1967.

67–06 "Importance of Temple Work." Regional Representatives Seminar Address, 27 September 1967.

67–07 Conference Report, 29 September 1967, pp. 11–14; "Is a Church Necessary?" *Improvement Era* 70 (December 1967): 44, 46–47.

67–08 *Speeches of the Year 1967–1968*, pp. 1–7, "Anniversary of Founder's Day." Devotional Address, Brigham Young University, 10 November 1967.

67–09 "How to Preside at and Conduct General Church Meetings." General Priesthood Board Meeting, 22 November 1967.

68–01 Regional Representatives Seminar Talk, 3 April 1968. Topic is the priesthood genealogy program.

68–02 "Seek Spiritual Maturity." General Primary Conference Address, 4 April 1968.

68–03 Conference Report, 6 April 1968, pp. 63–66; "We Owe Allegiance to Sovereignty." *Improvement Era* 71 (June 1968): 79–81.

68–04 "We Dare to Be Different." Staff and Faculty Address, Brigham Young University, 17 September 1968.

68–05 Conference Report, 6 October 1968, pp. 138–42; "Blessed Are Those Who Have Not Seen." *Improvement Era* 71 (December 1968): 105–8.

68–06 *Speeches of the Year 1968–1969*, pp. 1–11, "Gifts That Money Can Buy." Devotional Address, Brigham Young University, 15 October 1968; also titled "The Things That Money Can Buy."

69–01 "The Priesthood." Priesthood Board Address, 6 February 1969.

69–02 "The Children's Hour." General Primary Conference Address, 2 April 1969.

69–03 "Opening Remarks of Elder Howard W. Hunter." Regional Representatives Seminar, 3 April 1969.

69–04 "Genealogy." Regional Representatives Seminar Address, 3 April 1969.

69–05 Conference Report, 6 April 1969, pp. 135–39; "The Reality of the Resurrection." *Improvement Era* 72 (June 1969): 106–8.

69–06 "Temples—An Echo from the Past." Convocation Address, World Conference on Records, 3 August 1969.

69–07 "The Microfilming Program of the Genealogical Society." Welcome

Address, World Conference on Records, Salt Lake City, 6 August 1969.

69–08 "Temple Ordinances." Fourth Annual Priesthood Genealogical Research Seminar, 12 August 1969.

69–09 Conference Report, 5 October 1969, pp. 111–13; "Ethics Alone Is Not Sufficient." *Improvement Era* 72 (December 1969): 96–97; *MHJ*, ch. 30, pp. 175–79.

70–01 Conference Report, 4 April 1970, pp. 7–10; "The Reality of God." *Improvement Era* 73 (June 1970): 33–34.

70–02 Conference Report, 4 October 1970, pp. 129–32; "Where, Then, Is Hope?" *Improvement Era* 73 (December 1970): 115–17; *MHJ*, ch. 5, pp. 21–26.

70–03 Dedication Address, Benson Ward, Benson, Utah, 11 October 1970.

70–04 Christmas Message, recording sent to employees of Genealogical Department, 25 December 1970.

71–01 "Primer in Genealogy." *Ensign* 1 (February 1971): 4–5.

71–02 *Speeches of the Year 1970–1971*, pp. 1–4, "Unto All Men." Devotional Address, Brigham Young University, 16 March 1971.

71–03 Conference Report, 3 April 1971, pp. 48–51; "Prepare Every Needful Thing." *Ensign* 1 (June 1971): 51–52.

71–04 "The Pursuit of Excellence." Beneficial Life Insurance Company Convention, Shalishan Lodge, Oregon, 6 July 1971.

71–05 "Creation of the Fiji Mission." Given at meeting, presumably held in Suva, Fiji, where the Tongan Mission was divided to form the Fiji Mission, 23 July 1971.

71–06 "Keeping Priesthood Alive in Our Lives." Priesthood Meeting Address, British Area Conference, pp. 97–100, 28 August 1971.

71–07 "Talents." Conference Address, British Area General Conference, pp. 169–72, 29 August 1971.

71–08 Conference Report, 1 October 1971, pp. 51–55; "Elijah the Prophet." *Ensign* 1 (December 1971): 70–72.

71–09 "Friend to Friend." *Friend* 1 (October 1971): 10–11.

72–01 "Charge to a New College President." Church College of Hawaii, 11 February 1972.

72–02 Conference Report, 8 April 1972, p. 95; "A Teacher." *Ensign* 2 (July 1972): 85; *Friend* 16 (May 1986): ifc.

72–03 Conference Report, 7 October 1972, pp. 65–68; "Spiritual Famine." *Ensign* 3 (January 1973): 64–65.

72–04 *Speeches of the Year 1972–1973*, pp. 65–70, "The Deeper Meaning of

Christmas." Devotional Address, Brigham Young University, 5 December 1972; also titled "The Real Christmas."

73–01 Conference Report, 8 April 1973, pp. 172–76; "This Is My Gospel." *Ensign* 3 (July 1973): 118, 120–21.

73–02 "Apostasy and Restoration." Lecture to the Missionary Class, 17 April 1973. Note on typescript indicates that this talk was given to missionaries at the Missionary Home in Salt Lake City between 11 November 1960 and 17 April 1973. It was also given in the Missionary Training Center in Provo on 25 October 1988.

73–03 "The Need to Listen." Beneficial Life Insurance Convention, Xanadu Hotel, Bahamas, 7 June 1973.

73–04 "Genealogical Research and Jurisprudence." Genealogical Research Seminar, Brigham Young University, 2 August 1973.

73–05 "At Graduation." Remarks at Commencement, Brigham Young University, 17 August 1973.

73–06 Conference Report, 6 October 1973, pp. 64–67; "Of the World or of the Kingdom?" *Ensign* 4 (January 1974): 53, 55–56.

74–01 Conference Report, 5 April 1974, pp. 21–25; "His Final Hours." *Ensign* 4 (May 1974): 17–19.

74–02 "To the Last Graduating Class." Graduation, Mapusaga High School, 31 May 1974.

74–03 "Gratitude." Stockholm Area Conference, pp. 25–29, 17 August 1974.

74–04 "Parents' Example." Stockholm Area Conference, pp. 49–52, 17 August 1974.

74–05 Conference Report, 6 October 1974, pp. 137–40; "To Know God." *Ensign* 4 (November 1974): 96–97.

75–01 Conference Report, 5 April 1975, pp. 56–59; "Faith—The First Step." *Ensign* 5 (May 1975): 37–39.

75–02 "Prepare for Honorable Employment." *Ensign* 5 (November 1975): 122–24. General Conference Address, Welfare Session, 4 October 1975.

75–03 Conference Report, 5 October 1975, pp. 140–43; "The Tabernacle." *Ensign* 5 (November 1975): 94–96.

76–01 Conference Report, 6 April 1976, pp. 155–57; "That We May Be One." *Ensign* 6 (May 1976): 105–6; *MHJ*, ch. 9, pp. 47–51.

76–02 Conference Report, 1 October 1976, pp. 20–23; "The Temptations of Christ." *Ensign* 6 (November 1976): 17–19; *MHJ*, ch. 7, pp. 32–37.

77–01 "Four-Year Plan for Genealogy." Priesthood Board Meeting, 2 February 1977.

77–02   "That They May Be Redeemed." Regional Representatives Seminar, Salt Lake City, 1 April 1977.

77–03   Conference Report, 2 April 1977, pp. 32–35; "Thoughts on the Sacrament." *Ensign* 7 (May 1977): 24–25.

77–04   Conference Report, 2 October 1977, pp. 79–81; "Hallowed Be Thy Name." *Ensign* 7 (November 1977): 52–54.

78–01   Conference Report, 1 April 1978, pp. 51–53; "Bind on Thy Sandals." *Ensign* 8 (May 1978): 34–35; *Friend* 17 (October 1987); ifc.

78–02   "Obedience." Area General Conference for Hawaii, Honolulu, Hawaii, 18 June 1978.

78–03   "Marriage Insurance." Beneficial Life Insurance Company Convention, Tamarron, Colorado, 14 July 1978.

78–04   Conference Report, 30 September 1978, pp. 14–16; "True Religion." *Ensign* 8 (November 1978): 11–13; *MHJ*, ch. 27, pp. 158–63.

79–01   *Speeches of the Year 1978–1979*, pp. 32–36; "All Are Alike unto God." Fourteen-Stake Fireside Address, Marriott Center, Brigham Young University, 4 February 1979; *Ensign* 9 (June 1979): 72–74; *MHJ*, ch. 13, pp. 68–75.

79–02   Conference Report, 31 March 1979, pp. 33–36; "Developing Spirituality." *Ensign* 9 (May 1979): 24–26; *MHJ*, ch. 31, pp. 180–85.

79–03   "A Time for Wise Decisions." Commencement Address, BYU—Hawaii Campus, 23 June 1979.

79–04   "The Right Kind of Ambition." Beneficial Life Insurance Convention, Monterey, California, 12 July 1979.

79–05   Conference Report, 7 October 1979, pp. 91–93; "Reading the Scriptures." *Ensign* 9 (November 1979): 64–65.

79–06   "Sustaining in Unity." New Zealand Area Conference, Auckland, New Zealand, 25 November 1979.

79–07   "Permanent or Disposable." New Zealand Area Conference Women's Meeting, Wellington, New Zealand, 27 November 1979.

79–08   "Expression of Gratitude." New Zealand Area Conference, Wellington, New Zealand, 27 November 1979.

79–09   "Marriage Is Forever." Australia Area Conference, Women's Meeting, Melbourne, Australia, 28 November 1979.

79–10   "Unity Brings Peace." Australia Area Conference, Melbourne, Australia, 29 November 1979.

79–11   "Divine Creation of Woman." Australia Area Conference, Women's Meeting, Adelaide, Australia, 30 November 1979.

79–12   "To Sustain Builds Strength." Australia Area Conference, Adelaide, Australia, 30 November 1979.

79–13   "Daughters of God." Australia Area Conference, Women's Meeting, Sydney, Australia, 1 December 1979.

79–14   "Spiritual Strength of Youth." Australia Area Conference, Sydney, Australia, 2 December 1979.

80–01   Conference Report, 5 April 1980, pp. 33–37; "God Will Have a Tried People." *Ensign* 10 (May 1980): 24–26; *MHJ*, ch. 17, pp. 97–102.

80–02   "Follow the Light of the World." Los Angeles Area General Conference, Priesthood Session, Rose Bowl, Pasadena, California, 17 May 1980.

81–01   Conference Report, 5 April 1981, pp. 86–88; "No Man Shall Add to or Take Away." *Ensign* 11 (May 1981): 64–65.

81–02   "Courtesy." Beneficial Life Insurance Company Convention, Sunriver, Oregon, 9 July 1981.

81–03   Conference Report, 3 October 1981, pp. 14–17; "Conference Time." *Ensign* 11 (November 1981): 12–13.

81–04   "The Light of the World." Beneficial Life Insurance Company, Christmas Dinner Message, 15 December 1981. Note at end indicates that the talk was also given at the Correlation Department Christmas dinner, 19 December 1991.

82–01   Clarence H. Tingey, Funeral Service, Salt Lake City, Utah, 29 March 1982.

82–02   Conference Report, 3 April 1982, pp. 26–29; "True Greatness." *Ensign* 12 (May 1982): 19–20.

82–03   Conference Report, 3 October 1982, pp. 81–84; "Commitment to God." *Ensign* 12 (November 1982): 57–58; *MHJ*, ch. 26, pp. 153–57.

83–01   Conference Report, 2 April 1983, pp. 17–20; "Evidences of the Resurrection." *Ensign* 13 (May 1983): 15–16; *Friend* 16 (March 1986): ifc.

83–02   "Thoughts Make Us What We Are." Beneficial Life Insurance Company Convention, Victoria, British Columbia, 7 July 1983.

83–03   Conference Report, 2 October 1983, pp. 91–94; "Parents' Concern for Children." *Ensign* 13 (November 1983): 63–65; *MHJ*, ch. 19, pp. 111–15.

83–04   "Bethlehem at Twilight." BYU Mediterranean Cruise, Shepherds Field, Israel, 22 October 1983.

83–05   "An Apostle's Witness of Christ." *Ensign* 14 (January 1984): 69–71; Friendshipping and Fellowshipping Fireside, Salt Lake Tabernacle and Network, 30 October 1983.

83–06   "Revelation in Church Administration." Address delivered at General Authorities training Seminar, 30 November 1983.

84–01   Funeral Service for Edward La Vaun Clissold, Monument Park Stake Center, Salt Lake City, Utah, 17 February 1984.

84–02   Conference Report, 8 April 1984, pp. 87–89; "The Pharisee and the Publican." *Ensign* 14 (May 1984): 64–66; *MHJ*, ch. 23, pp. 138–42.

84–03   "Islands of the Pacific." Beneficial Life Insurance Company Convention, Waikokloa, Hawaii, 19 July 1984.

84–04   "The Learning Process Lies Within." Address to Administration, Faculty, and Staff, Brigham Young University, 30 August 1984.

84–05   Conference Report, 6 October 1984, pp. 40–43; "Master, the Tempest Is Raging." *Ensign* 14 (November 1984): 33–35; *MHJ*, ch. 8, pp. 38–43.

85–01   Conference Report, 6 April 1985, pp. 20–22; "Christ, Our Passover." *Ensign* 15 (May 1985): 17–19.

85–02   "Education with Spirituality." BYU—Hawaii Graduation Exercises, Laie, Hawaii, 22 June 1985.

85–03   Conference Report, 6 October 1985, pp. 92–95; "Fast Day." *Ensign* 15 (November 1985): 72–74.

86–01   "Make Us Thy True Undershepherds." *Ensign* 16 (September 1986): 6, 8–9; General Conference Priesthood Leadership Meeting, Salt Lake Tabernacle, 4 April 1986; *MHJ*, ch. 15, pp. 81–86.

86–02   Conference Report, 5 April 1986, pp. 17–20; "An Apostle's Witness of the Resurrection." *Ensign* 16 (May 1986): 15–17.

86–03   Conference Report, 4 October 1986, pp. 42–44; "The Lord's Touchstone." *Ensign* 16 (November 1986): 34–35; *MHJ*, ch. 24, pp. 143–47.

87–01   *Speeches of the Year 1986–1987*, pp. 110–16, "What Is True Greatness?" BYU Devotional, Provo, Utah, 10 February 1987; also excerpts in *Ensign* 17 (September 1987): 70–72; *New Era* 18 (February 1988): 4–7; *MHJ*, ch. 18, pp. 103–10.

87–02   "The Vital Role of Correlation." Regional Representatives Seminar, Closing Remarks, Salt Lake City, Utah, 3 April 1987.

87–03   Conference Report, 4 April 1987, pp. 18–21; "Am I a 'Living' Member?" *Ensign* 17 (May 1987): 16–18; *MHJ*, ch. 25, pp. 148–52.

87–04   Conference Report, 4 October 1987, pp. 68–71; "Opening and Closing of Doors." *Ensign* 17 (November 1987): 54, 59–60; *MHJ*, ch. 21, pp. 122–27; *Hope*, pp. 9–14.

88–01 Address to Law Students, J. Reuben Clark Law School, Brigham Young University, 28 February 1988.

88–02 "Continue to Minister." Regional Representatives Seminar, Church Office Building, 1 April 1988.

88–03 Conference Report, 2 April 1988, pp. 17–19; "He Is Risen." *Ensign* 18 (May 1988): 16–17.

88–04 "The Atonement of Jesus Christ." Mission Presidents Seminar, Missionary Training Center, Provo, Utah, 24 June 1988. Also given to mission presidents in the MTC in 1986, 1990, 1992, and 1994.

88–05 "Books." Beneficial Life Insurance Company Convention, Laguna Niguel, California, 13 July 1988.

88–06 Conference Report, 2 October 1988, pp. 68–71; "Blessed from on High." *Ensign* 18 (November 1988): 59–61; *Friend* 19 (November 1989): ifc; *MHJ*, ch. 20, pp. 116–21.

88–07 Letter on Resisting Pornography, 5 October 1988.

88–08 "The Voice of the Lord: The D&C Speaks to Us." Satellite Broadcast, 18 November 1988.

88–09 "An Apostolic Witness and Challenge." Concluding Comments, Satellite Broadcast, 18 November 1988.

89–01 "Eternal Investments." Religious Educators Night, Assembly Hall, Temple Square, 10 February 1989.

89–02 "The Church Is for All People." Single Adult Fireside, Satellite Broadcast, 26 February 1989; *Ensign* 19 (June 1989): 75–77; *MHJ*, ch. 10, pp. 52–57.

89–03 *Speeches of the Year 1988–1989*, pp. 111–16, "Fear Not, Little Flock." Brigham Young University Devotional, Provo, Utah, 14 March 1989.

89–04 Regional Representatives Seminar Remarks, Regional Representatives Seminar, Church Office Building, 31 March 1989.

89–05 Conference Report, 1 April 1989, pp. 18–20; "The God That Doest Wonders." *Ensign* 19 (May 1989): 15–17.

89–06 Conference Report, 30 September 1989, pp. 20–22; "The Golden Thread of Choice." *Ensign* 19 (November 1989): 17–18; *MHJ*, ch. 14, pp. 76–80.

90–01 Memorial Service for J. Talmage Jones, Pasadena Stake Center, Pasadena, California, 3 February 1990.

90–02 "The Mission of the Church." Regional Representatives Seminar, Church Office Building, 30 March 1990.

90–03 Conference Report, 1 April 1990, pp. 75–78; "Standing as a Witness of God." *Ensign* 20 (May 1990): 60–62.

90–04 "Building Church Institutions in Hawaii." Laie Community Fireside, Polynesian Cultural Center Theater, 1 July 1990.

90–05 "Walls of the Mind," *Ensign* 20 (September 1990): 9–10. Also given at Orem Regional Conference, Orem, Utah, 18 March 1990, and Richmond Virginia Regional Conference, 29 April 1990.

90–06 *Speeches of the Year 1990–1991*, pp. 1–7, "No Less Serviceable." BYU Eighteen-Stake Fireside, Brigham Young University, Provo, Utah, 2 September 1990; *Ensign* 22 (April 1992): 64–67; also titled "Out of the Limelight," *New Era* 21 (September 1991): 4, 6–7.

90–07 Conference Report, 6 October 1990, pp. 19–21; "Come unto Me." *Ensign* 20 (November 1990): 17–18; *MHJ*, ch. 3, pp. 11–15.

90–08 "Introduction to the Prodigal Son." Satellite Broadcast, Salt Lake City, Utah, 28 October 1990.

90–09 "Counsel to Students and Faculty." Church College of New Zealand, Hamilton, New Zealand, 12 November 1990.

91–01 "Teach One Another Words of Wisdom." Regional Representatives Seminar, Church Office Building, 5 April 1991.

91–02 Conference Report, 7 April 1991, pp. 82–85; "The Sixth Day of April, 1830." *Ensign* 21 (May 1991): 63–65.

91–03 "Declaration of Independence." Beneficial Life Insurance Company Conference, Lihue, Kauai, Hawaii, 4 July 1991.

91–04 Conference Report, 5 October 1991, pp. 22–24; "The Gospel—a Global Faith." *Ensign* 21 (November 1991): 18–19; *MHJ*, ch. 11, pp. 58–62.

92–01 *Speeches of the Year 1991–1992*, pp. 39–45, "The Dauntless Spirit of Resolution." Eighteen-Stake Fireside, Brigham Young University, 5 January 1992.

92–02 Conference Report, 5 April 1992, pp. 84–87; "A More Excellent Way." *Ensign* 22 (May 1992): 61–63; *MHJ*, ch. 29, pp. 169–74.

92–03 "Commencement Remarks." Brigham Young University, Provo, Utah, 14 August 1992.

92–04 "To the Women of the Church." General Women's Meeting, Salt Lake Tabernacle, 26 September 1992. *Ensign* 22 (November 1992): 95–97.

92–05 Conference Report, 3 October 1992, pp. 22–24; "The Beacon in the Harbor of Peace." *Ensign* 22 (November 1992): 18–19; *MHJ*, ch. 4, pp. 16–20.

92–06 "Thanksgiving." Primarians Thanksgiving Dinner, 17 November 1992.

93–01 *Speeches of the Year 1992–1993*, pp. 67–73; "An Anchor to the Souls of Men." Nineteen-Stake Fireside, Marriott Center, Brigham Young

University, 7 February 1993. *Ensign* 23 (October 1993): 70–73; *New Era* 24 (January 1994): 4, 6–7; *MHJ*, ch. 16, pp. 89–96.

93–02 Conference Report, 4 April 1993, pp. 78–81; "Jesus, the Very Thought of Thee." *Ensign* 23 (May 1993): 63–65; *MHJ*, ch. 2, pp. 6–10.

94–01 Conference Report, 3 April 1994, pp. 83–84; "What Manner of Men Ought Ye to Be?" *Ensign* 24 (May 1994): 64; *MHJ*, ch. 1, pp. 3–5.

94–02 "A Strong and Mighty Man." Memorial Service for President Ezra Taft Benson, Salt Lake Tabernacle, Salt Lake City, Utah, 4 June 1994. *Ensign* 24 (July 1994): 41–42.

94–03 "I Pledge My Life and . . . Full Measure of My Soul." Statement to the Press, Rotunda, Church Administration Building, 6 June 1994. *Ensign* 24 (July 1994): 2, 4–7; *Church News*, 11 June 1994, pp. 3, 14.

94–04 "The Pillars of Our Faith." Nauvoo Ward Sacrament Meeting, Nauvoo, Illinois, 26 June 1994. *Ensign* 24 (September 1994): 54–55.

94–05 "The Temple of Nauvoo." Nauvoo Temple Site, Nauvoo, Illinois, 26 June 1994. *Ensign* 24 (September 1994): 62–64.

94–06 "Come to the God of All Truth." Satellite Broadcast, Carthage, Illinois, 26 June 1994. *Ensign* 24 (September 1994): 72–73.

94–07 "Closing Remarks." Beneficial Life Insurance Company Convention, Lausanne, Switzerland, 15 August 1994.

94–08 "He Invites Us to Follow Him." *Ensign* 24 (September 1994): 2, 4–5.

94–09 "The Standard of Truth." Missionary Training Center Satellite Broadcast, Provo, Utah, 13 September 1994.

94–10 "Follow the Good Shepherd." Priesthood Leadership Meeting, Tucson Regional Conference, Tucson, Arizona, 17 September 1994.

94–11 "This Is My Gospel." Tucson Regional Conference, Tucson, Arizona, 18 September 1994. Excerpts in *Church News*, 24 September 1994, p. 4.

94–12 "Stand Firm in the Faith." General Relief Society Meeting, Salt Lake Tabernacle, 24 September 1994. *Ensign* 24 (November 1994): 96–97.

94–13 "The Great Symbol of Our Membership." *Ensign* 24 (October 1994): 2, 4–5.

94–14 Conference Report, 1 October 1994, pp. 6–9; "Exceeding Great and Precious Promises." *Ensign* 24 (November 1994): 7–9.

94–15   Conference Report, 1 October 1994, pp. 66–70; "Being a Righteous Husband and Father." *Ensign* 24 (November 1994): 49–51.

94–16   Conference Report, 2 October 1994, pp. 117–19; "Follow the Son of God." *Ensign* 24 (November 1994): 87–88.

94–17   "Our Unique Opportunity." Pasadena California Stake Conference, Pasadena, California, 16 October 1994.

94–18   "We Have a Work to Do." 100th Anniversary of the Genealogical Society, Salt Lake Tabernacle, 13 November 1994, *Ensign* 25 (March 1995): 64–65.

94–19   "A Charge to Build Faith." Inauguration of Eric B. Shumway, BYU—Hawaii Campus, 18 November 1994.

94–20   "The Gifts of Christmas." First Presidency Christmas Devotional, Salt Lake Tabernacle, 4 December 1994.

94–21   "The Light of the World." Mexico City Temple Lighting Ceremony, 11 December 1994.

94–22   "Our Responsibility as Members of the Church." Creation of 2000th Stake, Mexico City, Mexico, 11 December 1994.

95–01   "A Temple Motivated People," *Ensign* 25 (February 1995): 2–5.

95–02   "An Account of My Stewardship." 1 April 1995. Prepared as a general conference address but not given, inasmuch as President Hunter died prior to the conference.

SCRIPTURE INDEX

BOOK OF MORMON

PEARL OF GREAT PRICE

SUBJECT INDEX